THE PROCEEDINGS OF THE 15th INTERNATIONAL HUMANITIES CONFERENCE

ALL & EVERYTHING 2010

Stephen Aronson
Anestis Christoforides
Clare Mingins
Seymour Ginsburg
George Kazos
Dinitri Peretzi
Arkady Rovner
Andreas Zarkadoulas

Published by All & Everything Conferences
2010

First Edition Published 2010
Published by All & Everything Conferences (on behalf of the Planning Committee)
© Copyright 2010 by Seymour B. Ginsburg and Ian C. MacFarlane

The contents of this publication may not be reproduced or copied in whole or part in any book, magazine, periodical, pamphlet, circular, information storage or data retrieval system, or in any other form without the written permission of the Planning Committee.

Any profit from the sale of these Proceedings will be devoted to the funds for the organization of future Conferences of a similar nature.

Published by All & Everything Conferences

Website: www.aandeconference.org
Email: info@aandeconference.org

First Edition Print

ISBN-10: 1-905578-28-8
ISBN-13: 978-1-905578-28-3

Also Published as
First Edition eBook

ISBN-10: 1-905578-29-6
ISBN-13: 978-1-905578-29-0

Cover Photo © Copyright 2003 by Nathan Bernier
From: The Enneagrm - Symbol of All and Everything

Table of Contents

Table of Contents 3
Foreword 4
Conference Program 5
Planning Committee 13
Speakers 14
Egoism and Compassion: A Higher Perspective 16
   Ego and Compassion - Questions & Answers 25
The Structure of Laws 31
   The Structure of Laws - Questions & Answers 56
Seminar 1: Chapter 31, *Beelzebub's Tales* 59
Seminar 2: Chapter 6, Meetings with Remarkable Men 82
The Autonomous Nervous System in Ideas of Gurdjieff and Modern Neurophysiology 102
   The Autonomous Nervous System - Questions & Answers 113
There Is in our Life a Certain Very Great Purpose 116
   There Is in our Life a Certain Very Great Purpose - Questions & Answers 138
The Two Chief Motors of our Existence: Food and Sex 143
   The Two Chief Motors of our Existence - Questions & Answers 172
The Gurdjieff Tradition: To Be Continued 180
   The Gurdjieff Tradition: To Be Continued - Questions & Answers 192
Seminar 3: Men N1, N2, N3, N4, N5, N6 and N7: Levels of Beings in *Beelzebub's Tales* 199
Seminar 4: The Implied Mechanical Transformation in *Beelzebub's Tales* 213
Banquet Speaker - Democracy, Idiocy and the Esoteric Schools 228
Where Do We Go From Here? 232
Appendix 1: Concert Programme 233
Appendix 2: List of Attendees 237
Index 239

Foreword

The Planning Committee would like to take this opportunity of thanking all the Presenters for their help in producing these Proceedings. We have all done our best to produce a permanent record of what some of us believe to have been the fifteenth important and definite Conference under the title of All and Everything 2010.

It is hoped that this will lead to further creative interaction of those in the Work in the near future.

In the case of this Conference the individual Presenters have been responsible for providing a written paper covering the material they presented at the Conference and also for the transcription of the recording of their particular Question and Answer session.

The 15th International Humanities Conference - All & Everything 2010 convened on March 24, 2010 in Loutraki, Greece. The conference was attended by 44 delegates travelling from Greece, Russia, Crimea, Norway, Canada, Israel, the Netherlands, the United Kingdom and the United States.

From the Conference's inception, it's members have worked toward making this "gathering of the Companions of the Book" to become more and more just that - a gathering of people from all over the world who come together for the purpose of "fathoming the gist" of Gurdjieff's writings, of sharing our insights and experiences, our questions, and our efforts to understand and grow into becoming remarkable men and women.

Six papers were presented. Four Seminars were also conducted in which were discussed various issues and questions relating the books and ideas of Gurdjieff. A musical performance was presented by the RODA musical company.

The Conference Banquet speaker was George Kazos, who spoke on the subject of "Democracy, Idiocy and the Esoteric Schools".

Conference Program

all & everything

the 15th international humanities conference 2010

Wednesday, March 22 to Sunday, March 26

"Only then will you be able to count upon forming your own impartial judgment, proper to yourself alone, on my writings. And only then can my hope be actualized that according to your understanding you will obtain the specific benefit for yourself which I anticipate, and which I wish for you with all my being." AUTHOR – *Friendly Advice*

Conference Program

Hotel Pappas
Loutraki of Korinthia
Peloponnese - Greece
Tel. (0030) 27440/62782-4, 23936-8
Fax. (0030) 27440/23940
E-Mail: pappasae@otenet.Gr
Website: www.hotelpappas.gr/reservation.htm

Visit the All and Everything Conference website at: www.aandeconference.org

CONFERENCE PROGRAM 2010

8:00 - Every morning - Voluntary Sitting / Meditation

Wednesday
  8:30 PM - Informal Session: Getting to Know You

Thursday
  9:15 - Opening Remarks
  9:30 - Stephen Aronson: Egoism and Compassion – A Higher Perspective
  10:45 - Coffee Break
  11:15 - Paper: Dimitri Peretzi – The Structure of Laws presented in the Tales
  12:30 - Lunch
  2:30 - Seminar 1: Ch. 31 of *Beelzebub's Tales* - The Sixth and Last Sojourn of Beelzebub on the Planet Earth, facilitated by Terje Tonne
  3:45 - Coffee Break
  4:15 - Seminar 1: continued
Evening open for socializing

Friday
  9:30 - Seminar 2: Ch. 6 of *Meetings with Remarkable Men* - Abram Yelov facilitated by Ian MacFarlane
  10:45 - Coffee Break
  11:15 - Paper: Andreas Zarkadoulas & Anestis Christoforides – The Autonomous Nervous System in Ideas of Gurdjieff and Modern Neurophysiology
  12:30 - Lunch
  2:30 - Paper: Sy Ginsburg - There is in Our Life a Certain Very Great Purpose
  3:45 - Coffee Break
  8:30 - Cultural Event: RODA Musical Presentation

Saturday
  9:30 - Paper: Clare Mingins – The Two Chief Motors of our Existence: Food and Sex
  10:45 - Coffee Break
  11:15 - Paper: Arkady Rovner – The Gurdjieff Tradition – To Be Continued
  12:30 - Lunch
  2:30 - Seminar 3: Popi Asteri – *Men N1, N2, N3, N4... and N7* in *Beelzebub's Tales*
  3:45 - Coffee Break
  4:15 - Seminar 4: Mike Readshaw – To take the wrong road can be almost as long as a short cut – Or, what was Gurdjieff really doing?
  7:30 - Conference Banquet / George Kazos: Banquet Speaker
    Subject: *Democracy, Idiocy and the Esoteric Schools*

Sunday
9:30 - Seminar 5: Where Do We Go From Here?

Stephen Aronson
Egoism and Compassion: A Higher Perspective

In *Beelzebub's Tales to His Grandson*, Gurdjieff describes egoism as "abnormal and unbecoming to the essence of any three-brained being whatsoever" (p 107) and states "this said Unique-property egoism usurped the place of the Unique-All-Autocratic-Ruler in their general organization" (p 380). Yet any sincere observer of their inner world will admit that this tendency, even years after its overt manifestations have submitted to the direction of inner work, still flickers, off and on, in response to perceived insults to its' self-image. What are we to make of this tenacity and with what attitude ought we face the remorse it engenders?

Our current usage of the word ego to represent an immature, narcissistic self-focus is a narrow aspect of the original Latin meaning of the concepts I, me, myself. Metaphysical psychology broadly views ego as a conscious, thinking subject. Gurdjieff uses the term embedded in a number of neologisms that denote qualities far above ordinary psychological states. Is there a stage in the enneagramatic process of spiritual development that requires a broader understanding of ego in its possibilities as a representative of something higher?

This paper will attempt to explore egoism from a perspective that seeks to tame the battle between the higher wish for transformation, and the ego's wish for continued dominance of the inner world, by offering compassion, and perhaps even gentle humor, for the suffering of the ego.

Biography
Stephen Aronson received a BS from Penn State University in 1965 and MA and PhD in clinical psychology from the University of Connecticut in 1970. He has been a practicing psychotherapist for nearly 40 years with a background spanning cognitive-behavioral, psychodynamic, inter-personal, gestalt and Jungian training. He was co-author of The Stress Management Workbook, Appleton-Century-Crofts, N.Y. 1980, one of the first publications on stress management. Life interests have included photography, science and baseball. He has been a student of the Gurdjieff work since 1982. Inner world interests are his passion for 'The Work' in all its forms and manifestations, but particularly the method of Gurdjieff since his first encounter in 1982.

Dimitri Peretzi
The Structure of Laws

The powerful image of the hierarchy of the Worlds in the Ray of Creation that appears in Ouspensky's *In Search of the Miraculous* poses a number of questions in relation to the various formulations of a number of Laws given in quite an exact way by Gurdjieff in *The Tales*.

Is there a relation between the two presentations? How are we to view the connection with the Laws in *The Tales* with those in the Cosmoses? How does the concept of the "First and Second conscious shocks" fit with the structure of the Laws described in *The Tales*? The basis of this study revolves around the investigation of relation between Microcosms and Tetartocosmoses. Its aim is, not only to connect the two presentations, the one found in the Tales with the one articulated by Ouspensky, but to also connect these formulations with practical observations about the Work.

Biography

Mr. Peretzi is the president of the Gurdjieff Foundation of Greece. With reference to his personal contacts with eminent students of Gurdjieff, Lord Pentland, Madame de Salzmann, Dr. Welch and others, he has authored a number of books and articles that study the problem of consciousness, relating views from the esoteric traditions to those of the contemporary philosophy of mind. Mr. Peretzi did graduate work in Philosophy, at Yale, where he received his Master of Architecture. Having settled since 1974, he established his own Construction and Prefabrication Company.

Seymour B. Ginsburg
There is in our Life a Certain Very Great Purpose

At the end of *Beelzebub's Tales*, Gurdjieff tells us: "There is in our life a certain very great purpose and we must all serve this Great Common Purpose – in this lies the whole sense and predestination of our life." He goes on to say that a man or woman who is conscious, "acquires the possibility, simultaneously with serving the all–universal Actualizing, of applying part of his manifestations according to the providence of Great Nature for the purpose of acquiring for himself 'Imperishable Being'." *(BT* pp1226-27)

This gives rise to several questions:

(1) What is Gurdjieff's status to tell us that there is in our life a certain very great purpose, and is he connected to the esoteric conscious inner circle of humanity about which he spoke to Ouspensky and others?

(2) What is the certain very great purpose in our life to which we are all slaves?

(3) What makes it possible for us to acquire imperishable being while fulfilling the certain very great purpose in our life?

(4) What is the lot of those who fulfill the certain very great purpose in their life consciously and who thereby acquire imperishable being?

This paper addresses these questions and proposes answers in the context of theosophical teaching and Gurdjieff's role as a Bodhisattva, a member of the esoteric conscious inner circle of humanity along with others whom H.P. Blavatsky and J.G. Bennett have called "the Masters of Wisdom". In this respect the paper exposes the close link between Gurdjieff and these other Masters.

Biography

Sy Ginsburg was born in Chicago in 1934 and currently resides in Florida. He was introduced to the Gurdjieff Work by Sri Madhava Ashish, an eminent theosophical scholar and Hindu monk, who became his mentor over a 19 year period. Ginsburg was a member of the Gurdjieff Society of Florida and later a cofounder of the Gurdjieff Institute of Florida. Currently, he is a Director of The Theosophical Society in Miami and South Florida and facilitator of the Gurdjieff Study Group at The Theosophical Society.

Andreas Zarkadoulas and Anestis Christoforides
The Autonomous Nervous System in the Ideas of Gurdjieff and Modern Neurophysiology

This presentation includes a parallelism of Gurdjieff's ideas with the modern neurophysiology, mainly with regard to the autonomous nervous system. In *All and Everything - Beelzebub's Tales to His Grandson*, Gurdjieff refers to the nerve ganglions of sympathetic nervous system, defining them as the centre of feeling. On the other hand, modern neurophysiology has proven that the autonomous nervous system has direct relation with what we call feeling.

In other points of his work, Gurdjieff considers that the biggest value for the Work with his system has the conscious contact with subconscious. He refers that the contact with subconscious is attained with the modification of blood circulation in the blood vessels. From the physiology we know that the change in the circulation of blood is subject to the autonomous nervous system.

From the parallelism of these opinions, it appears that Gurdjieff had acquaintance of subjects that became much later known in science, causing us to study his work with greater attention and in combination with modern scientific discoveries.

Biographies
Andreas Zarkadoulas is a Medical Doctor, General Practitioner of Alternative Therapies, member of Liga Medicorum Homoeopathica Internationalis.
Anestis Christoforides is a Mechanical Engineer and he has been involved in a variety of activities including research and engineering in alternative and renewable energy systems. Both were introduced to the Gurdjieff Work by Dimitri Peretzi.

Clare Mingins

The Two Chief Motors of our Existence: Food and Sex
According to Gurdjieff, sex energy is the final result of the transformation of our ordinary food and drink. It is also the source of all higher energy and of Will, and is necessary to create a soul.

The ordinary person carries out incomplete absorption and transformation of active elements from the three being-foods. The small amount of energy produced is either automatically used up, wasted, or tainted. Ordinary human physiology is the physiology of abnormality. Orage pointed out that work on oneself produces fifty percent more mental energy and three times more emotional and sex energy than before.

Here I look at various questions concerning the transformation of the three being-foods with reference to material in *Beelzebub's Tales* and Gurdjieff's oral teaching, and that of Bennett, Ouspensky and Orage. Information from the various sources often appears discrepant, perhaps intentionally so. Subjects considered include a composite food diagram, 'food for real man,' vegetarianism, 'the most important part of the second-being food,' evolution and involution of sex energy, 'half-beings,' and others. This paper is part of a broader piece of work looking at 'Gurdjieff's Medicine.'

Biography
Clare Mingins is a member of the Leeds Gurdjieff Society and lives in Cumbria in the north of England. Interests include fellwalking, sheepdog training, singing, playing the organ, food and medicine.

Arkady Rovner
The Gurdjieff Tradition – To Be Continued

Gurdjieff's tradition, generally known as the Fourth Way, has come to a lengthy pending stage after almost one hundred years of its history. Today, when those who met G.I. Gurdjieff in person and who studied under his supervision are no longer among us, the tradition appears to be without a commonly recognized center of gravity. Various groups and individuals all over the world practice the Fourth Way as they see fit, thus taking full responsibility for their interpretation of Gurdjieff's teaching. Some of the adherents of the Fourth Way along the road of rediscovering for themselves such respectable ancient traditions such as Sufism, Advaita-Vedanta, and even Christianity as being the real sources of Gurdjieff's tradition. Still others have chosen the way of creation of new syncretic teachings based on the Fourth Way and other traditions. As a result of this discord, Gurdjieff's tradition has been gradually reduced in practice to the Gurdjieff Movements, an essential but by no means a central element of his teaching.

Thus we have the following questions before us, which require urgent answers. What are the most essential components and what is the core element of Gurdjieff's teaching? What could be the continuation or the new shape of the Fourth Way? What attracts the modern spiritual seeker to the Fourth Way and what no longer does? Finally, what type of a person is this seeker who is capable of understanding and following Gurdjieff's path in earnest?

The answers to these questions could be found by means of research, experiments and examination of Gurdjieff's writings, which encourage us to seek independent solutions for any arising problems. One must keep in mind that we are dealing with the problem of paramount importance, namely, with the future destiny of Gurdjieff's tradition.

The following quotation from Gurdjieff's early talks hits the point precisely: "…now we speak in a language which two hundred years hence will no longer be the same, and two hundred years ago the language was different." *Views from the Real World* p 211.

In his *Beelzebub's Tales*, chapter 30, Gurdjieff broadly elaborates on the subject of transmission of the Knowledge by enlightened members of the club of "Adherents-of-Legominism," tying this transmission with the Law of Sevenfoldness and other phenomena. The problem in question is dealt with numerous times throughout this book. The author's sincere and strong objective lies in addressing those questions in his presentation.

Biography

Arkady Rovner was born in 1940 in Odessa, USSR and spent his youth in Tbilisi, Georgia. He studied at Moscow State University and Columbia University, New York. He taught numerous courses on world religions and contemporary mysticism at the New York University, the State University of New York, the New School for Social Research and the Moscow State Humanitarian University. He was introduced to Gurdjieff's ideas and practices in Moscow, Russia in 1965 and has been an adherent of the Gurdjieff Work ever since then. During the years 1975-1984 he was in constant communication with Lord Pentland, the head of the American branch of Gurdjieff

Foundation. In the summer of 1980, with a letter of reference from Lord Pentland, he travelled to London and Paris where he met and interviewed a number of Ouspensky's and Gurdjieff's former disciples, including Mr. Tilley and P. L. Travers, as well as Michael de Salzmann.

Seminar Facilitators notes and biographies

Popi Asteri-

Men N1, N2, N3, N4… and N7

In Beelzebub's Tales there is a continuous reference to the terms three-centered and three-brained beings, and to the fact that human beings - while they are three-brained beings and have the potential to perfect themselves spiritually - due to the unnatural conditions of their usual existence, do not develop harmoniously. It is also mentioned that the quality of existence of humans and the state of their consciousness depends on the harmonious function of all three centers and that when this balance does not exist, the way we perceive our self and the world is one sided and imperfect. The study that I will present sets off those imperfections of perception of men N1, N2 and N3, as they are described by Gurdjieff in Beelzebub's Tales, through certain characters that appear mainly in the first three descends of Beelzebub on earth. I will also refer to the qualities of man N4, who is mainly described in the fourth descend, through the inner pursuit and actions of Belcultassi - the founder of the Akhaldan society. Man N7, who is the man that has reached complete development, is described in Beelzebub's Tales mainly through the Deliberations and the activities of Ashiata Shiemash.

Biography

I live in Greece and I have been in Gurdjieff's work since 1990. My group is in Thessaloniki and we work with the support and the guidance of Dimitri Peretzi. I wrote a book published in Greek with the title: *Beatitudes and the Lord's Prayer within the Enneagram*.

Ian MacFarlane

Ian was born in Niagara Falls, Canada, in 1949 and in 2001 moved to England where he lives with his wife near London. He first became acquainted with the Gurdjieff Work in 1973 and joined his first group in Toronto in 1977. In 1979 he studied Movements at Daglingworth in England. In 1980 he became a member of a group called The Search at Northeon Forest in Pennsylvania, USA, that was lead by Paul Beidler, a former student of Gurdjieff. After two years residential training, he returned to Toronto to assist and eventually lead the satellite Toronto Northeon Group. Since Mr. Beidler's death in 1998, he has been working to bring the practical side of the Work to a wider audience through the medium of an internet website and an online Work group.

Michael Readshaw

To take the wrong road can be almost as long as a short cut –
Or, what was Gurdjieff really doing?

The mind that wakes up is not the mind that is asleep. Gurdjieff was not teaching ideas but was initiating in his pupils a transformation, or awakening, that takes place of itself, automatically, by itself, mechanically (Gurdjieff's words! *BT* pp 24/25) and which takes place outside the person, without the awareness of the person, and takes about 30 years (my experience). *Beelzebub's Tales* consists of a ladder of teachings, none of which appear in any of the established literature, with the bottom rung being the comparison between the 'vices' at the start of this transformation, the ordinary man, (using the words ordinary, abnormal, external) and the 'virtues' at the end (normal man). The second rung consists of the 64 'essences of certain real notions' (*BT* p 24-25 again). Third rung, Gurdjieff's use of remorseful rhythm, and so on.

Biography

Mike Readshaw first read *Beelzebub's Tales* at University, where he obtained a degree in Mathematics, specializing in Mathematical Logic. A meeting with Rina Hands indirectly led to him producing a number of audio talks, the first of which, Reading Gurdjieff, exposed the difference between Gurdjieff's own writings and the established Gurdjieff canon of thought. This was much praised by Mrs. Annie Staveley, but after a serious climbing accident in the Alps, Mike was distracted and had to re-learn to walk, married, and trained as a teacher. He lived in France for a number of years before family circumstances forced him back to England. Mike is a widower, with five children in his care, and teaches Mathematics in the north of England. Knowing that personality has ideas whilst essence has insights, his most recent work consists of devising 365 completely original sayings with the intention of raising the overall level of awareness of those in contact with him, based upon the principle that: A good saying. stops all thought so that understanding can fill that vacuum.

Terje Tonne

Terje Tonne, born 1951, was educated as a Conservator at the Kent and McMint Fine Art Restorers in 1974. For the last 30 years he has had his own Restoration Studio where he has specialized in restoring fire and water damaged oil paintings for private collectors, museums and insurance companies. While studying in London in the early 70s he came across the Work ideas. He lives in Oslo, Norway and leads a group there along with his wife Ulrike.

George Kazos

I was born in 1957, I am married and have two children. I am an electronic engineer and a PMP (Project Manager Professional). For more than 20 years I have been responsible for large scale IT projects in Greece and abroad, as a Senior Project Manager for Intracom IT Services. I participate in the Work in Greece since 1983 and conduct my own groups. I have been present in two A&E conferences in Bognor Regis.

ADVISORY BOARD
Nick Bryce, Dr. Keith A. Buzzell, Seymour B. Ginsburg, Dimitri Peretzi, Prof. Paul Beekman Taylor
Music advisor: John Amaral

READING PANEL
Dr. Michael Pittman, Rev. José Tirado, Terje Tonne

PLANNING COMMITTEE
Paul Bakker, Ocke de Boer, Marlena O. Buzzell,
Ian MacFarlane, Robert Ormiston, Bonnie Phillips, Farzin Deravi

Planning Committee

Ocke de Boer - Netherlands
Marlena O. Buzzell - USA
Ian MacFarlane - UK
Robert Ormiston - UK
Bonnie Phillips - USA
Paul Bakker - Netherlands

Reading Panel

Terje Tonne - Norway
Dr. Michael Pittman - USA
José Tirado - Iceland

Advisory Board

Seymour B. Ginsburg - USA
Nick Bryce - Canada
Dr. Keith Buzzell - USA
Dimitri Peretzi - Greece
Prof. Paul Beekman Taylor - Switzerland
John Amaral - USA (Music Advisor)

Speakers

Stephen Aronson
Stephen Aronson received a BS from Penn State University in 1965 and MA and PhD in clinical psychology from the University of Connecticut in 1970. He has been a practicing psychotherapist for nearly 40 years with a background spanning cognitive-behavioural, psychodynamic, interpersonal, gestalt and Jungian training. He was co-author of The Stress Management Workbook, Appleton-Century-Crofts, N.Y. 1980, one of the first publications on stress management. Life interests have included photography, science and baseball. He has been a student of the Gurdjieff work since 1982. Inner world interests are his passion for 'The Work' in all its forms and manifestations, but particularly the method of Gurdjieff since his first encounter in 1982.

Anestis Christoforides
Anestis Christoforides is a Mechanical Engineer and he has been involved in a variety of activities including research and engineering in alternative and renewable energy systems. He was introduced to the Gurdjieff Work by Dimitri Peretzi.

Clare Mingins
Clare Mingins is a member of the Leeds Gurdjieff Society and lives in Cumbria in the north of England. Interests include fellwalking, sheepdog training, singing, playing the organ, food and medicine.

Seymour B. Ginsburg, J.D.
Sy Ginsburg was born in Chicago in 1934 and currently resides in Florida. He was introduced to the Gurdjieff Work by Sri Madhava Ashish, an eminent theosophical scholar and Hindu monk, who became his mentor over a 19 year period. Ginsburg was a member of the Gurdjieff Society of Florida and later a co-founder of the Gurdjieff Institute of Florida. Currently, he is a Director of The Theosophical Society in Miami & South Florida and facilitator of the Gurdjieff Study Group at The Theosophical Society.

George Kazos
I was born in 1957, I am married and have two children. I am an electronic engineer and a PMP (Project Manager Professional). For more than 20 years I have been responsible for large scale IT projects in Greece and abroad, as a Senior Project Manager for Intracom IT Services. I participate in the Work in Greece since 1983 and conduct my own groups. I have been present in two A&E conferences in Bognor Regis.

Speakers

Dinitri Peretzi
Mr. Peretzi is the president of the Gurdjieff Foundation of Greece. With reference to his personal contacts with eminent students of Gurdjieff, Lord Pentland, Madame de Salzmann, Dr. Welch and others, he has authored a number of books and articles that study the problem of consciousness, relating views from the esoteric traditions to those of the contemporary philosophy of mind. Mr. Peretzi did graduate work in Philosophy, at Yale, where he received his Master of Architecture. Having settled since 1974, he established his own Construction and Prefabrication Company.

Arkady Rovner
Arkady Rovner was born in 1940 in Odessa, USSR and spent his youth in Tbilisi, Georgia. He studied at Moscow State University and Columbia University, New York. He taught numerous courses on world religions and contemporary mysticism at the New York University, the State University of New York, the New School for Social Research and the Moscow State Humanitarian University. He was introduced to Gurdjieff's ideas and practices in Moscow, Russia in 1965 and has been an adherent of the Gurdjieff Work ever since then. During the years 1975-1984 he was in constant communication with Lord Pentland, the head of the American branch of Gurdjieff Foundation. In the summer of 1980, with a letter of reference from Lord Pentland, he travelled to London and Paris where he met and interviewed a number of Ouspensky's and Gurdjieff's former disciples, including Mr. Tilley and P. L. Travers, as well as Michael de Salzmann.

Andreas Zarkadoulas
Andreas Zarkadoulas is a Medical Doctor, General Practitioner of Alternative Therapies, member of Liga Medicorum Homoeopathica Internationalis. He was introduced to the Gurdjieff Work by Dimitri Peretzi.

Egoism and Compassion: A Higher Perspective

Stephen Aronson

Abstract

In *Beelzebub's Tales to His Grandson*, Gurdjieff describes *egoism* as "abnormal and unbecoming to the essence of any three-brained being whatsoever" [p 107] and states "this said Unique-property egoism usurped the place of the Unique-All-Autocratic-Ruler in their general organization" [p 380] Yet any sincere observer of their inner world will admit that this tendency, even years after its overt manifestations have submitted to the direction of inner work, still flickers, off and on, in response to perceived insults to its' self-image. What are we to make of this tenacity and with what attitude ought we face the remorse it engenders?

Our current usage of the word ego to represent an immature, narcissistic self-focus is a narrow aspect of the original Latin meaning of the concepts *I, me, myself*. Metaphysical psychology broadly views ego as a *conscious, thinking subject*. Gurdjieff uses the term embedded in a number of neologisms that denote qualities far above ordinary psychological states. Is there a stage in the enneagramatic process of spiritual development that requires a broader understanding of ego in its possibilities as a representative of something higher?

This paper will attempt to explore egoism from a perspective that seeks to tame the battle between the higher wish for transformation, and the ego's wish for continued dominance of the inner world, by offering compassion, and perhaps even gentle humor, for the suffering of the ego.

Egoism and Compassion: A Higher Perspective

The Impression

I am aware inside myself. Opening attention to the sensation of the surrounding body, I feel its outline. Within that form are sensations of tingling, movement, a kind of 'buzzing' or 'humming.' There is the beat of the heart, the rhythmic pulse of blood in motion. There is the breath moving through the nostrils, with the accompanying movement in chest and abdomen. There is the impression of body as a wall, a porous membrane separating material outer from the subjective interior. In the mind, words and images appear in conjunction with this direct experience followed by an evaluation of their accuracy. The 'world' of experience at this moment is directly perceived as having three levels or concentric rings. There is the outer world, including the physical body as its closest representative. In the middle is the world of thought, image, valuation. Most interior is a level directing, dividing and holding attention on the other two experienced as exterior to its locus of perception.

Something else is now felt, something deep in the body's interior; a sense of constriction, density, sharpness. Words of irritation, jealousy, offense appear. Another voice observes these words with further evaluation, naming them vanity, hubris, egoism. Immediately a different quality is tasted with associations of shame, disappointment, ruefulness, disgust; the remorse of conscience. How can it be that after so many years of inner work, such deep and seemingly sincere longing to transform this ordinary self, that this manifestation of wanting credit, this wishing to seen of men, continues to linger in the depths? Am I not working hard enough, meditating enough, studying enough, worthy enough? Why continued resistance from this representative of ordinary self to my highest inner aims? How can this exist in the midst of a state of three centered attention?

Initial Response

A choice is perceived. Will remorse feed the wounded pride of self-image or illuminate its delusions? At this moment, there is sufficient quality of presence to access the time-body of Work impressions. Memory of countless efforts of work with negativity blend to suggest direction. Divided attention is refreshed, this time between the taste of remorse, with its object of perception, and the wish to...... to what? There seems to be the possibility of different wishes. One is recognized as the wish to be free of suffering the burden of contamination from egoism within my psychological body; but, is the aim of Work to free myself from 'suffering' the reality of imperfection?

Attention moves back to the envious complaint initiating this question: how can this be understood? A glance down reaffirms the confirmation of 'levels' within this inner world. Here is the wish for self-oriented, mental/emotional forms to leave me and never return. I can see them, feel them moving within, subsiding now but not yet quiet. Their aspirations reach out through me into the world, wanting from others recognition of their imagined sense of importance. They don't appear to see me looking at them. Where is this place of looking down? It certainly feels higher, or deeper, in some way to the object of its interest. The wish from this higher location is to be free of attachment to rewards from the outside world. The wish feels sincere, yet, obviously is not shared universally within. Something is now noticed between these two levels, something not focused on recognition from outside, but rather, seeking recognition inside. It has taken this image of itself and divided it in two. It wants to see itself the way it wants others to see it, while pretending, both to itself and others, that outer recognition is not important. This attempt at self deception is interesting.

Pondering

Mr. Gurdjieff describes egoism as "abnormal and unbecoming to the essence of any three-brained being whatsoever" and states "this said Unique-property egoism usurped the place of the Unique-All-Autocratic-Ruler in their general organization." [p107,380] Egoism seems to be the attitude of pretending to be what is not, taking credit for what one has no role in creating. It is theft. Reflecting on this multi-layered inner world of psychological experience as corresponding, in some way, to the division of cosmoses, then everything would have its own level and function within that location. Perhaps this constellation of feeling and thought we call egoism, also has a place and function at its own level. Gurdjieff says it is "abnormal and unbecoming to the essence," but, is it unexpected and unlawful to the personality under the circumstances of its own level?

What do I know about the 'levels' below this location from which this inquiry is taking place? I know from experience and study that the body has a built in mechanism for survival, instinctively distinguishing safety from danger. My body's preference for avoiding discomfort is a constant reminder. I can see how this function is echoed subjectively in my relationships: discomfort when feeling unwanted by others or concerned about acceptance of ideas and opinions by those to whom I give significant valuation.

Itoklanoz

This first subjective body of meaning comes into existence through what Gurdjieff calls "first education" or "Itoklanoz," the cumulative impact of all intentional and unintentional influential people and surrounding events during growth towards "responsible age."

Initial stirrings of self-awareness, distinct from the surrounding world, will immediately be confronted by the Itoklanoz process, blending with the program for biological survival and social imperative for security among people on whom survival depends.

What will aid in this lawful, programmed social/biological quest? The physical body, instinctive processes in place, mechanically matures following its inherited pattern. This pattern of muscular, hormonal and nervous system responses becomes shaped by the influence of environmental and social feedback. An adaptive sensitive psychic body, personality, as its capacities begin to appear within the developing mind, forms around the essential pattern of potentialities, utilizing or suppressing these qualities dependent on their functionality for the process of safety and survival.

Thus inevitably develops an outer layer of the inner world of feeling/thought, as distinct from sensation. Like the rind of a fruit surrounding a deeper, richer, juicier interior, gifted with capacity to conceptualize about the body's relationship with its surroundings, it seems lawful that a portion of psychic capacity would become dedicated to assisting the preservation imperative. Unable to compete with the instincts for quickness in the moment, this psychic assistant could contribute to the survival mission by devoting its capacity to plan for moments to come by reviewing moments past. Thus the physical body would live in the moment while the psychic body of personalized memory and interpretation would contribute its imaging capacity to straddle subjective past and imagined future to assist the body in protecting its existence. How could it not be so ---- and how could it possibly transform? I can no more eliminate my personality than I can get out of my body. I live inside both. The potential for freedom must lie in a different direction.

Egoism and Compassion: A Higher Perspective

Sense Of Self

A subjective increase in quality of inner experience, beginning its penetration into the material mind, can be symbolically represented by both the vertical line of the cross and the upper triangle of the six pointed star. As this energy descends from above the life of the material body, it is first experienced as sensitivity to the world outside perceived though the sensory organs. As it develops, new functions of memory, interpretation and creating meaning appear. These are clearly different levels of potential carrying different qualities of awareness and possibilities for understanding. When a minimally sufficient level of the vertical penetrates, automatic conditioning and sensitivity become blended with higher levels of awareness. I become aware of myself in the process of experiencing.

This nacent tip of self-consciousness learns to believe itself good or bad, competent or incompetent, clean or unclean, through interaction with its surroundings, primarily direct and indirect attitudinal and verbal indications from others. Underneath either positive or negative self attitude is the conditioned belief that I "can do," or ought to be able to do, and that the ultimate aim of this doing potential is to be projected into the outer world, rather than sought in relationship with the non-sensual world hiding behind its conditioned gaze. It doesn't know that it has been trained to look for its source and sustenance in the wrong direction and that to know itself requires looking in two directions simultaneously. Awakening into an Itoklanoz dominated level of sensory and human interaction, who or what can help consciousness understand the mystery of itself?

In Gurdjieff's ideal, Foolasnitamnian world, this dawning light within would be greeted by sensitive recognition. A real teacher, an Oskianotsner, would offer joyous initiation to the arrival of this self-recognizing, initiating guidance towards relationship with the true source of awakening, calling forth a sense of responsibility to use the light for service to others, to the life of the planet and to God. Without such support, our little body and little essence are alone in their struggle with the pressure for conformity in behavior, reaction and thought to the outer world view. The question of who I am becomes entangled with the sense of survival. Seeking to gain favor, and thus safety with our surrounds, we draw from the essential qualities given at conception to shape ourselves into a form that will ensure these pragmatic ends.

If sufficient success occurs, the sense of self accrues positive value labels. I will begin to think of myself as a "somebody." I will need this developing image fed sufficiently to become stabilized. Its maintenance confirms a sense of reality and safety. If my efforts and qualities are defined as unattractive or unsuccessful, this insufficiency will suggest weakness and consequent danger to myself. If, in particular, I come to believe that what I am is unlovable or incompetent, I will conclude my interior, itself, is insufficient and a threat to my survival. Turning on myself as the source of my problems, an object to be feared or despised, becomes a type of auto-immune reaction that will make the later inner spiritual search that more difficult, if possible at all. Regardless of either hypothesis about my value, the underlying question, "Who am I"?, continues to haunt. It seems to have an independent component, not tied to the biological/ social question, but emerging from increasing self-awareness.

All & Everything Conference 2010

Here appears a sense of Gurdjieff's Theomertmalogos as interactive energy levels reverberating below as above. His cosmology posits an "atom of God" inside everything such that descending levels of the creation are composed of more and more individual atoms of God held together in increasingly complex forms. The essence of God must lie at the heart of everything, including the awareness of what I call "myself." At the level called "myself," the breath of Theomertmalogos, the word of God, can be experienced along a continuum, from moments self awareness inside the body to increasingly deeper levels of waking inside feeling, inside thought, inside the ongoing flow of life. Surely these deepening levels of experience will differentially illuminate questions about myself.

Ego and Egoism

Gurdjieff continually reminds us of the necessity for specificity in discussing inner work. His system stresses distinctions between inner and outer, higher and lower, finer and courser, lighter and denser such as essence and personality, real I and false I, waking and sleeping, conscious and subconscious. This quality of relativity clearly refers to different levels of potential psychic experience. Does the term egoism refer to the same level or quality as Ego? Gurdjieff does say our "Ego-individuality is sharply dual". [p 595]

Dividing attention again confirms the reality of "two personalities" in me as Gurdjieff describes. Are all wishes for myself "egoistic"? If so, why does Gurdjieff have Hassein defend himself against this accusation from Ahoon at the very beginning of *Beelzebub's Tales*, by exploring the role of motivation and context in self expression? [p 59]

Gurdjieff uses "egoism" and "egotist" to indicate the worst in man that both blocks spiritual growth and is a continuing source of disharmony for the universe and suffering for Endlessness. Gurdjieff urges for "struggling unceasingly with one's subjective weaknesses... and defects in one's established subjectivity... and combating them, strive for their eradication without mercy towards oneself." (p 1209) Such powerful directives ought to be aimed with precision.

"Ego" is the sound assigned by Greek to the experiential sense of "I", by Latin to the feel of "I", "me", "myself", and is referenced in metaphysical psychology as "the conscious, thinking subject." In this sense, at its beginnings, it appears to carry no inherent trace of the narcissistic qualities we attach to egoism. It enters incarnation, descending with the penetrating vertical dimension from "above," carried into heart and mind as innocent potential for self-awareness.

If Ego refers to the sense of I-myself, the experience of self-consciousness can't be "abnormal and unbecoming" to the essence. What is it am I to strive to eradicate without mercy towards "myself"? If Ego refers to the sense of I-myself, how is this to be done? What then, is aware of being an "I" becoming aware of its egoism? Is egoism the same as Ego?

In the birth pangs of awakening, when unfed and unsupported, insufficiently midwifed by its human community, the young subjective self-awareness invariably misunderstands the potential

Egoism and Compassion: A Higher Perspective

behind its sensory interface with the world. It is understandable that the growth of this capacity might lead to the assumption that the existence of this power represented the ultimate level possible within the individual.

Viewed from the horizontal line of life, this psychic capacity to influence ones own manifestations and those of others is, arguably, the supreme ruler within the animal world and a powerful tool in the struggle for acceptance in the emotional universe of personalities. If this young "conscious thinking subject" doesn't have the support of appropriate education to recognize itself as but the growing tip of a larger Self lying above its current awareness, it can't help but take credit, or blame, for its situation. Feeling it must hold its sense of self together against the outer world by its own efforts, ignorant of the help available from within, its lower part becomes encrusted with this misunderstanding. The descending conscious entity, Ego, develops, at its tail, an 'ism,' as Gurdjieff would say. Egoism becomes a belief system, an ideological world view believed necessary to maintain its existence. Affixing the suffix 'crat', which Gurdjieff says means to 'hold' or to 'keep," the lower part of Ego becomes an Egocrat", holding its sense of self together only by means of mistaken understanding of who and what it is. Becoming part of its sense of survival, this belief must be defended at all costs. [p 764]

In many theologies, and parts of the Gurdjieff work community, the problem created by egoism seems to have blended with the larger question of Ego. Applying the standard of relativity, this self reflectivity would lawfully experience fluctuating intensity with differing levels of understanding. If Ego is viewed as the subjective experience of I, the subject conscious of itself, then the term feels related to Gurdjieff's third state of consciousness and the potential for higher being bodies.

Throughout *Beelzebub's Tales* to His Grandson, the term Ego, in combination with other prefix and suffix combinations, is used in contexts suggesting a multitude of meaning for this root. In relationship with only one other term, such as egoism, egocrat, egoist, the sense is pejorative. An expanded potential is suggested when Ego is embedded within neologisms that denote higher beings, higher states and Endlessness Itself. Egoplastikori has the flavor of increased flexibility of attitude and perception. Egolionopties resonates with the feel of enhanced vision, the cognizance and feeling of courage and faith in one's might symbolized in the legs of the Akhaldan Sphinx and Gurdjieff's praise of the intelligence and courage of "Mr. Lion." [p 199, 308] "Egoaitoorassian being-will" is 'something' engendered from "the excess of its third holy force, namely, the 'Holy Reconciling,' obtained during the assimilation of cosmic truths." [p 563] Inclusion in the terms Autoegocrat and Trogoautoegocrat lift Ego into the highest realms. There seems the implication of a seed planted to differentiate Ego, as awakening consciousness, from the misuse of its power when applied to the aim of self-calming in life.

From the level only of experiencing wish for better within myself, the way forward is unclear. If it were clear, there would be awareness of more than wish sensed at this location. This wish must be a resonant taste of something lying above, otherwise there would be no intuition that there is more to seek beyond this current position. Here now is the sense of relationship with a third element. The view must shift to what is above to find help with what is below.

Beelzebub's Tales are filled with exhortations for non-violence, forgiveness and pardon. Excluding only the Eternal Hasnamuss, all errors, miscalculations, mistakes and unbecoming manifestations are forgivable. "It goes without saying, GOD forgives everything -- this has even become a law in the World." [198] Angels and archangels are promoted despite miscalculations of cosmic proportion. Higher being bodies are given the most beautiful planet on which to continue work on lingering imperfections. Beelzebub, even during his exile and prior to his return home in honor and recognition, is asked for help by Endlessness Himself. Beelzebub comes to understand that "even such great events as wars, civil-wars and other similar misfortunes of a general character, proceed simply on account of a property in the common presences of ordinary people who have never specially worked on themselves, which property I... would call "the-reflecting-of-reality-in-one's-attention-upside-down." [p 1233] Recognition of the implications of the unfathomable energy that makes consciousness possible is blocked when Ego-consciousness looks outward, rather than inward, for its understanding.

When deepening experience begins to inform these questions, the sense of something new growing into the interior, or upward, starts to solidify a different understanding. Belief in what the world suggests I am is now seen as an image reflected back from life. From where does the light that illuminates this reflected image originate? With such questions, egotistic reactions weaken.... but they do seem to linger. Perhaps the depth of remorse at their persistence indicates the distance of growth away from life values. Yet, there seems to be another more subtle level of misunderstanding at this point.

Gurdjieff describes the experience of remorse as occurring when "every part that has arisen from the results of any one Holy Source of the Sacred Triamazikamno, as it were, revolts and criticizes the former unbecoming perceptions and manifestations at the moment of another part of its whole." [p 141] Here is the tension between what I wish to be and what I see still contained in my inner world, but there is more to be discovered in this reaction. Are revolting and criticizing, by themselves, facilitators of digestion or indigestion? How is this meal to be digested?

Remorse is also referred to as the "sacred process, Aieioiuoa" that "always proceeds with the Omnipresent-Active-Element-Okidanokh...when in immediate touch with the emanations either of the Sun Absolute itself or of any other Sun." [p141] Is it the light of my inner sun that illuminates the egoism for me to see below? I must not turn the taste of remorse into an attack on my whole Self. Nor ought I to attack the lower part of my psychological nature that has fallen into a misguided understanding of itself.

Words accompanying remorse over lingering manifestations of egoism often take a recriminative form, such as "Why I haven't outgrown this reaction"? Behind this question is still a semblance of continuing supposition that "I can do" -- or "I ought to be able to do." There is still attachment to a sense of individual I-ness. Is this not itself a reflection of egoism, the belief that I, myself, can direct the work of moving back towards the origin of consciousness and creation? The mystery of myself grows more profound as it becomes more directly experienced. How can I assume I ought to know how to direct what I do not understand when I do not even know who or what I am? Only egoism could make such an assumption.

If I anathamatize Ego for its immature misunderstandings, am I not engaging in the same type of division, hubris and third force blindness attributed to sleeping humanity? The egoist's weapon of choice is dividing others into castes and attacking those lower than itself and fawning at those it deems higher. If viewed as something without logical explanation in my inner world, the desire to separate from the misunderstanding of 'egoism' likely leads to an attitudinal attack on these qualities when seen from above. Ironically, attack is the tool of egoism.

Compassion and Reconciliation

Gurdjieff tells us not to use violence to facilitate transformation but to withdraw from identification, to separate our sense of Self from impressions. *Beelzebub's Tales* indicates our approach to change must be indirect, patient, based on observation and reason, held within a state of three-centered presence. If I am to separate from identification with my unbecoming parts, I must recognize that egoistic qualities remain below as conditioned potential reaction, reflection of an immature level of understanding continuing to live pressed up against the belief that the body is all I am. Attack requires identification as a prerequisite and strengthens this belief. Why attack the whole of my Self for lingering consequences of Itoklanoz education not of my own doing? The very existence of my wish demonstrates that understanding has already matured far beyond the Itoklanoz perspective. If I attack what lies below, the power and potential coming from above is stolen and driven downward into life, the potency of the attack lawfully provoking an equivalent defense.

Now another question appears. Do "I", 'me" and "myself" refer to the same levels? The term "myself" has a quality of possessiveness: my self, mine,... as distinct from what.... others "selves"? If this self belongs to "me," can it be lost? Must it be protected and defended? Who would be able to take it away? What about "me" and "I"? Does "me" have the same resonance as "I AM"? Which self and whose self is being referred to? Instead, I must ask, what is awareness of I-ness to serve? Is its growing presence for my individual maturation alone, or is something deeper to emerge from the ripening sense of Self?

Gurdjieff says, " 'the highest aim and sense of human life is the striving to attain the welfare of one's neighbor,' and that this is possible exclusively only by the conscious renunciation of one's own." [p 1186] What inside my psychological world would have the wish and will to renounce my own welfare? The Five Strivings outline duty to Endlessness as the use of consciousness to serve life and the development of higher being bodies, not to attack the lower world. [p 386] The power of self awareness is a reflection of the creative potential to modify understanding and the course of events.

What an unfair dilemma for the awakening Ego-consciousness, born into a hypnotized world deep in sleep, struggling for years to fathom itself on a foundation of misunderstanding implanted from the outside, constantly fooled by the overpowering energy of the senses, commanded by instinct to serve the body's desire for comfort and survival. This is truly the origin of myth and fairy tale. No wonder Ego, the conscious sense of I-ness, becomes trapped in identification with the material world at an immature stage of growth where it tragically believes itself solely responsible for holding itself and its entire world together. It must be a frightened child indeed, hiding, equivocating or puffing itself up to avoid glimpsing its non-existence.

If I am to develop the ableness to tolerate the unpleasing manifestations of others towards myself, I ought to begin with tolerating the insults to my spiritual self-image when offended by the appearance of lingering immaturity unbecoming to higher aims. To do otherwise is spiritual egotism.

Gurdjieff has St. Buddha say that to assist Endlessness in His suffering, we are to choose the non-desires over the desires. He says our mechanical suffering stands between us and our spiritual possibilities. Desiring results leads to frustration when their manifestation cannot be controlled or maintained.

To forgive means to release from debt. If I believe I am owed, and that this debt limits my freedom, then I am a slave who must wait for repayment to be free. If I cancel the debt myself, the moment I free my debtor I am simultaneously released. I see that I contain within my being, conditioned, unintentional, youthful misunderstandings imposed from outside and nourished by my fears and suggestibility. Can I forgive my Self for being a manifestation that encompasses lower as well as higher worlds stretching from earth to Heaven? Can I intentionally suffer laboring to remain conscious within my Self at all levels?

I need to experience and accept my Self in the middle, half way up the ladder, crucified at the point of penetration from above with the world below, helpless to force my will, challenged to have only the courage to see. I must serve below and above by looking simultaneously, with compassion downward and essence-hope and faith towards the love flowing from above. If the world below suffers and I suffer here in the middle, how much must the world above suffer also? May joining my Self consciously to this intentional tension connect me to Endlessness and decrease the sorrow of us both.

References

All quotes from G.I.Gurdjieff, *All & Everything: Beelzebub's Tales to His Grandson*, E. P. Dutton Company Inc., N.Y. 1964

Ego and Compassion - Questions & Answers

Participant 1: Thank you very much. I want to ask whether you believe that the aim of the Gurdjieffian work, as you put it, has to do, just as in Buddhism, with releasing from suffering, or through conscious suffering in the world as you describe, below oneself and higher worlds, that the aim is a release from suffering? Is that the motive why Gurdjieff brought these teachings to the world? That is my question.

Stephen Aronson: I hope I am prudent enough not to try to speak for Mr. Gurdjieff. (Pause) So, I will just speak from my own experience, which I think is the only place any of us ought to speak from, or try to. The reduction in suffering seems to be a result of these kinds of efforts. I don't know that I would say it is primary aim. That would be self oriented, I think. But, certainly, the diminishment of dependence on a defense system, the reduction of a sense that there is anything of value that can be taken from me, or that what I am is really subject to anything in the outside world, brings with it a tremendous relief from the imagined suffering that comes from the illusion that I am a body, and that I can be attacked if you don't agree or you don't like me When that begins to diminish, the suffering induced by that is seen as really the result of imagination and a mis-formulation about the mystery of what is happening. It is clear, I think, that all of the traditions wish for a reduction in suffering. As a practical matter, clearly, when people suffer, they squirm around trying to get out of it and, will either attack themselves or somebody else or their environment, because there is pain. So, a reduction of pain leads to a lot more quiet, and when things are more quiet, it seems as if whatever is coming to us from behind the scenes, or higher above, is able to find a more appropriate manifestation that is not filtered by all this squirming and trying to get out of difficult situations. So, the elevation of self-calming, as a major impediment, plays a very large role in Gurdjieff's thinking and presentation; that to aim to make ourselves comfortable, in the moment, is not the aim because that would, of necessity, quell the voice of conscience, would reduce my openness to seeing contradictions within myself, or my negative impact on other people.

The discomfort that has come for me, personally, over the years of seeing those (contradictions), seeing what happens when the buffers fall down and seeing these parts of myself that I would not wish to be there, that also is based on an image. Now, I carried a blueprint that I should be a certain type of person and when I saw internal or external manifestations that did not conform to this blueprint, there was suffering. But, where did the blueprint come from? It is quite arbitrary. There were other times of my life when I forgot about the positive blueprint and I was reading off the negative blueprint... so there wasn't anything good in me and if I got a compliment I would not hear it or I would think the person was teasing me. Having these two, the positive and negative image, come together gives a much greater picture of the whole, but it is all a conditioned whole. It is really all imaginary.

All & Everything Conference 2010

What do I really know about myself? Well, I live inside of this (gestures towards the body). I don't know how it works. I don't know how this happens (raises arm). I don't know how the voice comes out. I don't know where the thoughts are coming from. I have no idea what 'he' (speaker gestures towards himself) is going to say next.

How can I tolerate that if I am concerned for making this apparatus have a certain appearance for a certain effect? So, being able to dis-identify whatever I am from all of that, does bring many more degrees of freedom, maybe operating under fewer 'laws' as Gurdjieff also phrases it.

Participant 2: "I", the image, I found very dramatic that you painted about this frightened child living in this flat world, not being able to see and recognize things happening from another level and being afraid of losing himself because he feels obliged to defend everything he sees happening on this flat level. This is a very dramatic image and one I think that we can recognize. Now, it seems that real balance, real equilibrium, cannot occur unless somebody frees himself from this picture, becomes aware of a higher level or of higher levels, and in that way eases the blame of him having to deal with everything he sees in front of him. I understand this. I have a question on that. You are a psychotherapist. Surely therapy must have to do with finding some sort of balance. To what extent does this image, the image of this particular balance, of being balanced because of recognition of higher levels, to what extent would this image enter your practice? Does it affect your practice at all?

Stephen Aronson: One of the core issues for all of us is the discovery of what we are truly responsible for and how we have been operating under illusions of what we thought we were responsible for, that we are not. So, with most of the people I work with, who are very normal people, like everyone in this room, but they come with a certain tension, primarily because of this imbalance, a misunderstanding of where responsibility actually lies, and, either feeling that we are responsible for things outside of us, or even things we've inherited, that are not true. There is a lack of understanding about what inside myself I can, should, actually be responsible for. Feelings of blame and guilt and shame, I see as an extraordinarily unhelpful and crippling introduction from external morality.

The issue is real responsibility. I see there is something in me that is not developed appropriately. All right. That, perhaps is my responsibility to attend to. What do I wish to do about it? But, am I to accept that I am also responsible for 'something' in someone else, who is telling me that they believe I am responsible for the feelings and reactions they are experiencing inside them? If I believe them, this now gets me feeling badly about myself, because this other person has convinced me I am the cause of, and must take responsibility for, their thoughts and feelings so they need not take responsibility for themselves. There is this sense, for everyone, that the fluctuations in my inner world appear to be the result of events out there (gestures towards the world around). Someone says one thing instead of another, something unexpected happens instead of something else. There is a reaction in here (gestures towards body), and it looks as if, and feels as if, I am being tugged and pulled in here, by things moving around out there. What I don't see is that the reaction in here, is in here. It doesn't have to be that reaction to this event. The event, itself, is not responsible. The event is a stimulus that triggers a response in me, but, if that conditioned response were not already in me, this particular event, would not elicit that particular response.

It is very tricky because many people who have concerns about themselves already feel guilty or insufficient in some way, so to say, "Look, your feeling of inadequacy is your responsibility," could easily get translated by that person, to themselves, as: "I knew I was right about deficiencies. I really am no good." So, sufficient groundwork has to be laid to first distinguish where this pattern of self assessment and reaction came from, and to recognize that I am not personally responsible for being born into a certain family, at a certain time in history, in a certain political situation, with a certain religious orientation, that is Itoklanoz. Everybody is dealt a deck of cards. That is what you got. You didn't ask for them, but that is the hand you have to play. That's not our fault. How we play it does become our responsibility. What our interest in finding a sacred tradition may, in part, be about is our sense that there may be an extra card or two lying around that I've missed and it could make a big difference. There is something more going on than just this apparent 'reality' I've come to accept as myself and my life. Is that an adequate response?

Participant 3: You have spoken of two appropriate attitudes in two directions: faith, hope directed upwards and compassion addressed to the lower parts of reality, and this attitude implies sort of a classical, philosophical tolerance, acceptance, self-pacifying. If we have this attitude, then we understand, and understanding becomes sort of a key to solving all problems. My question is, do you see a role of Will, of effort, overcoming, or, do you suggest, in a psycho-therapeutical way, of pacifying our place, our relationship with outer and inner world; by pacifying this, we can mature, we can grow, we can reach the level of freedom? So, where is the Will, will-power? How does it works in your scheme of understanding?

Stephen Aronson: The question is about Will. This grows more and more mysterious the more there is an impression of catching a glimpse of it in the peripheral vision. What is that? There is something, something, but it really seems intangible. One of the things that really interest me is that all the effort and the writings and in the life of many of the groups I have been in, for a long, long time, "Effort, effort!" Gurdjieff talks about "super-effort," about creating friction. And, all this in retrospect was colossally helpful in many, many ways. It helped develop a "something" that could hold itself together for a little while in the face of what would, otherwise, have been very distracting and would have dispersed it. So, whatever that is, seems somewhat like a muscle that can begin to strengthen if it tries not to express negativity or makes an attempt to remember itself whenever it passes through a doorway or tries to not identify with something. Where would this effort come from, if not Will? It's not part of life. It's not part of anything the culture says is necessary, unless you want to try to be an athlete or develop a certain discipline to make money. It comes from inside and doesn't seem to serve any real purpose out here, unless you want to put it towards dominating the outer world in some way. So, there is all this effort.

In another way, I think that all this emphasis on effort like a Zen Koan. What is the sound of one hand clapping? What is the effect of trying to exercise 'my will' all these years? Virtually nothing!

What's going on here? So, could it also be, or it was for me whether Gurdjieff intended it or not, it got me to a point of intense frustration, self delusion that, with all my years of effort that, yes, sometimes I remember myself walking through a doorway and yes, I could hold negativity in and I was learning a lot about it, but I couldn't stay awake. Why can't I stay awake? And, then the thought occurred to me, "Maybe it doesn't work that way! Maybe, I can't make myself stay awake!" Maybe there really is something else that rises and falls, carries "me" up and carries "me" down, as it flows through me from whatever dimension it originates. But, perhaps all these efforts have opened me, quieted the interior, sensitized the sense of the body, thereby delineating the psychic experience from the physicality. With greater quietness and sensitivity there is more awareness of the rise and fall of this something. Perhaps the fall isn't as deep. Perhaps the crests last a little longer.

And then, in the kind of experience I am attempting to point to in the end here, there is a very different kind of strange and subtle change where it is almost as if one needs the Will to not to try to exercise Will. For instance, if we are really to study ourselves, we must allow our ordinary self to be its ordinary self. Now, after all these years of learning to have a certain Work posture and language and really be on guard, which did require a lot self remembering,........ what now? Is that the Aim? What does it take to be aware inside and watch the voice and the body and the personality manifest in ways that would not be according to the 'higher script' that one would write if one were actually, already, what one wished to be? How to be present and not interfere with manifestations, to trust the state of Presence sufficiently that the quality that will emerge will be a reflection of that State, and that anything I would call "my" will is at a lower level and would only get in the way? To just "let it run", but be present to it. To trust that the seeing of it, in itself, that the 'presence', in itself, produces the change. "I" don't change anything, but change occurs because of the quality of whatever this energy of 'presence' is. So, if the effort is towards that State, in the moment, then there need be little to no concern about the outer manifestation. And, that is a very different kind of "Will" for me, to try and keep my hands off the steering wheel of this apparatus of personality and watch it.

Participant 4: You referred to one of the qualities of the egoism to be a thief and a thief without arms is unthinkable. The arms I can see in my life is the thinking apparatus running by itself. What seems to be necessary for me is to recognize this sensitivity which is available for just seeing and through seeing I would mainly look for two things: and that is the motivation for that thinking and the consequences of that thinking. My question was, what emphasis would you put on just watching? And you just answered that.

Stephen Aronson: It is so difficult to try to watch thought, an image, because it is so magnetic. Almost from the moment the attention says, "I can look at this without loosing myself," (snaps finger), it is gone. But, the continued effort is so enormously important, and in my experience, I see the attention is like a little balloon. Thinking and motion and imaging are like the wind and so they just blow this little balloon all over. Unfortunately, I am my attention, or seem to be mostly my attention. Wherever the attention is, there I am. So, if this balloon can be tethered, if it can be tied to something that won't blow around, maybe it won't blow so far away so often. Here is where I have found the practice of sensing the body to be invaluable. The body is like a tree. It doesn't blow around. It is right here. So, if I can practice anchoring part of my attention into the sensation of the physical body, then it is a little easier for short times to see when a thought comes in and says, "Come with me." If I can feel the body at that moment, I can respond, "I don't think so," and look past it. For years I read literature that said thoughts are like clouds floating through the sky.... and they are! They really are. My wife and I were sitting on the balcony. We were sitting in our bodies on the balcony and here is the water and the mountains on the other side and we can see, between our body and the mountains, thoughts floating through, and images and associations going back and forth. For short moments, one can see all three layers. It would be wonderful to live that way, but being able to be in that state with some frequency is marvellous beyond expectation. But, it is the thought that produces the "reality." There is just the mountain. There is just my body here. It is the thought that says, "You ought to be reading something." It is the thought that says, "You don't deserve to be here." It is the thought that says, "You paid a lot too much for that rental car." That is what produces my "reality." It is the thought. The thoughts are thieves. I have the right to think the thoughts I want to think when I want to think them. It's not right that I should have to be pick pocketed constantly by these thieving thoughts that come through. But, I have to start by recognizing that that is the case. I would rather it won't be, but that is the hand we have been given. That's where I have to start, but it is not hopeless and persistence begins to show results. Then, instead of being frustrating, it becomes really interesting. The more one sees, the less one understands. It is quite paradoxical. Now that I actually have no idea who or what I am, I feel terrific. (Laughter) The less I know, the dumber I am, the more interesting things are.

Participant 5: Concerning forgivefullness, I think you said, "God is forgiving. Forgivefullness is even law." Can you enlarge on that please? I am wondering who is in charge.

Stephen Aronson: Gurdjieff said that, I didn't say that. I was quoting him. The quote, I believe was, "God forgives everything. This has even become a Law of the World." [p. 198] So, you would have to address that to Mr. Gurdjieff. We can talk about it, but I can't speak for him or for God.

It is absolutely clear to me that if I have a grievance, I am in prison. Even if I can get a jury of my peers to agree my grievance is legitimate, even if I can get a court to say that judgement should be for me, it doesn't matter. I am still a prisoner of my grievance, because until I get paid what I think I am owed, I am unsatisfied. So, my debtor actually ends up being my prison guard and I wind up in a prison of my creation because I've given my debtor the power to hold me captive, to hold my attention captive, with all the emotional arousal that is stimulated by fixing my attention on this grievance. I cannot, and I will not move on until I am paid. Why should I go out and work if you owe me a lot of money and the check is supposed to arrive in the mail? I'm not going to go get a job. I am going to sit by the mailbox every day because as soon as your check arrives, I can retire! And, I'll be damned if I am going to go out and get a low paying job when all that money is due me. But, what has happened to my life? It would make much more sense to say, "Well, it's probably not coming. It would be nice if it did. Silly me, I should not have loaned him the money.

I had better go get a job, because those are the cards I hold in my hand. Everything else is thinking and imagination. As soon as I write it off, I am free. But, I have to really write it off. I can't just say it. I have to believe it. I have to realize I am helpless. I cannot make that check appear in the mail. I can't do anything about it, whether it is right or not. In some cases, standing on my sense of justification makes it much worse for me because then it is just harder to back down. So, I don't know about God but, if I forgive, I am better off.

The Structure of Laws

Dimitri Peretzi

Abstract

The powerful image of the hierarchy of the Worlds in the Ray of Creation that appears in Ouspensky's *In Search of the Miraculous* poses a number of questions in relation to the various formulations of a number of Laws given in quite an exact way by Gurdjieff in the *Tales*. Is there a relation between the two presentations? How are we to view the connection with the Laws in the *Tales* with those in the Cosmoses? How does the concept of the "First and Second conscious shocks" fit with the structure of the Laws described in the *Tales*? The basis of this study revolves around the investigation of relation between Microcosms and Tetartocosmoses. Its aim is, not only to connect the two presentations, the one found in the *Tales* with the one articulated by Ouspensky, but to also connect these formulations with practical observations about the Work.

The Structure of the Laws Presented in the *Tales*

Slide # 1

> **A&E Conference 2010**
>
> **The Structure of the Laws
> Presented in the Tales**

The presentation today aims to make a specific point. The intent is to show that,

All & Everything Conference 2010

Slide # 2

> The Laws of Three and Seven can be viewed as Laws of Perception.
>
> That is, beyond those two basic Laws being Laws of the World,
>
> They are Laws of how human beings perceive the World.
>
> And this makes them to be Laws of Perception
>
> It makes them, that is, Laws by which Human Perception works
>
> This is one of the important points reached at in the *Tales*, one that is necessary to…
>
> 1. Connect the Work ideas with current science
> 2. Understand the Work and how to Work in a practical manner
> 3. Understand what is meant by "Man becoming God"

The question has been brought up many times, why it is that Gurdjieff never mentioned the enneagram in the *Tales*. Was it because he didn't think it to be important enough? This is certainly not so. The truth is quite contrary.

Indeed the fact is that Gurdjieff never ceased to talk about the enneagram. Through the period he was writing the *Tales*, as well as up to the end of his life, he composed several multiplication movements. Multiplication makes no sense, of course, without the structure of the enneagram behind it.

He also had people often construct enneagrams with varying materials. At least one of them, about three feet in diameter, made out of the fur of different animals, still hangs on the wall of the living room in his apartment.

Stanley Nott in his memoirs explicitly states that Gurdjieff made constant references to the Law of three, to the Law of seven and to the enneagram, and to the fact that the keys to their understanding are to be found in the *Tales* (p. 119 in the Greek text).

To support the view that Gurdjieff believes the study of the enneagram to be of great importance, let me quote from Purgatory:

The Structure of the Laws Presented in the Tales

Slide # 3

> I repeat my boy: Try very hard to understand everything that will relate to both these fundamental cosmic sacred laws, since knowledge of these sacred laws … will help you in the future to understand very easily and very well all the second-grade and third-grade laws of World-creation and World-existence … Likewise, an all-round awareness of everything concerning these sacred laws also conduces to this … that the three brained beings … acquire data for the elucidation and reconciliation in themselves of that … "individual collision" which often arises in three-brained beings from the contradiction between the concrete results flowing from the processes of all the cosmic laws and the results … expected by their "sane logic"; and thus … they become capable of … impartiality.
> *(Purgatory, pp755-756)*

I fact it seems that the enneagram can be found "hidden", so to speak, in many spots in the book, to the point that one may begin wondering, whether the "dog" Gurdjieff said that is "buried" in its pages is the enneagram. One may end up wandering whether the enneagram is buried there, not in just one place, but all over the text of "All and Everything".

One such place has to do with the enneagram structure of the Laws presented in the chapter on Purgatory, which I shall use here as an example of how we might think of the use of the enneagram in the *Tales*.

Gurdjieff is quite specific in the *Tales* when he refers to the various Laws. In his narration he mentions Laws of Physics (like "*the law of gravity*"), but he also mentions laws that sound like laws of "psychology" (like the "*law of the flow of associative movements*") or others that sound like laws of the "social sciences" (like the "*law of the aggregation of the homogeneous*").

Slide # 4

Laws specified by Name	**Laws given through a description**
Examples: • Litsvrtsi • Aieioiouoa • Retarnotoltoor • Harnel-Miatznel … • Triamazikamno • Heptaparaparshinokh	• "The Law of the balance of vibrations" • "The Law of the affinity of the total of the vibrations" • "The Law of the flow of associative movements"

All & Everything Conference 2010

Some of those laws he specifies by name, for others he just gives a description.

Slide # 5

Laws that are referred to by just one name	Laws referred to by more than one name
Examples: • Litsvrtsi • Harnel-Miatznel and most others	For the so-called "Law of Three" • Triamazikamno • Law of the Holy Trinity • Law of Three For the so-called "Law of Seven" • Heptaparaparshinokh • Law of Seven • Law of Nine For the Law of "*law by which planetary bodies decompose*" • Again-Tarnotoltoor • Retarnotoltoor
	The two phenomena referred to by the same name of Aieioiouoa
• Light-of-day (Darkness-of-night) • Remorse-of-Conscience	

Some laws he refers to by just one name, for others Gurdjieff uses two or more names. And there is at least one case when he refers to several phenomena as being the result of the same law: By the same name, Aieioiuoa, he seems to refer to three different laws: that of the creation of light, of darkness and of remorse. And as it was discussed in a previous conference, one can think of this as a "lawful in exactitude", by which a number of interesting aspects about one's Work on himself are revealed.

And here we come up against a real question. Do the *Tales* include, not just theories about the world, but also real practical advice about the Work, about how is one to Work?

Slide # 6

Another interesting differentiation made in the *Tales* is that the Laws presented fit in one of three categories, they belong to one of three levels or "grades". There are the two "fundamental" or "primordial" Laws, that of Triamazikamno and of Heptaparaparshinokh…

The Structure of the Laws Presented in the Tales

Then there is a number of Laws that are mentioned as "Second Order Laws"…

And there's a number of Laws of unspecified order, which we can assume to be of a grade lower than both the primordial and the second order ones.

Slide # 7

Second Order Laws			
#	Name of Law	Chapter	§
1	Aieioiouoa	17 / 22	0810
2	Tenikdoa	39	3810
3	Aggregation of the homogeneous (Litsvrtsi)	39	3955
4	Mutual attraction of the similar	39	3964
5	Retarnotoltoor	39	4000
6	Harnel-Miatznel	39	4076
7	Attraction-and-fusion-of-similarities	39	4069
8	Tetetzender	39	4132
9	Urdekhplifata	39	4140

The Second Order Laws that Gurdjieff mentions in the *Tales* are shown in this table. They are placed here in the order in which they appear in the text (first column). In ***this*** next column we have the name he gives to the law, in ***this*** we see the chapter and in ***this*** the paragraph in which each appears.

The fact that there are nine of these Laws, coupled with the fact that almost all of them appear in Chapter 39 (Purgatory), in a unified, dense narrative, clearly suggests that Gurdjieff intended to present in this instance a strong, coherent image. And of course, since the number of those laws is nine, the mind immediately goes to the enneagram.

> Are these laws to be thought of as composing an enneagram?
>
> Can they be placed on the enneagram?
>
> And what would be the meaning of that?

Before we attempt anything, let us first have a closer look at these nine laws:

All & Everything Conference 2010

Slide # 8

The Table of Second Order Laws

	A	B	C	D	E	F
1	Litsvrtsi Ch. 39 § 3955	**Aggregation of the homogeneous** Sexual attraction and Procreation.	Forces generated in the species, by Man	T (3)	**T**	T
2	No Name Ch. 39 § 3964	**Mutual attraction of the Similar** (the law according to which microcosmoses concentrate into Tetartocosmoses)	Forces that are generated within the wider spectrum of Organic Life	T (6)	**T**	T
3	No Name Ch. 39 § 4069	**Attraction-and-Fusion-of-Similarities** Possibility of acquiring certain active elements automatically	Forces that are implanted from above, to secure the development of higher being bodies, even independently from the individual's efforts	T (9)	**T**	T
4	Aieioiouoa Ch. 17 § 816 (and two other places)	**Remorse** Light	Law of yearning to develop… which gives a… …sense of direction and meaning in life	1	**1**	1
5	Tenikdoa Ch. 38 § 3810	**"Sometimes called the "law of gravity""**	Laws of Physics or of the Physical World (In a general way)	2	**2**	4
6	Retarnotoltoor Ch. 39 § 4000	Disintegration Decomposition	Inevitability of Death Death as the Provider of Meaning The monks' Skull and Bones	3	**4**	2
7	Harnel-Miatznel Ch. 39 § 4076	**"Mixture and Fusion according to the "affinity o vibrations"** **The higher blends with the lower to actualize the middle**	Digestion, Assimilation, the alchemical processes of both bodily growth and esoteric growth, growth of higher being bodies	4	**5**	8
8	Tetetzender Ch. 39 § 4132	The grievous phenomenon Add what is needed	The Work as Organic Need. One has to move to "Planet Purgatory", as it were	5	**7**	5
9	Urdekhplifata Ch. 39 § 4140		Good old personality never dies	6	**8**	7

The Structure of the Laws Presented in the Tales

This Table shows that three of these laws are given through an almost identical description (attraction of the similar). The remaining six are placed on this table in the order that they appear in the text.

Column A: Name of the Law and location in the text
Column B: The way the Law is defined in the text and the sense it makes
C: Its possible meaning in everyday terms and understanding
D: Placement of the Six Laws by the order of their appearance in the text
E: …by their placement on the enneagram (coincides with the order of their appearance in the text and it makes the most sense when their meaning is examined in the order they form when arranged as 142857)
F: …their order, assuming that they were presented by the order of 142857

	A	B	C	D	E	F
1	Litsvrtsi Ch. 39 § 3955	**Aggregation of the homogeneous** (thanks to this law there began to be grouped on the planets themselves, from the mentioned "relatively independent" new formations named "similarities-to-the-already-arisen, yet other also "relatively independent" formations.[1]	Sexual attraction and Procreation. Eros Love Basic Urge	T (3)	T	T
2	No Name Ch. 39 § 3964	**Mutual attraction of the Similar** (the law according to which microcosmoses concentrate into Tetartocosmoses)	From Microcosmoses to Tetartocosmoses Forces that hold the organism together, that make cells cooperate	T (6)	T	T
3	No Name Ch. 39 § 4069	**Attraction-and-Fusion-of-Similarities** (according to this law it is possible for certain active elements to arise automatically [and not only through the conscious intention of some individual] and, according to what form of functioning of the fifth Stopinder of the Sacred Hepta… was flowing during their arising are actualized certain subjective properties and their what are called "proportions of vivifyingness")	Possibility of acquiring certain active elements automatically We are talking about the creation of substances that are necessary to create substances of "another Okhtapanatsakhnian class" through Harnel-Miatznel.	T (9)	T	T
4	Aieioiouoa Ch. 17 § 816	Remorse Light	Urge-Force to develop Sense of direction Meaning of action	1	**1**	1

[1] Note that he seems to define "feeding" as a process, not as a law ("Iraniranumange")

5	Tenikdoa Ch. 38 § 3810	"Sometimes called the "law of gravity"" In consequence of the fact that the body Kesdjan of the being is coated with those substances which in their totality make this cosmic formation much lighter than the mass of cosmic substances which surrounds the planets and is called the planetary atmosphere, then, as soon as the body Kesdjan of the being is separated from the planetary body of the being, it at once rises according to the cosmic law called "Tenikdoa", or as it is sometimes called the "law of gravity"…	Law serving for a formation to find its place within the context of physical laws and conditions	2	**2**	4
6	Retarnotoltoor Ch. 39 § 4000	Disintegration	Decomposition Inevitability of Death Death as the Provider of Meaning The monks' Skull and Bones	3	**4**	2
7	Harnel-Miatznel Ch. 39 § 4076	"Mixture and Fusion according to the "affinity o vibrations" **The higher blends with the lower to actualize the middle** Note the relationship of Harnel-Miatznel with the law of the Attraction-and-Fusion-of-Similarities	Digestion, Assimilation, the alchemical processes of both bodily growth and esoteric growth, growth of higher being bodies	4	**5**	8
8	Tetetzender Ch. 39 § 4132	The grievous phenomenon	The Work as Organic Need. One has to move to "Planet Purgatory", as it were	5	**7**	5
9	Urdekhplifata Ch. 39 § 4140		Good old personality never dies	6	**8**	7

By accepting that the first three refer to laws that give rise to three forces interacting with each other and that the other six refer to laws that give rise to six processes, we can attempt to put these concepts on the enneagram.

This is one way of doing it:

Slide # 9

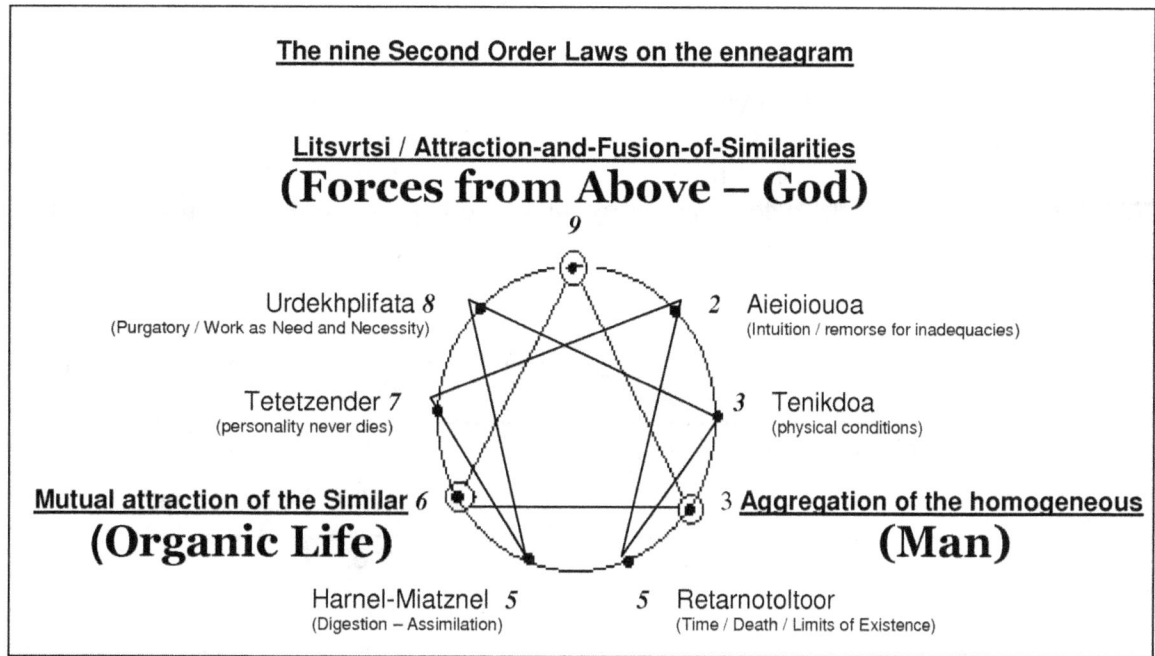

Did actually Gurdjieff mean these Laws to be read as an enneagram? A study of what each Law represents shows that we have every reason to believe so. And the fact is that if one chooses to see them structured by the enneagram, many interesting relationships are revealed to exist among them.

About this enneagram:

Firstly, on the nine points on the circle are placed the only nine "second order laws" that Gurdjieff mentions in the *Tales*. These laws are not scattered; all except one appear together in chapter 39. So we have every reason to assume that he was very much aware of naming "nine second order laws" and that by doing so he wanted to say something.

The next issue has to do with determining the three main forces. Here, in places (3, 6, 9) there have been inserted the notions of "man", "organic life" and "god", as three forces that correspond to the three Laws of the "aggregation of the homogeneous". This has come about from the way Gurdjieff describes the three laws. They seem to constitute three forces (or wills), that are very similar, and yet distinctly different from each other. We can see this by the way Gurdjieff speaks about them:

Let me make a note at this point: We can go a long way into discussing these three Laws and why they are to be placed at points (3, 6, 9). There is also much to be said about the specifics of this enneagram. Maybe there's a need to go deeper into all these, and we might do that at the end of

39

the talk, if there is the interest. But, perhaps we should not spend too much time on it now, so as not to lose the overall picture, which has to do with the general structure of the Laws in the *Tales*.

The next issue has to do with determining the location of the six laws. Where exactly shall we place on the enneagram Aieioiouoa, Tenikdoa, Retarnotoltoor, Harnel-Miatznel, Tetentzender and Urdekhplifata? That issue seems to have an easy answer. The way they have been placed here at points 1, 2, 4, 5, 7, 8 follows the exact order by which Gurdjieff gives them in the *Tales,* and we know of the determination by which he kept this order in things related to the "multiplication" in the movements:

Slide # 10

The sequence 142857 in the Multiplications			
Multiplication by	…results in…	This starts the sequence at the	…which happens to be…
1	142857	1st digit of the esoteric flow	1
2	285741	2nd digit of the esoteric flow	2
3	412857	3rd digit of the esoteric flow	4
4	574128	4th digit of the esoteric flow	5
5	741285	5th digit of the esoteric flow	7
6	857412	6th digit of the esoteric flow	8

Multiplication by 1 results in 142857 and this starts the sequence at the first digit, which happens to be "1".
Multiplication by 2 results in 285714 and this starts the sequence at the second digit, which happens to be "2".
Multiplication by 3 results in 428571 and this starts the sequence at the third digit, which happens to be "4".
Multiplication by 4 results in 571428 and this starts the sequence at the fourth etc.

The Structure of the Laws Presented in the Tales

So we have strong reason to place these nine laws onto the enneagram in the way and in the sequence in which they were shown.

Slide # 11

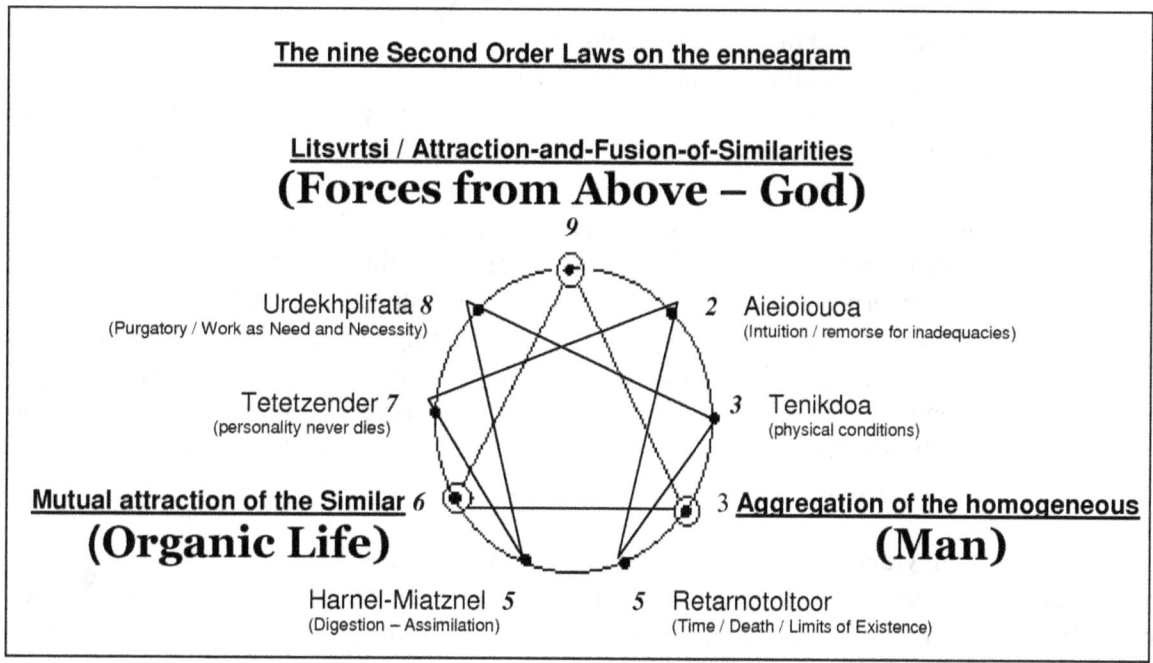

There are interesting results to be had by investigating this enneagram under the light of the "Law of Relativity", to investigate, in other words, the way this enneagram can relate to practical advice about the Work and the way the Work proceeds with man:

(A) <u>**The sequence 124578 of the outer circle**</u> follows the flow of linear time, the sequence of realization of the meaning of Work:

Work starts at point 1. It starts through intuition, through the remorse felt "for things not being as they should be with me". This is best exemplified in the *Tales* by Belcultassi (check) and by the conditions that end up with the institution of the society Akhaldan. It is remorse that starts the process…
…in the physical world…
…the realization of the inevitability of death and the time limitations of life…
…the realization of the importance of the food diagram…
…of struggle with personality that never really dies…
…but continues if and when it has become a need.

This can be said to be the "exoteric" deployment and development of the Work.

(B) The sequence 142857 of the inner circle refers to the esoteric development of the Work, and here we can point out some major issues in the Work, such as the relationship between,
- Remorse about how one lives his life in relation to the Limits of his Existence,
- The Limits of Existence in relation to Physical Conditions,
- Physical Conditions in relation to the possibility of Work,
- The Work in relation to the Food Diagram,
- The need for food in relation to the development of Personality
- Personality and Remorse, an area in which we can detect the possibility of studying the idea of neurosis and of mental balance.

Of course, we cannot forget that all of this is presented in Chapter 39, the one on "Purgatory". The whole of this chapter reads like some kind of "map" for the Work. And the axis of this presentation, the one incorporated in this structure is one of Gurdjieff's most basic ideas: That the whole of Existence is inexorably linked to Work, to developing consciousness and to the process of forming Higher Being-Bodies. In the general economy of the Universe, *Being and Working are closely connected*, and, in fact, ***Working is the Meaning of Being***. All images in the *Tales* are to be understood in relation to the Work. This is, in all probability, the most basic key to the text, and it is clearly reflected on the structure of this enneagram.

What is interesting in viewing these ideas through the enneagram is how
practical their study becomes. One can use them for his Work and for structuring the Work of a group. This enneagram contains information, how the flow of group exercises and effort can proceed.

So this enneagram is like a "dog buried", to be found by the reader and used appropriately.

There are many dogs buried in the *Tales*, I believe.
- One of them is the little big secret about who are the Germans, of whom Beelzebub tells Hassein "a wee bit more" in chapter 36.
- Another one is Aieioiuoa, and the lawful inexactitude by which it is defined as remorse-of-conscience in one chapter, as the light-of-day in another, but also as the darkness-of-the-night in yet a third one.
- Another one is the enneagram above, the one that involves the second order laws and, in actuality says that "Being is Working", or gives a universal dimension to the principle of relativity.

The fact that Gurdjieff mentions nothing about the enneagram in the *Tales* is yet another "inexactitude", to say the least. How is one to take the fact that in his book entitled "All and Everything" he does not mention once the symbol to which he gives such a central place in his teaching?
To understand in what way this "inexactitude" is a "lawful" one, this must certainly have something to do with one of the big dogs buried in the *Tales*.

The Structure of the Laws Presented in the Tales

This "Purgatory Enneagram" is not the only enneagram we can trace in the text of the *Tales*.

We can structure around the enneagram the contents of chapter 40, the one on Heptaparaparshinokh. The breakdown of the three octaves there, "opium", "light", "sound", is spelled out in every detail and this facilitates the application.

One can be certain that there other places in the *Tales*, as well, where Gurdjieff intended to make a statement through the use of a hidden enneagram structure.

Keith Buzzell addressed the issue of the enneagram in the *Tales* in his talk "The Enneagrammatic Structure of the *Tales*", which he presented in one of the early conferences. His view is that the very structure of the *Tales* is enneagrammatic in form, the symbol to be found in many different aspects and many different spots within the text.

Such thoughts pose questions.

Slide # 12

- Is the relationship between the enneagrams that are to be found in the *Tales*, themselves, structured in some way?
- Is there in the *Tales* a top enneagram, a main enneagram, to which all other enneagrams somehow fit?
- Is the relationship between the enneagrams to be found in the *Tales*, themselves, structured in some way?
- Is there in the *Tales* a top enneagram, a main enneagram, to which all other enneagrams somehow fit?

Slide # 13

Enneagrammatic structure of the Ray of Creation

Enneagrams within Enneagrams

(Drawing of Nathan Bernier – from "The Enneagram, Symbol of All & Everything")

The thought is not extravagant. In the image of the Ray of Creation, there is the structure of the Worlds 1, 3, 6, 12, 24, 48 and World 96, the last one, 96, being the one our mechanical society lives in. Since the Worlds are somehow connected, every event is connected to all other events. The existence of the "lateral octaves" gives us the image of the world being composed of a mesh of energy flows: the lateral octaves act as shocks to the events flowing in the linear time of our everyday understanding. Things happen at the points where the shocks are applied, and they always happen according to the Law of Triamazikamno and Heptaparaparshinokh. That is,

All & Everything Conference 2010

enneagrams appear at the points where lateral octaves meet with the octaves of linear time. This is the mesh that gives rise to the image of enneagrams within enneagrams.

So, is there in the *Tales* a top enneagram, a main enneagram, to which all other enneagrams somehow fit?

Slide # 14

- The story of the Beelzebub's six visits to Earth ("**six visits**")
- The story of Beelzebub's exile ("**exile**")
- The story of Creation of Trogoautoegocrat ("**creation**")

The way these three stories are presented in the *Tales*, one can be viewed to be within the other. They are like the basic containers of the narrative; they are like "stories within stories". Each story is an enneagram in itself, as all stories are. So these stories form "enneagrams within enneagrams". They refer to a hierarchy of "worlds within worlds".

Slide # 15

Story (enneagram)	Ray of Creation	Corresponding Triad	
Six Visits On Earth	World # 6	1. Narrator 2. Listener 3. Third Force	Beelzebub Hassein (Me) Ahoon
Beelzebub's Exile	World # 3	1. Narrator 2. Listener 3. Third Force	Gurdjieff The Reader (Me) Mullah Nasrudin
Story of Creation (Trogoautoegocrat)	World # 1	1. Narrator 2. Listener 3. Third Force	God Man -Tetartocosmos (Me) Work

Assertion	All ideas of the Fourth Way must be verified	The action of Triamazikamno and Heptaparaparshinokh is to be found in everything	The Principle of Relativity, which boils down to "*Working is the Meaning of Being*"
But...	How can one verify ideas such as these?	How can one verify the action of these Laws at the level of World # 1, 3 and 6?	In what way are these particular ideas of practical use for one's Work?

The whole of Beelzebub's narrative about how he acquired his knowledge of the human affairs is structured around his six visits onto Earth and his use of Tescooano. Gurdjieff is using the succession of six events, which is certainly connected to the structure an enneagram.

Here, Beelzebub is narrating the story to Hassein, and he addresses Ahoon, as the Third Force, to verify his points. This narrative would correspond to World number 6.

The story of Beelzebub's six visits is contained within the story of Beelzebub himself, of how he was exiled and is now returning to the planet of his origin. This is clearly an allegory for the fate of Man, how he is exiled from the bosom of the Father, with a mandate: to spend a useful life on Mars as an observer, so as to deserve his return home. As an independent narration, this sequence can be viewed as an octave (or as three octaves), and that can be mapped on an enneagram, also.

Here, it is Gurdjieff who is narrating the story directly to the reader, with constant references to Mullah Nasrudin as the Third Force, to verify his points. This "higher", so to speak, narrative, would correspond to World number 3.

And this narration is contained within another one, the one that involves Creation, OUR ENDLESSNESS and HIS objectives when he created the World, and the Laws by which it is maintained. Beelzebub and his existence are a result of this divine action. All these enneagrams are connected according to the way they belong to different worlds, according to the hierarchy of those worlds, as this hierarchy is expressed by the Ray of Creation.

The knowledge of this story can only come through revelatory means. Only God can be said to know this story, only He can reveal it to Man. The only means of verification Man has is the Work, which acts here as the Third Force. This is a way for us to look at World number 1,

At the same time, these correspondences have to be viewed under the light of the assertions Gurdjieff makes, that,

- Everything related to the Fourth Way ideas must be verified. *The question here is, how can one verify such ideas?*
- The action of the primordial Laws Triamazikamno and Heptaparaparshinokh, the action of the Enneagram that is, is to be found in everything and in anything. *But how can I verify that this is so on the level of World 1, 3, 6?*
- The Principle of Relativity exemplified by the enneagram shown before, which boils down to "**Working is the Meaning of Being**". *The big question here is, in what way are these ideas of practical use to one, to his Work?*

The answer to all these questions, I believe, is yet another "buried dog", the "dog" that is hidden in another of Gurdjieff's assertions:

Slide # 16

> Of all the things those unfortunates know about the world, they do not even suspect that the one that is closest to reality is that each of them is an exact image of OUR ENDLESSNESS".

Of all the things those unfortunates know about the world, they do not even suspect that the one that is closest to reality is that each of them is an exact image of OUR ENDLESSNESS".

The key to approach the meaning of this, I believe, is the Ray of Creation, a form of which is given in "Purgatory" (§ 3960, 3961, 3962, 3963)

The Structure of the Laws Presented in the Tales

Slide # 17

Ray of Creation Presented in "Purgatory"		
Name of Cosmos	**Reference**	**World # Correspondence w. "Search"**
Protocosmos	Sun Absolute	World # 1
Defterocosmos	Second Order Suns	World # 3
Tritocosmos	Planets	World # 6
Microcosmos	Organic life	World # 12
Tetartocosmos	Man (Perfected Man)	World # 24

This is the image of the Ray of Creation in "Purgatory".

And when we view this in the light of the assertion that "Man is an exact image of God" and that "the difference between each Tetartocosmos and our common great Megalocosmos is only in scale" (§ 4026), this same Ray of Creation takes a similar form,

Slide # 18

Ray of Creation "Man is the image of God"		
Name of Cosmos	**Reference**	**World #**
Protocosmos	Sun Absolute Inside of me	World # 1
Defterocosmos	Second Order Suns Inside of me	World # 3
Tritocosmos	The world of Planets Inside of me	World # 6

Microcosmos	Organic life Inside of me	World # 12
Tetartocosmos (Man)	Man Me as man # 5	World # 24
Magnetic Centre	Man Me as man # 4	World # 48
Personality	Man Me as man #1, 2, 3	World # 96

We could call this the "Ray of Creation Inside Man".

But on the other hand, it is important to see that this is the only Ray of Creation that Man will ever know. This is his personal Ray of Creation, the one that passes through him, this ***is the Ray of Creation for him***. This is my Ray of Creation.

Slide # 19

Chapter, Paragraph	**Text**
9 491	…there then first arose just those biped "Tetartocosmoses" whom you a while ago called "slugs".
39 3963	…those formations… which also became concentrated on the planets, this time thanks to the second-order cosmic law called "mutual attraction of the similar", were named "Tetartocosmoses"
39 3970	The radiations issuing from the "Tetartocosmoses" they called "Hanbledzoin"
	Etc. etc. etc.

There can be no doubt that the word "Tetartocosmos" refers to individual human beings. Gurdjieff's repeatedly returns to the issue.

The Structure of the Laws Presented in the Tales

- …there then first arose just those biped "Tetartocosmoses" whom you a while ago called "slugs" (9.491).
- …those formations… which also became concentrated on the planets, this time thanks to the second-order cosmic law called "mutual attraction of the similar", were named "Tetartocosmoses" (39.3963).
- The radiations issuing from the "Tetartocosmoses" they called "Hanbledzoin" (39.3970).

To go back to the Diagram of the Ray of Creation,

Slide # 20

Ray of Creation		
Name of Cosmos	**Reference**	**World #**
Protocosmos	Sun Absolute	World # 1
Defterocosmos	Second Order Suns	World # 3
Tritocosmos	Planets	World # 6
Microcosmos	Organic life	World # 12
Tetartocosmos (Essence)	Man (Me as man # 5)	World # 24
Magnetic Centre	Man (Me as man # 4)	World # 48
Personality	Man (Me as man #1, 2, 3)	World # 96

The Ray of Creation does not just "pass through Tetartocosmos"
Tetartocosmos is not "Mankind" or some abstract, faceless "Man"

Man is Me. I am Man.
I am Tetartocosmos. I am the only Tetartocosmos I will ever know from the inside.
The *Ray of Creation* passes through *Me*.
My Ray of Creation, the only Ray of Creation I shall ever know, passes through Me.

This is my world. The only world that exists for me. The only world that exists.
I am idiot (the original sense of the word: *inhabitant of a private world*)
I am alone (monachos-monk). I am the only person that exists.
I am the only inhabitant of my world and there is no other world for me.
There is no other world
When I die, this world dies with me
To become God in this world, this is my practical Work.
I have to work to be perfect, just like God is perfect,

All & Everything Conference 2010

What is important about this seemingly familiar diagram is that the *Ray of Creation* is not just "one sequence" that comprises all the possible worlds, which is what readers of Ouspensky's *In Search of the Miraculous* often come to believe. The Ray of Creation does not just "pass through Tetartocosmos". Tetartocosmos is not "Mankind" or some abstract, faceless "Man".

"Man" is Me.

- I am Man.
- *I am Tetartocosmos*.
- I am the only Tetartocosmos I will ever really know.
- The *Ray of Creation* passes through *Me.* Through me, personally. It is my personal Ray of Creation, the one that connects me with God. I am in closer and more direct connection to God than to any other being. I am God, even though my consciousness is not free enough to experience it.
- My Ray of Creation, the only Ray of Creation I shall ever know, passes through Me.
- *This is my world*. The only world that exists for me. It is the only world that exists.
- *I am idiot* (the original sense of the word: *inhabitant of a private world*)
- *I am alone (monachos-monk)*. I am the only person that exists.
- *I am the only inhabitant of my world* and there is no other world for me.
- There is no other world
- When I die, this world dies with me
- *To become God in this world, this is my practical Work.*
- *I have to work to be perfect, just like God is perfect,*

Slide # 21

A direct result of this is that the Law of Three and the Law of Seven can be seen as Laws of Perception, as Laws of Human Perception:

- Everybody lives in his / her own "Ray of Creation"
- Everybody lives in his / her own World.
- Everything that happens in the World is what happens in my World.
- The World I see, everything I sense, I perceive, is lit through my own Ray of Creation.
- Everything that I can ever perceive happening is happening in my World.
- The Law of Three and the Law of Seven govern everything that is happening in the World; they govern everything that is happening in my World; they govern everything I perceive happening.
- The Law of Three and the Law of Seven are not Laws of things happening "out there" somewhere in the universe. It is Laws of things happening in my universe, Laws of how I perceive what is happening.

The Structure of the Laws Presented in the Tales

> - It is in this sense that the Laws of Three and Seven are Laws of Human Perception; they are laws of the way I perceive the World.
> - It is important that I experience this possibility, this dimension of being. It is important that I work toward this possibility.

Stanley Nott quotes Gurdjieff having said that "…he who studies a symbol and gets to understand it, he perceives the symbol within himself. All in the world is one and is governed by the same, uniform laws. The closest object for man to study is his own self".

Slide # 22

> Did Gurdjieff have any reason, not to have mentioned explicitly the enneagram in the *Tales*?

Was it for some reason that Gurdjieff never mentioned explicitly the enneagram in the *Tales*?

The answer I personally have to that is, yes. Gurdjieff did not want to give a description or an explicit account of the enneagram in the *Tales*. And the reason is that, if he did, he would have to say something about the enneagram's origins.

I believe that any comprehensive reference to the enneagram inevitably reveals its origins. And Gurdjieff did not want to have the origins of the enneagram revealed, at least not within his lifetime.

And I think that we are dealing with a major dog buried here.

Slide # 23

> The Enneagram

- The *Aggregation of the homogeneous*. Gurdjieff defines this as the law by which *there began to be grouped on the planets themselves, from the mentioned "relatively independent" new formations named "similarities-to-the-already-arisen, yet other also "relatively independent" formations*. Here we have the description of procreation, of people willing and being able to have offspring.

- The *Mutual attraction of the Similar*. Gurdjieff defines this as the law according to which *Microcosmoses group together to form Tetartocosmoses*, or by which independent cells are held together to form the human body. Here we have the will of being that defines organic life, the possibility to form complex beings with specialized parts, that is, organs.

- The *Attraction-and-Fusion-of-Similarities*. This is the law according to which *it is possible for certain active elements to arise automatically* [and this means, not exclusively through the conscious intention, efforts and intentional suffering of individuals] *and, according to what form of functioning of the fifth Stopinder of the Sacred Heptaparaparshinokh was flowing during their arising, are actualized certain subjective properties and their what are called "proportions of vivifyingness"*. What we have here is a law by which higher being bodies can develop, not only through the conscious efforts of individuals, but also through the automatic action of certain cosmic substances. This observation underlines the fact that development is a process favoured by the higher forces. Something high up in the hierarchy of the cosmoses wills the development of consciousness. When man works, he is in fact helping this process. Nevertheless, the process can be put into action by itself, at least to some extent, and this supports two more aspects of Gurdjieff's ideas - one, that there are "messengers sent from above" and two, that a hasnamuss may be in possession of a higher being body.

- As if Gurdjieff wanted to underline this fact, that higher being bodies can also develop through the automatic action of certain cosmic substances, he writes in chapter 40, "*How People Learned and Again Forgot About the Fundamental Cosmic Law of Heptaparaparshinokh*", (p.815), explicitly intending, as he says, *to clarify some seemingly unimportant details that are important for Hassein to understand the Law of Heptaparaparshinokh,*

Slide # 24

> …at the arising and the beginning of the formation of each one of them, there are always in their presence the germs of all possibilities for the crystallization … of corresponding being-data, which later, during responsible existence could serve for the engendering and functioning of objective-Reason…

The Structure of the Laws Presented in the Tales

Slide # 25 - Back to the Enneagram

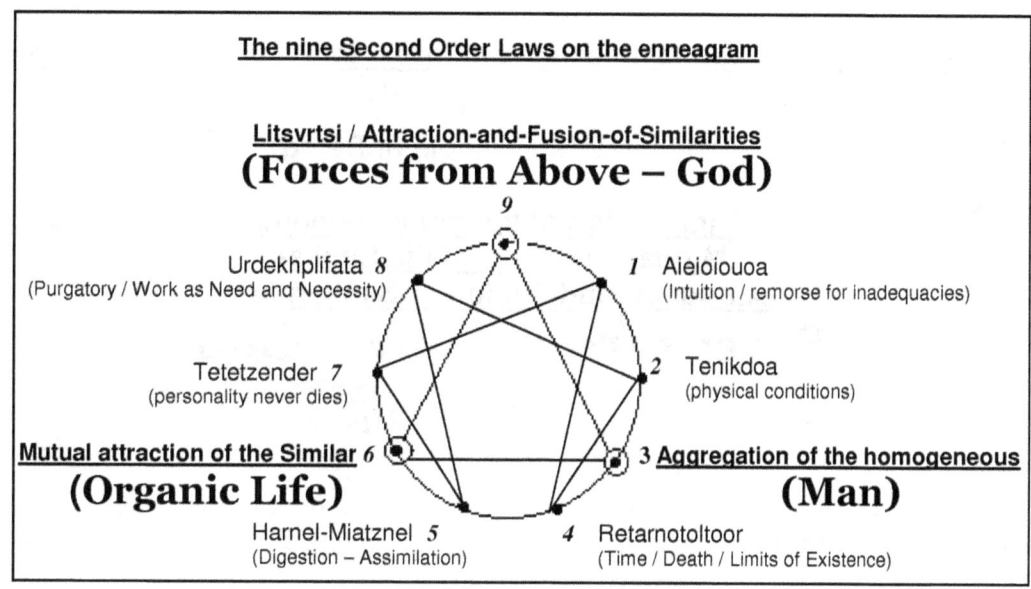

The general image here, common to those three laws, is that their action causes similar things to get together, to fuse and to become one. Nevertheless, Gurdjieff clarifies that each of these three laws defines a force that causes a different kind of action. By giving details of the way they operate, he makes it clear that each one involves a different aspect of the-will-to-be, so to speak. Gurdjieff's idea here of using terms and definitions that are so similar and yet so different cannot be a mere coincidence, as those terms and definitions he presents in Chapter 39, within the literary space of only a few paragraphs (from §3955 to §4069).

Keeping all these in mind, there is at least one more way of configuring this enneagram:

Slide # 26

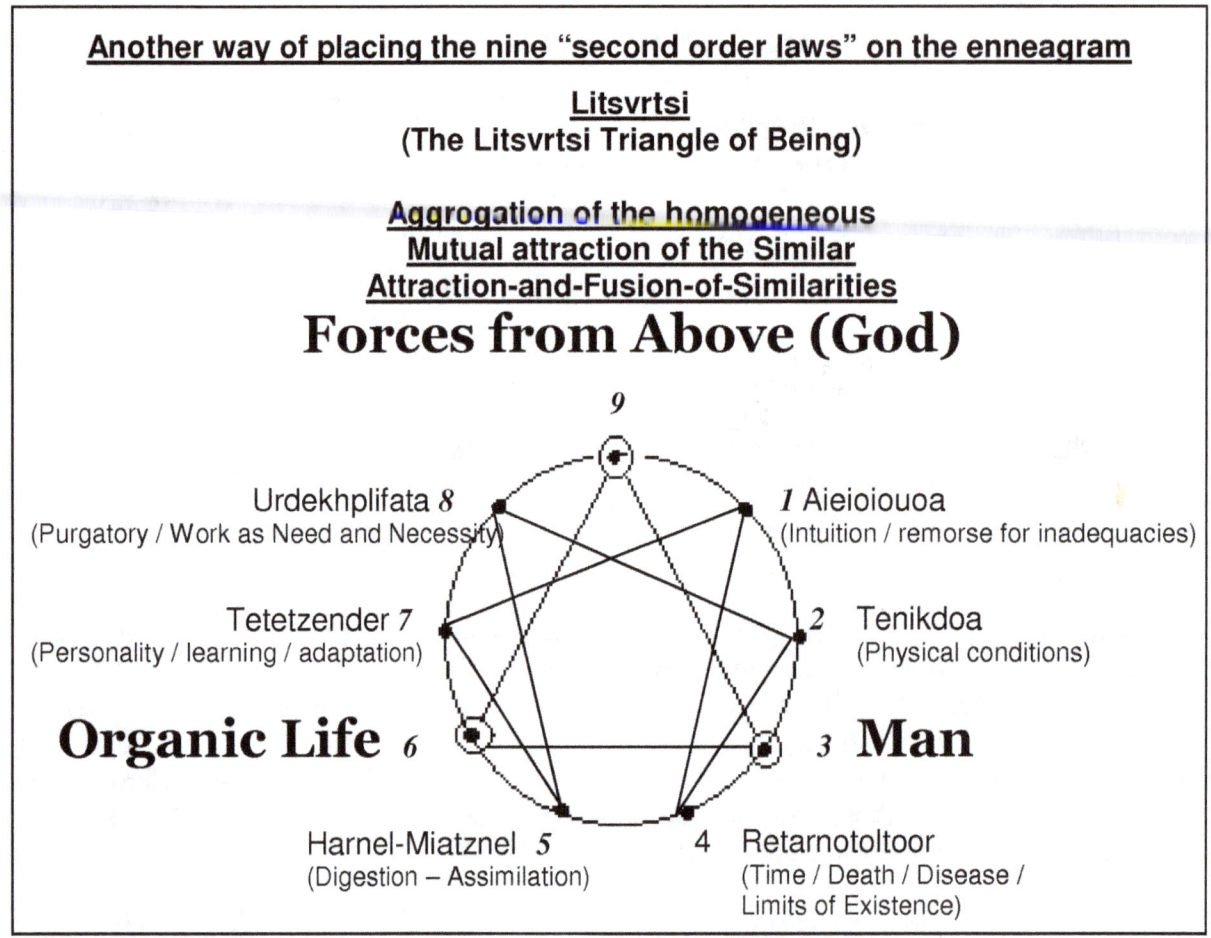

(Litsvrtsi / Man / Organic Life - the three laws of the Triangle placed on 9, 9, 9, denoting the deployment of the enneagram in three octaves)

The interest of this (of seeing Litsvrtsi as having three aspects) is that it clearly implies the existence of three level or three octaves in the action of this structure, even more clearly and explicitly than the previous enneagram does.

Slide # 27

> The idea of the "Three Consecutive Octaves" conforms:
>
> - to Gurdjieff's remark in "Fragments" that the enneagram can be seen to be unfolding in three octaves
> - to his remark that his writings are to be interpreted on three levels
> - to the specific analysis about the multiple meanings of Aieioiouoa
> - and to the way that the Law of Heptaparaparshinokh is shown in chapter 40 to be the object of the study of the science "Tazaloorinono", which considers the three domains where it suffices to study the Law: the total of the substances derived from "Opium", from the "White Ray" of light, and from "Sound".

And this conforms:

- to Gurdjieff's remark in "Fragments" that the enneagram can be seen to involve three octaves,
- to his remark that his writings are to be interpreted on three levels
- to the analysis about the multiple meanings of Aieioiouoa
- and to the way that the Law of Heptaparaparshinokh is shown in chapter 40 to be the object of the study of the science "Tazaloorinono", which considers the three domains where it suffices to study the Law: the total of the substances derived from "Opium", the "White Ray" of light, and "Sound".

© Copyright 2010 - Dimitri Peretzi - All Rights Reserved

The Structure of Laws - Questions & Answers

Participant 1: The Laws... I feel they can be understood as what Gurdjieff says, "The Objective Science" but the idea of objective implies the idea of subject. So then the question comes, who is the subject?

Dimitri Peretzi: Of course.

Participant 1: And that means God. I mean for all of this comes that the subject of this is God himself.

Dimitri Peretzi: Well, you can say that, but you can also say that the subject is Man, and that he is juxtaposed to organic life in the sense that he has to find his food, and everything, and that there is a force coming from above.

Participant 1: Yes, and that Man being the image, of course. So what we are doing here is objective science.

Dimitri Peretzi: If you are doing something, which is not necessarily true.

Participant 2: The approach to understand the difference aspects in the *Tales*, seems to me to also move according to the law of three. There are things that have puzzled me for long time, in *The Tales*, which has only been made accessible, if I think in Triads. So, what I am trying to get at is this; that not only is it found, as you have presented like this, but it is also something that we have to be able to apply in our search, according to a law. I am thinking specifically to the law of three. For example in the presentation of the difficulties that they had to find a new language, which they really needed, and they recognised the need. Gurdjieff said, of course, it came to nothing. When I look at it, the other way around, how would they be able to come to something? They would need to use the triad of regeneration, where the form is active, the new idea of a language, and the passive position there is the matter, the old language, which is worked upon, which is seen in a completely different light; and the neutralising factor is life. That is a new language. So, if we put it again the other way round, you see that the reason why it didn't work was because the triad that was used was that of crime. So, to approach different aspects of the book through trying to see it in one of the six triads has to me personally revealed some of the nature of what he says and is behind why things work, why things do not work.

Dimitri Peretzi: I have a feeling that what you say is very important. Of course, one has to be always aware of the fact of being lost into words. One question that I had when I was working with this enneagram, is, to the extent to which the processes can be viewed to conform to the idea of one-two-three, two-three-one, three-one-two, etc, the idea of them, six basic processes covering the idea of regeneration, elimination, etc. It seems that one can draw such equivalent ways of

The Structure of the Laws Presented in the Tales - Questions & Answers

thinking quite clearly, and in fact, in the sequence of my presentation I eliminated a whole part, because I would have to be talking for quite some time. That was the next topic I wanted to discuss, in this direction.

If one keeps in mind, that he has to avoid losing himself in the words, then I think this is the next thing to be explored, in fact. At least, with this enneagram.

Participant 3: Can I ask a rather technical question? In BT, I have never found any connection between the term remorse, and the term remorse of conscience. I noticed that S, earlier, used both terms, and I noticed that during your talk you used both terms. I wondered if there was a connection, and if you saw a connection between the two things.

Dimitri Peretzi: Actually, I am not ready to verify this, that there is no connection. I take your word for it. I see it is possible. Yet in my mind there is connection in the sense that we have explicitly the word remorse. The word remorse, connected to AIEIOIUOA. As something that is allegorically, something that arises allegorically the moment that there is light, there is "light" in ones life. Then of course, the very explicit way that Belcultassi faces the issue of realising that something is not perfect with him. So, I have no hesitation in connecting these two, and saying that remorse, refers to remorse of conscience, at least to what I understand, in everyday life, as remorse of conscience.

Participant 3: Yes, I think remorse, as you have it there, I see it as one part sees and criticises another, so it is the origin of self-knowledge.

Dimitri Peretzi: Yes, yes.

Participant 3: I find that remorse of conscience does not lead to self-knowledge, it is just saying, "oh, its all my fault" It is a ...

Dimitri Peretzi: Is it the same thing?

Participant 3: I don't think so...

Dimitri Peretzi: Well, if you want to see it differently, I will go with this thing, that you pointed out.....

Participant 3: Okay, that's fine, I'll take your word for it...

Dimitri Peretzi: … but somehow they are also connected.

Participant 4: I like that using this enneagram, and I think that, as you are implying, there is a lot more to it than meets the eye. Looking at it now, I see, I think what troubles me is these lines which pass through the Law of Three. So I see it from practical point of view, and you were saying that this has a real practical application in work, and the way I see it, that if I begin at 1, where I see myself as I am, so I have a wish to change, so in order to get energy from my wish, I have to go from 1 to 4, which passes through the Law of Three, so as I enter the Law of Three, I pick up energy, and as I leave the bottom section between 3 and 6, I deposit that energy, I pick up emotional energy from 4, and return, doing the same thing to 2, which crosses over to 8, because now I wish to have something of a higher nature to observe me, impartially, and that requires more energy, so I have to go back down to 5, where I pick up energy from my heart, which goes back to 7, and then I have to start the whole sequence all over again. But each time it passes through the triangle I am depositing energy for future use so it is like money in the bank, that I can draw on, at a later time. For me, the right side of the enneagram is how I am, and the left side of the enneagram is how I could be.

Dimitri Peretzi: Quite possibly. Now I want to say something about that. How to actually read the enneagram?

To agree on that is a complicated issue. I can juxtapose to what you just said, a reading of this enneagram, and how I see it. In my mind what happens is, that, this triad, defines somehow identity. How I understand myself, how I understand the world, how I understand God. This has different levels. Lets say that I am fixed on one level, whatever this level is, if it is the level of personality, or the level of the magnetic centre, or the level of essence, whatever it is, I am fixed on a certain level. Then my work proceeds, that is the way I read this enneagram, like this, and I do indeed, back-up energy, to move to a next level, the next level being a change of the triad of identity. Being another person, another identity, that might still be working along this kind of energy flow. To accumulate the energy needed for the next level. Now, this practicality in the way I work, and there is also practicality, I can see, in hindsight, looking back, there is practicality in the identity changing. For example, the person who is in the church praying, he still might be sensing the same kind of triad. Person 1,2,3 can be in the church praying, and still ... asking God for something, you know, other people in my life, being no 6, going against me, I want to go beyond them. Yet, one can see, one can imagine another level of this reality, when I realise I am the only inhabitant of the world, and all this is decoration, part of the war (?). When I realise, and I live experientially my aloneness that is quite another level of the person who just wishes to gain over his neighbour something, and prays for that in the church. So I think that this enneagram could be applied in both cases. What happens through the inner energy accumulated in the dynamo of the interior could help push up the triad of identity; and it is the identity that changes on a new level, a new level of work, a new way of working, everything is new on that new level. This is the way I read this enneagram. I am sure that one can find ways of projecting this idea of what is, versus what can be, to the left, also on it, my first reading is what I just said.

Seminar 1: Chapter 31, *Beelzebub's Tales*

The Sixth and Last Sojourn of Beelzebub on the Planet Earth

Facilitator: Terje Tonne

Introduction

MC: Hope you all had a good lunch. This is our afternoon seminar period. This afternoon we'll be having an open group discussion of chapter 31 of *Beelzebub's Tales*: "The sixth and last sojourn of Beelzebub on the planet Earth".

The seminar will be facilitated by Terje Tonne. Terje runs an art gallery and a Gurdjieff group in Oslo, Norway, and is a long-time supporter of the conference.

The protocol here - for people who are new - will be that Terje will most likely give an introduction to this chapter, with some of his observations and possibly questions that he has found interesting about the chapter, and then the discussion will be opened up to everyone, as a sort of a large round for floor discussion. And, as I mentioned earlier, if you want to speak, put up your hand, and the microphone will get passed around the circle, and to try to speak clearly into the microphone, so that when we go to transcribe this for the proceedings, that we'll have a clear record of your voice, to make an easy transcription - and I think at this point, I'll just turn everything over to Terje.

Terje Tonne: Thank you. I'm sure that there will be many different views on certain aspects of this chapter, and maybe different views on the core of the chapter. And that would, at least partly, be in accordance with the idea that is put up in this chapter, in regards to language and the problematic nature of not having one language. Maybe even such a discussion can indirectly support one language - something that goes in the direction of one language.

For me at this moment this chapter is about suggestibility. And reading it and re-reading it, it almost becomes like a warning. In this chapter, it is said that the need for reciprocal destruction initially is due to past generations. Although instinctively they refrained from this killing, but due to their environment they continue.

In another part, the mooring of "Occasion" was done at the North Pole, in order not to be bumped into by ships constantly fleeting about, and representing a constant danger.

Now, a "North Pole", without a "North Pole" in my life, I am subject to all kinds of impulses. I will be at the prey of what is suggested from the outside world, and from the parts in me which is programmed, and from where I am acting mechanically. Without a silent point in me, a place where I am separated from that which constantly, more or less, attacking me by means of suggestibility, I have no possibility to exist.

And this chapter for me is, and the whole book, is about the support for my existence. It is the support for having a life, even though I am bumped into now and then. Without this silent point, I know I can not return, and return, and return.

So, I thought that this "North Pole" would be a good place to start maybe. This is my take on this "North Pole".

What is yours?

Seminar Discussion

Participant: Yes, that's a big question for me, too. Six descents mean for me, that there is an "I", my "I", has to come closer to me, to solve certain problems that are connected with this chapter. And this "I" is going to give me cold facts about myself. So this is how I relate this to this business of the Occasion, which I think in French means "opportunity" - this is an opportunity for me to work, by just receiving objective cold facts about my existence, and my behavior.

And the six descents comes up the position of "la" on the octave, and "la" on the octave for me, means experimentation. And he says, in the book, that he's going to experiment, and he goes into that in quite detail.

Another thing I just wanted to mention about - at the very beginning, he says he's moving from the atmosphere of the planet "Revozvradendr", and he falls in the direction of the solar system "Pandetznokh". And Revozvradendr is at the periphery of my life, I think for me, and "dendr" is the famous astrological Egyptian scheme of things, and that's where I am. I'm subject to all my astrological influences, but now I'm escaping from that, close to the center. So this is my - this is how I feel about this "North Pole".

Participant: I'd like to put a completely different viewpoint on this chapter. In my opinion, Gurdjieff, in this chapter, is speaking about a psychic peculiarity of human beings you reach at a certain stage in the Work, which he calls the processes - periodic processes - of reciprocal destruction. And in this chapter he's providing a remedy - if you read this chapter carefully, he's providing a remedy for that psychic property. I'm sorry to change the tone of it - I can explain further if anyone wishes, but I don't want to hog the floor.

Terje Tonne: No, if you can go on -

Participant: Right, what I can say is that the minute - the minute Gurdjieff starts to say something that you think you recognize, that's when you should start to pay attention, because he says in this chapter, and he says in virtually every chapter of *Beelzebub's Tales*, the same thing - he says that man has two consciousnesses: our ordinary consciousness and the subconscious. And he says that the subconscious should be our true consciousness, our real consciousness.

My assumption based upon that, is he's writing a book for both consciousnesses, which is not a very easy thing to do. Now, in order to speak to the subconscious, which is what he's trying to do in this book, one of the easiest ways to do that, is to switch off our ordinary consciousness, and speak to the subconscious. Now, I don't know whether this is a part of psychiatry or psychology, or is well known, but one of the easiest ways to switch off a person's ordinary consciousness, is to start to tell them something they already know. If someone starts to repeat themselves, or tell you something that you recognize, immediately you switch off. And, I think, in this chapter, Gurdjieff tries to give to our conscious mind, for example at the start, the idea that he's talking about war - the periodic processes of reciprocal destruction, he doesn't say "war" - and what he's actually talking about, is something quite different.

Now, the psychic property that he mentions is very difficult to talk about, which is why he doesn't actually do it - consciously. It's something I think you come across, we all know what it is, but it's in the area of what he might call the "idiot mind", that is, there is no structure to it - it's very difficult to talk about because it has no structure, it has no form. So, my opinion is that, without going into further details about what this psychic property is, that's what this chapter's about. Right - I can answer any questions, if people want to put them, or I'll move on.

Terje Tonne: I don't want to give up this "North Pole"-thing. Is there anyone who has a view on that?

Participant: Since you've come back to it. I've always noticed that reference to parking at the North Pole, and there's a reference somewhere else to the Pole Star, I think, earlier in the book. Those have always stood out for me, but I had no idea what to make of them, so I didn't.

So this is somewhat interesting, and - in terms of the North Pole, the poles are, you're standing at the poles, they're the place on the Earth with the least rotational movement. Everything else is spinning faster and faster the further away you get from that place, where things don't move. I found that interesting to think about in terms of the still, silent place we're trying to father in ourselves, to park our observational viewpoint, to hold us steady, while we venture further out into this spinning world inside of us and outside of us, and trying to investigate it.

And, just to comment about Mike's observation, as I recall the beginning, Beelzebub noticed something peculiar, he thought he had already come to an understanding of war, based on fear and proximity of someone you didn't understand, and so there was a sense of threat. But now he notices something completely different - killing at a distance, out of boredom. And that doesn't make any sense. So, in addition to the suggestibility, an impression that I got reading the chapter, was that he's also exploring again the issue of where did conscience go - how can people do one thing, with the understanding that they're only pretending what they're doing, and that's not what they're doing, or maybe even not notice that - what happened?

All & Everything Conference 2010

Participant: It's Steve, isn't it? I think what Steve said is important, because it's an example of how Gurdjieff can say one thing and mean another thing. Because he talks about a certain person does a certain something, and another person, at a distance, there's a puff of smoke, rather, and another person at a distance falls down, injured, dead or maimed. And - the impression is that he's talking about the invention of rifles or weaponry of some kind, so the conscious mind thinks: "I understand that, that's fine, no problem with that." But, if you then read it as I've tried to do - a bit more carefully, because I'm always suspicious when I understand something - then he doesn't actually say that. My impression - I might be wrong - is that he means something else. He's saying one thing for the ordinary conscious mind, but he's saying something else, that we pick up on, sorry, we pick up on, with the subconscious mind. Because in the subconscious mind, we are very, very clever, subtle, discriminating - and we recognize the difference. Sorry to keep harping on about this.

Participant: Well, he also gives this marvellous little speech on page - ah, probably everybody has a different book to me, but - about the way beings wish in fear for the destruction of other beings, in order to protect themselves. And I want to see the book about myself, really - what is it in me that always wants to protect myself from destruction from external forces. And I think my ego has all the fear in the world, and wishes to protect itself at all costs, no matter what. So I think that's one of the other central points of these first two or three pages.

Participant: It's just occurred to me, that this issue of influencing at a distance, even killing at a distance, is not one just for the soldiers. Because here we have the doctor who does not see how he influences people at a distance, and the pharmacist, and the advertisers, and the chemist. And because everything is connected to everything else, we don't - we think that maybe we're just making a little puff of smoke, and we don't see where the effect goes.

Participant: Can I just, the part of it, a bit deeper. Terje mentioned that the question of languages, and for me, personally, this again is a bit of a sticking point. Because I seem to remember one particular paragraph in this chapter, where I understood, my conscious mind understood, exactly what was being said. It was about the many different languages and different dialects, and it occurred to me that, actually, there was no mention in that paragraph of countries or nationalities, and it occurred to me that actually what Gurdjieff was saying, was that internally, we are divided, we are divided into many different areas, and that in fact, there is - the problem of human beings - is that there is no communication between all the different inner parts of ourselves. They all speak different languages, they all have different dialects, and therefore, we do not communicate within ourselves, which, in many ways, sort of sums up much of what Gurdjieff said to Ouspensky, I believe.

He says, in, I think, the same paragraph, that this is a property unique to the Earth. It does not happen anywhere else. Everywhere else, the beings existing there, whatever form or however we understand that, have one common language. So the Earth, he says, is the only place where we are so divided. Each part of us speaking a different language, unable to communicate with each other part within us. Thank you.

Terje Tonne: I think this is interesting, to look at the languages and perspective of something which is going on inside. And he said that when he couldn't get fodder for his horse, although he could speak eighteen languages, he couldn't manage to get fodder for his horse. And I've been pondering this, what is this eighteen languages? And if one finds out, then there are still more languages, because it is due to the languages which is not of those eighteen, that he couldn't get fodder for his horse. So it's not only eighteen, but there are eighteen he knows. Now, if one looks at the centers as they are presented, to example in "Oragean Version", where the moving center and the instinctive center is taken as one, then you have emotional center and intellectual center. They are all divided into three, that makes nine. One can either see that the missing nines are the subdivisions, but it is also possibility to see the missing nines as the negative halves, including the negative halves which is in the emotional center, which has no negative halves. But, one must remember, that we are speaking about the mechanical man, who has artificial negative halves, and that makes up eighteen exactly.

Either way.

And another connection here is with language, and a thing that goes on inside, which is difficult to understand. About lack of sincerity towards oneself, he says, it is due to the lack of coordination of centers. Now these subdivisions and these divisions and negative halves, et cetera - they are not connected. They are unknown. But they were known to him, if one takes it as those eighteen being centers, negative halves or under-divisions. That means, indirectly, that he would have those qualities for having an ability to be sincere with himself. It's good we don't go in details about the under-division, I think.

Participant: Yeah, he's talking about parking there. The space on the northern pole, which could have some relation also with the magnetic center, through the magnet of the north. And also that the thing that is the spacecraft, is there. The spacecraft is somehow his vehicle, which in the esoteric language is the psychosomatic body. Our body and our lower mind, which should have some mechanical, some steady, orientation. Otherwise, I will be lost in space. I need some stability, I need to have my feet on the ground. And also that the problem with the languages, also it reminds me, the tower of Babel, where all the division came from.

Participant: Hello. I must confess I didn't read the sixth chapter, but I am trying to get into understanding what he's talking about. And I would like to take you back to what is said in the beginning, okay, which I found very curious, and I would like to ask you about it and maybe have a dialog about it. I don't know if I understand what you are saying, but it seems to me that you're saying that there's great difficulty, or great destruction, going on in the human being - yeah? And that without a certain "North Pole", which I understand you use it as an analogy of something, it's going to be very difficult, if not hopeless at all. Am I understanding you?

Terje Tonne: Yes. I think so.

All & Everything Conference 2010

Participant: Can you enlarge on that, can you say what is the great destruction, great difficulty, the great war that we stand in front when we try to develop, and what is this "North Pole"?

Terje Tonne: I don't think I used the word "war", but -

Participant: No, I used it.

Terje Tonne: Yeah, all right. No, I mean, we are sitting here right now. We have been entrusted with a life. And we exist whether we will or not. And the difficulty is to raise the consciousness to a level where we recognize that we actually are somewhere, and to start to get serious about living. And in order to deal with other people, which we very easily blame for all kinds of things, and all the impulses that we have been imprinted with, which wants us - as an organic being - to remain as an organic being, but this is not what Gurdjieff said, this is not what any of the great traditions says. They say that Man is on Earth for a higher purpose than the organic one, and this teaching has a very clear information about what the organic purpose is. There is this energy coming down, and we are a part of that organic belt that receives it. But that is not the end of human life. Now, if we don't take up this - I don't like the word "war", but I almost used it - if we start looking at our situation in this perspective that we have a potential, then we find out that we are daydreaming, that we are indulging in inner talking. So much inner talking, even, in a conversation, that we cannot hear what the other person say - there are no communication. And, if you look at this in perspective of sincerity, how can Man be sincere to himself? Well, the reason for being sincere - the source of the reason for being sincere - must be in the fact that I actually exist, but I'm not aware of it. So there is where my effort has to go, to see what in me is hindering this.

Participant: And the North Pole?

Terje Tonne: And the North Pole is a place where I am not so easily bumped into. What is the word - locomotions...

Participant: I think a place of stability. You understand what a gyroscope is? A gyroscope would be like myself, rather the whole of life is revolving around me, but I have in myself a place of stability, which is completely impartial to my behavior. That it has no judgment of my behavior, and not only that, it has no descriptions - because if I'm objective, it means there's no analysis, and there's no descriptions of it. It's just the fact that I exist in this state, and - but it's in a state of impartiality, and it's quite different from an ordinary state in my ordinary life, where I'm certainly not in a state of impartiality, or objectivity. So I exist in chaos, I exist in reciprocal destruction, I exist in all these languages that I - live in chaos within me. But if I have this place of stability, it doesn't matter any more, because that's a representative of the universe. So I have this clash of "yes" and "no", but I have the reconciling principle, which is impartiality. So there I have Okidanokh, and that's how it functions.

Participant: Absolutely. One word that I want to add to your exact words, is being neutral.

Participant: It's a neutralizing principle.

Participant: Yes. And being neutral towards your life, which is absolutely opposite than identifying.

Participant: Yes.

Participant: Thank you.

Participant: Perhaps there is a connection between the North Pole as a place of stability, and the actual spacecraft as an analogy for the vehicle - the mental vehicle that one creates. The other body that we create through doing conscious work, whether it's a meditation or a system, which is like a vehicle which helps one to travel. Because unless one creates such a vehicle, one is likely to perish within the chaos that surrounds one, within the complexity, within the mass hysteria in society that one lives in. So, to create a firm center within oneself, or another body, which is like creating a vehicle which is a spacecraft, and then, perhaps, the North Pole - one should have created such a vehicle, it's like a - gives bearings. So, yes, the "North Pole" is something within ourselves and external to ourselves. Perhaps, perhaps.

Participant: <inaudible> have recently read this chapter, in a group. I kept thinking, all the time, that in this chapter, Gurdjieff says specific things, like there are too many languages, and the psychic tension of the war. And there are other things that I can not understand at all - how he begins this chapter, with this North Pole, as you said. I can not quite clearly understand that, but I kept thinking that he's trying to hide something. Beelzebub is trying to hide something. He says that old people, right now, are going on and on to the North Pole, too. They didn't use to go, but now they reach the North Pole frequently, so he's trying to hide the ship - the vehicle. I thought that the vehicle is a teaching, and he's not teaching, Beelzebub is not teaching, coming to Earth. He's trying to realize how man is like this - to communicate, to feel compassion for this kind of state that Man is. The real teaching is something - how to say - dangerous. Because he says that we could make the spaceship not to be seen, if we would like, but then, some of the other vehicles of men would have to crash in it.

Terje Tonne: He says it's a danger, he used the word "danger" two times there. It is a danger, yes.

Participant: So, Beelzebub himself knows the dangers of the teaching itself, and he tries to understand the real meaning of the state of Man, before to - to give the teaching.

Terje Tonne: Yes, I agree that the teaching is dangerous, but for whom? Not for those part in us that is seeking to be sincere with oneself and others, but it is dangerous for those parts in us that bumps into us. Because they only have function when they bump. My negativity has only possibilities to manifest itself and have the function of holding me on an organic level, if there is nobody who have attention on it. Sometimes attention, to just recognize, without having any other method, or an ableness to fix things - the attention on my negativity, for me, sometimes is enough to put those things out of function. So it's very dangerous for the lives of those who we are not. That's what makes it so precious, isn't it?

Sounds like we're stuck on the North Pole, or?

Participant: A few moments ago, there was passed out this idea that we have been entrusted with a life, and the lack of, in a way, responsibility we take for that life which we have been given. And I wonder if the short part on page 536 is related exactly to what has been said just a few moments ago. He mentions the word there, or the term, "half-dead terra firma", which, I guess, is maybe to be understood that there is life lacking in me, and if we take this little paragraph, which is in short this promising beginning of theirs in this business of establishing one common planetary language, changed nothing there in their height of absurdity, and everything remained as before, down till now. That is, this comparatively petty planet, with a petty half-dead terra firma, continues to remain, as again, our dear teacher Mullah Nassr Eddin says, "a thousand-tongued hydra". I don't know what the word "hydra" means - anyhow, maybe that could be commented on this, that could be understood in the way I was trying to present it.

Participant: I also was very struck by Terje's observation that we've been give the responsibility of a life - in fact, I felt a shock. I'd never felt it that way before. I've been given responsibility for this life - each of us, for this life, for the care of this body, for the care of this psyche, for the development of this potential, we've been given that responsibility. And it reminded me of something Dimitri said this morning that also touched me deeply. It's more profound than that, it's not just that each of us had been given the responsibility of a life, we'd been given the responsibility of a universe.

Can I say, that the thought forms that are created in me, don't have a life, they don't suffer pleasure and pain, and clash with each other? How do I know that when I permit certain things to take form, or encourage them or feed them, or go create them on my own initiative, that I'm not giving life to something? They certainly profoundly affect how I feel, what I do, the puffs of smoke that I admit, that influence other people. Dimitri quoted a Gurdjieff saying that "they don't realize that we're made in the image of God". Do we not, actually without realizing it, have - are we not the God of our inner universe? Totally oblivious, irresponsible, not knowing the language, not knowing the what to do, how to do it - within ourselves, to bring order to this <inaudible> universe, as Dimitri said: "Who will ever know?"

So, our cosmologists are very excited about the theories of multi-universes, or multiverses, whatever they call them - well, here they are. Each one of us. So, I'm quite stunned with this revelation. And one more thing about the North Pole - we look at images of the electromagnetic field - these are the doorways, this is the place where the electromagnetic field flows in and out, these two big donuts we're told of, all this flowing energy. And I think it's the second space drive that has something to do with what he calls "elekilpomagtistzen" - something like that. And what is it flowing around our nervous system with, to our brain - is that not electromagnetic energy?

Seminar 1

Are we not aspects of the electromagnetic spectrum ourselves? So, this sense of responsibility, now, has just really stunned me.

Participant: When I read this chapter, the first word came to my mind, was the division we have - all our parts are divide, our personality is divide, in many different parts. So, too many nations, too many people, too many languages - we can't communicate it with the personality. So, I think that all this that we leave as war, is because we can't communicate as human beings. And, it's only with Work we can do it.

I also want to point out some things about this chapter. The events concerning Ashiata Shiemash, became known to Beelzebub during his sixth descent on Earth. Also, all the events concerning Saint Buddha. This is in page 361, in other chapter. And, it is also interesting to mention that the sixth time Beelzebub had come to Earth, was a while before he was pardoned, and was permitted to return to planet Karatas. It was the year 223 after the creation of the world, according to the objective time measurement. As they would say here on Earth, the year 1921 after the birth of Christ. This introduction - this make me sense Gurdjieff was alive, in that time. This is a question, also: What was the meaning of all this, that you see in introduction - it's the first thing that he say.

Participant: Can I just say thank you, that's an amazing question - why 1921? Thank you. I have the microphone, but not the answer.

Terje Tonne: Maybe we could, for the sake of efficiency, move to another part of this chapter, and maybe return if there is something to this what we have been discussing up to now? What about the pharmacist?

Participant: Continuing from before, I feel somehow that - <inaudible>, who said, "what's the worst", he said yesterday, and what comes up today now, he go the, somehow the - the instrument of where he go is the mind, and the instrument of compassion is the heart, in some way. Either one of them is not enough, cannot do the job - our Work - alone. We need cooperation of the two. Not a fight between the two, the reconciliation force, which, of course, can happen only inside me. And in some way also, this is the main reason for war, is the inside not understanding; fight. And there is also, in some movements, the talk about the "intelligent heart" - Muslim, Buddhist - and they talk also about the "wisdom heart", and this is that we don't have; the language. That the heart doesn't understand the language of the mind, and the mind does not understand the language of the heart. And this results into the problems - and what he said - the hydra is from the tales of Hercules, the animal with the many heads, where he would cut one, and there would spring out two? You know the fable? This is an ancient Greek myth of Hercules. In that myth, the hydra, that simile animal that he was impossible to kill, was his main, his root, let's somehow say, ego. He would cut the head of - one of the heads of the animal - and two other heads would spring out. Killing the one, this divides into duality, into two - the positive and the negative.

Participant: There are two things I have observed in this text. The first one is that the duration of the sixth descent is three hundred years. This is exactly the same duration as the life of a developed man, according to "Life is Real". This is mentioned in this book. And the second observation is that Beelzebub, in this chapter, speaks eighteen languages, which is exactly the same as the number of languages spoken by Gurdjieff in the chapter for Yelov <inaudible>. Beelzebub in this chapter speaks eighteen languages, Gurdjieff in Yelov-chapter speaks eighteen languages. I do not know what does that mean, but it's a kind of peculiar - there is an identification between Gurdjieff and Beelzebub in this point. Maybe this goes with Popi's comment earlier. I can not explain it further, but this is something I'd like to observe. Thank you.

Participant: I think my conclusion would be that the number eighteen occurs twice. My conclusion would be that there are eighteen, Gurdjieff thought there were eighteen different parts of the psyche, speaking different languages inside. And he could speak the language of each part. That's how I would understand it.

Terje Tonne: He says several places in the book that the information that is needed for getting an objective view of the situation, has to be not only observing the single individual, but also the individual as a mass. And he also says that the observation of the past generations has to be included, in order to get the picture of what is really going on. And my idea was that that would count for those 300 years. Not seeing these individuals as a mass at one moment, but over a period of time, so that the consequences of their actions can be recognized, from one generation to another.

And as it was pointed out earlier here, and this is my understanding also, that I am not responsible for my mechanics. I am responsible to the degree that I have an awareness of these mechanics, and a choice. So all these things that has been put into me, they are things I will have to live with, and they are things which has been passed on. And in order to find out what has been passed on, and the nature of this passing on, it is needed more than an instant observation, but long observation of the generations and so on. So I see it.

Participant: Can I suggest that the question of time, is Gurdjieff perhaps pointing out, of these divisions within us - the different languages - all these different parts of us are working in different time zones, they're working in different times, different rhythms. It's just an idea. That's perhaps why they can't communicate, because they're working in different time, some in very long spans of time.

Participant: I mean, Gurdjieff - I don't know if Esperanto was actually invented around that time when Gurdjieff was writing his Beelzebub's, but there seems to be this question as to, you know, why don't all humans have the same language. Perhaps there's an analogy with ourselves, with all the different disparate I's and parts that we have, whether we can even communicate with ourselves. Because, surely Gurdjieff must be aware that it's impossible on Earth for all human beings to speak the same language, because that's the way it is - there are different countries with people who don't know each other, different geographies. How can you expect for there to be one language, and as we know, I mean, there is no one language today we recognize - there is no one language that's better than another. They're all - the whole science of linguistics and philosophy,

Wittgenstein and all the rest. But we do have, through our skills, common language. And I'm reminded of an example - a friend of mine said that they were in Germany, and their car broke down, and they went to the garage to have their car fixed, and he said to the man there: "We're very sorry, but we don't know how to speak German, to explain to you what happened," and he says "Never mind - the car speaks German."

Participant: Can I just say that my mother-in-law in France has learned Esperanto, but she's not yet found anyone who can understand her.

Terje Tonne: If you look at this question of Esperanto in a psychological perspective, the reason he seems to give for Esperanto being no good, is that there is a lack of understanding of that a language needs, as I understand him, experience - some practical experience. You cannot just cook it up. And if I am to understand something of my own nature and my potentiality, it has to be a living experience in the moment, and that is far from anything I cook up. And that would be the material to create a language from.

Participant: On the subject of language - we do have a common language, all of us. We don't need to learn Esperanto. The problem is that we forgot this language, we have a mother tongue, we're all born with this language, but we move away from it. And I talk about body language. It's a universal language, it's the language of our emotions, and we are divorced from it. And I think that if we relearn this language, all human communication could be different.

Terje Tonne: I partly agree with you, if we are speaking about something externally. Partly, because it will be very difficult for a Scandinavian to understand why the French is using their hands, and the Italians is almost tearing their hair off. There will immediately be some attitude.

Participant: Yeah, I just want to say that according to researchers, the differences between cultures in terms of body language, is no more than ten-fifteen percent. Body language is universal. Even a French person understands when a Swedish person or Norwegian person is nervous, or angry, or amusing. The basic human emotions are universal by body language.

Participant: But surely, this is the problem, isn't it - where we're using one center to be expressed by another. So my body is expressing my feelings, instead of them being separate and disconnected from that, so I have no real language of the emotional center, and my feelings in my solar plexus are spread throughout the whole of my body. So my feelings are using my body to express themselves. So consequently, the speed which this takes place is quite incredible, but it's a complete waste of energy. So if I can learn to separate my centers, and have a real emotional language, then I won't use my body any more to express my emotions. So all this thing about body language, in Work, for me would be the reverse - that I don't want my body to express my feelings. I want my feelings to be one center and my body to be another center, and my intellectual center to be another center. So at least they are separated, and at least there's a potential for them to grow.

All & Everything Conference 2010

Terje Tonne: Yes, and that which is rightly separated, seems to fit together.

Participant: So - just to elaborate a bit more on that, for me to sense my body, would mean that I give my body an attribute where it has a sense of its own existence. And then, if I practice enough, a sense of impartiality comes in. But then, I have to give - because I've withdrawn the feelings from my body, I have to replace that with something else. And I have replaced that with energy from my heart, that replaces the energy of the feelings. So now, I have a real possibility that my body can become a real servant to the other two centers. And I think, for me, this is what Ahoon represents in the book. Ahoon represents the body, which is always present at the meetings between Beelzebub and Hassein. So this business about body language, as far as Work is concerned, would be something the opposite of what you just described.

Participant: I don't agree. I think basically, the body is separated from the emotions because of lack of awareness. People speak body language all the time, but they don't know what they're doing. They speak mechanically. And this causes them to express what they identify with. Now, if you put awareness into it as a neutralizing vector, then you actually cause a unison between the body and the emotions, that they will express the higher aspect of you, and not the lower aspect of you.

Host: I think on that note, that it's coffee break time, and if we convene back here in approximately half an hour, to continue this conversation.

*** Coffee Break ***

Terje Tonne: Is everybody here, Ian?

Participant: I think so. <inaudible>

Terje Tonne: So, if we could take one minute to collect ourselves, before we go ahead?

Participant: Well, I have been carefully listening, observing the first part of this lively conversation, discussion. And I want to share with you some <inaudible> observations and opinions - my opinions regarding several aspects of the discussion. I would like to start with the problem of a common language. I think that the common language that we have, at least in this room, is not only the language of the body and not the English, but the language of Gurdjieff's teaching. You may remember P. D. Ouspensky's report in his *In Search of the Miraculous*, of Gurdjieff saying that the true knowledge needs true language, and that, as Gurdjieff said to his disciples, you have to learn this language, you have to slowly develop it within you. And he gave them several concepts that were shocking to them, so this was the beginning of Gurdjieff's mission, and he presented his version of the language of tradition. Now, this is not the first time that tradition presented itself using different concepts and different language. Actually, all great world religions are successful esoteric traditions. There are esoteric traditions that were rejected by history, but Christianity, Buddhism, Islam, et cetera, became successful. They brought to the world their language, and it was completely new language, extremely rich, and dealing with the same issue, namely developing in human beings their higher potentials, their higher being-bodies. Gurdjieff's tradition stands in the line, and with Judaism, Christianity, Islam, and so on. But those religions, they produced new understanding, but then this new understanding emerged again into the heavy waters of common understanding and language of masses. So they have these great concepts, but they lost their profound meaning. And Gurdjieff came to remind us of the essential things. He reminded us that tradition serves the task, the goal of human awakening. And now this great book that brought us together, is not the last book, not the last expression of great eternal tradition. Probably, later on, we will have another revelation, and so we should not think that this is the final book, like Qur'an according to Islamic theology is the last revelation - no more revelations will come - and Arabic language is the language Allah spoke himself. He stated this to Muhammad.

Terje Tonne: I'm sorry to interrupt you, but, I'm curious to see how you put all this wonderful information in the context of this chapter.

<inaudible>

Participant: I have been replying to, reflecting on, the discussion that took place here about the language. <inaudible>

Participant: Well, regarding this chapter, I want to remark that Beelzebub's last sojourn to the earth is being dealt with not only in this chapter, number 31. Next several chapters deal also with his last sojourn. And many things that are just tentatively outlined in this chapter, are continued in the next chapters, about hypnotism, about Beelzebub as a master of hypnotism, about Russia, and other places that Beelzebub visited. This chapter is very interesting chapter, and it has many, many secrets - some of them were discussed here - and let me touch on one of them, namely the North Pole, where according to Beelzebub, the space ship was placed. According to Sufi tradition, there is a special function that is ascribed to the north, and especially the North Pole. It is the place related to the source of spirituality, while the southern pole is just the opposite, a place where there is division and destruction and multiplicity. So that's the meaning that we have to have in mind while reading this chapter. Well - and finally, with your permission, I wanted to remark on Beelzebub being not a carrier of tradition. He is in exile, he was sent away from the Sun Absolute, and he was actually a tourist. From time to time he helped some Archangels, some saintly beings, to solve certain task. But mainly he sees himself as a free being, travelling and interested in studying peculiarities of three-brained beings. So he is sort of a detached observer with his own interest. It was not a task that was given to him, it is his personal, individual interest. What are those beings, why they are so strange, and I think that behind this curiosity, stood compassion. There was compassion, and definite desire to help. And therefore, he studied so thoroughly and so carefully - us. Well, thank you, I didn't want to say more than I said.

Terje Tonne: Thank you. What about the "Dover's powder" - let's return to the chapter. Or the chemist - what are they? Who are they, what are they doing? Is there in their business some kind of information for us? Or is it a warning, the way they handle business? What is it?

Participant: It strikes me that it's a warning for each of us to look at how we conduct our own business. And not just with other people, but with ourselves, how often is a prescription given us - but we take short cuts, and tell ourselves that we're actually following the prescription. And then we can even analyze it and confirm that we're following the prescription, even though we know we're not. In any case, the substance that was <inaudible>, that might really have had an effect on us - the dangerous part - was taken out.

Terje Tonne: Uhm-hm.

Participant: So I certainly see in my own life this tendency to take shortcuts, not go all the way - you know, to stop partway around the Enneagram, not go from seven back to one. So, finishing has been a work of my own that I've been watching for a long time. But I think that it says something about our tendency to self-deception and insincerity with ourselves. The traditions give us remedies do we follow them, or only go through the motions?

Participant: Yeah - I have several takes on this, and I haven't really arrived at one that satisfies me, but I agree with what Steve says. I see the laboratory is myself -

Participant: The what?

Participant: Laboratory, where he says that he went to the laboratory and he met this chemist, and the chemicals, for me a code for behavior. And it's interesting in the chapter on Russia that he was also looking for an laboratory, and I think it's a very important part that all laboratories have instruments to observe objectively. And I like what Steve says that the main part was eliminated - opium - and opium being one of the "polormedekhtian" classes of elements. And opium, as Gurdjieff said, is fantasy, and I still haven't got a take on what quinine is, or the other chemical that goes into it. But it's what Steve says, it's right that we don't follow the prescription for Work. There is a definite prescription for Work, for the method, and we ignore it. So that's an important part of this -

Terje Tonne: Yeah.

Participant: … chemistry.

Terje Tonne: If we look at this in the perspective of what he says about what it takes for us to be sincere to ourselves, it is this: To be able to tolerate ourselves, to accept ourselves. And the reason why we are not, is because we have different parts in us which is pulling in different directions. Now, this pull in different directions might be this insincerity, which is thoroughly in this part where he is appearing, this chemist, and the content of the powder is not what it is said to be. How it is made is made secret, and it is taken precautions to reveal its content. And this attitude of the pharmacist, when he's asked about - "but isn't it analyzed?", and he just answers sarcastically, and he even smiles. The whole business of this "Dover's powder" business, is to me an - from one end to another, a very insincere business. All the way, even the justifications, and I think on page 520, he - I can find it - maybe 550, have you got that?

Participant: I've got another book <inaudible>

Terje Tonne: Oh, yeah. He puts this into one sentence: As regards how the remedy is made, and what it contains, what does it matter? There is no responsibility, there is no valuing, there is no levels, everything is operating on the same level. What does it matter? And I try to see some of these aspects in perspective of triads, and if one looks at what the chemist has of qualities, Gurdjieff say, the whole help for the physician consists in remembering names of the medicine. It's not the quality of the medicines that matters, it's the names - it's an outer thing. The ability of the medicine, and the proper use of the medicine, is of no importance. Neither are the real need for the medicine, that's very serious, the need is not taken into consideration. Social status of the patients is what counts. And if you look at this in the triad of corruption, the triad of corruption being form - life - matter, then you will see that the social status is the active part, and the sickness - our situation - is parked in the passive position. And the neutralizing factor, what is it? It is a medicine that does not work, and even can be dangerous. A medicine that, looking at it from a medical point of view, a medicine that would be proper to use, would be a medicine used in the triad of healing. And the triad of healing is matter - form - life. And if you look at what in that triad is the active part, it is the right medicine, and the sickness itself is parked, it is not active, it is acted upon by the right medicine, and the help that one gains through taking this medicine is the neutralizing factor. So the triad is matter - form - life. Now, if you just look at the positions, the different position of life in these two triads, you will see that in corruption, life is not taken into account, it is parked in the second position. But as in the triad of healing, it is the result, it is the neutralizing factor. So, if we are seeing this business, this corrupt business of this business of Dover's powder - it is a very strong warning to me.

Participant: Another aspect of that, that I kind of see, with the Dover's powders and the changing of the formula over time, as you say, the corruption of it, or the involution of the formula. And if one takes the analogy that Dover's powders is like the teaching, the Work, and one could conceive that over time, the Work itself will involve, and will lose some of its essential elements. And in fact, I think even Gurdjieff mentions this some place, that all the teachings do involve, devolve - start to lose important parts of the teaching. So I think maybe this is a question many of us have about the Work, and maybe why a lot of us come to a conference like this, to sort of compare notes with people from other groups, and say, you know, have we been fed real Dover's powders, or has someone fed us a fake teaching. How do we all know that we've all received real Dover's powders on our groups, that we come from.

Terje Tonne: In that perspective, the pharmacist would be who?

All & Everything Conference 2010

Participant: A teacher?

Terje Tonne: No... <laughing>

Participants: Or someone who, possibly, yes? A group leader, an author of a book -

Terje Tonne: Yes.

Participant: Or any of us ourselves. As someone mentioned the other night - the man makes the system, the system doesn't make the man. A system is just the map. The formula for Dover's powders was a map. The map is not the territory.

Terje Tonne: What's the territory?

Participant: Our inner life. Our inner being. Our North Pole.

Participant: Can I suggest a different interpretation of this chapter? I think earlier in this chapter, Gurdjieff speaks about the caste system, or the system of classes. And we have a saying that society is a sedimentary rock - it's in layers. And the whole chapter, I see it linking together with these processes of reciprocal destruction. Gurdjieff is pointing out the conditions in which this takes place, and the caste system then links with the - Gurdjieff criticizes doctors, to the point of suggesting that the word "doctor" should be used as a swearword. And this then links to the Dover's powders, I think. And the Dover's powders are the various elements of the caste system, and we exist in a caste system because we believe there are experts out there who know what they're doing. Gurdjieff links the doctors, whose job, he says, is to write out prescriptions with the Dover's powders, which is then the medicine that they give out. And in fact there is no quinine in the formula, there is no expert there. What the significance of all that is, I don't know, but that's my understanding of it, as an alternative viewpoint.

Terje Tonne: Does that bring us back to suggestibility in one way, you think?

Participant: I don't know in this context, I know that suggestibility is one of the great vices that Gurdjieff points out.

Terje Tonne: What you just said, do you see that it brings suggestibility into the perspective?

Participant: Oh, yes, I see what you mean - yes. We are suggestible because we believe there are experts out there who know what they are doing.

Terje Tonne: Exactly.

Participant: And we rely on them, and so we, in a sense, accept our level in whatever caste system we belong. Not necessarily outwardly, but inwardly, we have some idea of our place in things. We live according to that, because we believe there are experts out there who know what they're doing, when we do not. So there is suggestibility, but he also suggests that - I think for the quinine, I seem to remember he suggests that any medicine, I think it's the pharmacist says it, any medicine can be effective, all you need is faith in it.

Terje Tonne: Who says that?

Participant: I think it's the pharmacist.

Terje Tonne: Yes -

Participant: Something - says that. Maybe it's Beelzebub, I can't remember.

Terje Tonne: No, it is the pharmacist.

Participant: But, he says, it doesn't matter that there's no quinine in it, because what really counts, is that the patient must have faith in the medicine.

Terje Tonne: Yes.

Participant: Which I think is an interesting comment as well.

Terje Tonne: Yes.

Participant: But that does link to suggestibility.

Terje Tonne: Yes, to me that points direct to suggestibility.

Participant: Yeah.

Participant: Pharmacist also tells Beelzebub that the powder is in such demand, because everybody has heard from somebody else that it's an excellent medicine. And there would not be enough of, whether it is the quinine or opium, on the planet, to fill all these orders anyway. But I'm finding it very useful that we're exploring this question of mixing, and the necessity for appropriate sequencing of mixing what's got to be mixed with what. In *In Search of the Miraculous* , Gurdjieff gives Ouspensky a chemical allegory of a retort, a flask, with different powders, and they have to be put in the right order, because when the heat is finally applied, they will crystallize. And a man who crystallizes with an inappropriate mixing of his understanding and his development, is in a very difficult situation - has got to be melted down and he has to start all over again. So, this brings up for me the feel of everything we've been talking about today in terms of our different levels and our understanding and looking at the laws of healing and...

All & Everything Conference 2010

Terje Tonne: Corruption.

Participant: Corruption. Here we have the subtlety of knowing where to place the emphasis, the attitude. So all the factors can be there, but if you put them in the wrong order, or have the wrong emphasis, or they're not connected appropriately, then it looks like the real thing on the outside, but it really is corrupted on the inside. Both in terms of organizations as well as one's own inner life.

Participant: Yes, absolutely. I believe that in Gurdjieff's lifetime, many times he disbanded groups, because he felt that even though <inaudible> they were using were similar to what he was doing, the motivation perhaps was wrong, and that, he mention, would lead to madness. So, pharmaceutics is a dangerous business. So I also agree with you like <inaudible>, on the surface of it a lot people do a lot of work on themselves, but their motives are often allied to financial gain or fame. And they do put enormous amount effort and detail, and the religion of today has become this constant working and putting all one's energy in life and oil into promoting these socially acceptable values.

And they're putting just as much work as people following perhaps spiritual path, maybe even more - but to me it seems that the motivation is misguided. And the question of eternity or <inaudible> - the perspective on things is very short term. So that's all.

Terje Tonne: You touched upon motivation. Now, all the difficulties that we have, if we look at being a pharmacist and operating a very dirty business, like this, as I see it, the Dover thing, what would motivate us in such - is there anything in this chapter that points in the direction that we don't have to go down with this powder, but can be motivated, and in that case, by what?

Participant: What that implies, below the surface of that, and he spells out, I think, very clearly here, is to make as much money as possible with as little effort. The deception of the pharmacist and the analyst reminded me of the deception that he found in Chicago, with the slaughterhouses - with the false advertising. And at a restaurant, was that New York or Paris, where they were serving all of these wonderful meals, and he goes into the kitchen, and there's one old guy in a t-shirt with a cigarette hanging out of his mouth, opening cans and dumping them all in the same pot. So again it seems to me, try to get something for nothing if possible, or very little in the way of effort or disturbance of my self-calming. And whether that's literally money, as is usually the case, or recognition, or approbation... or whatever it is we want. I remember, he said to Ouspensky early on, payment is always in advance. But here, most of the time, most everybody is trying to get the advance without the payment, or the product without paying something up front.

Terje Tonne: Seems to me that these corruptive processes in us, they must be turned into, somehow, to become something we don't run away from, but accept, and can be nourished by, through accepting it, not explaining it away. But that is very difficult to see, how this - by the head, with the intellect - how this nourishment can come about, from my mechanism. But that is what we have got - our negativity, that is what we have got. Everything which is mechanical in us, so that is to me what we have to be motivated by, not be pressed down by. It has been shown to us in moments when we have some awareness, not in order to be misused, but also again as a trust. In trust that we should use it to something.

Participant: I thought about the question you asked, and what comes to my mind, is the necessity of keeping a critical attitude. Both to one own I's and also to what other try to teach you. And this business of trying to verify what is suggested. Did the mike function?

Terje Tonne: Uhm-hm.

Participant: It's just a little wiseacreing on my part, but it's not the first time that powder's been mentioned. In the third descent, the beings of Atlantis took the horn of the animal, the "pirmaral", and made a powder of it to heal people. And they went far and wide to find this animal in order to extract the powder from it. And that was in Atlantis, which for me is essence - my essence. Now we have another powder, and I think Steve mentioned a retort - and a retort is what the alchemical process is used to mix these powders. And the powders that are mixed in this laboratory are ersatz, so they're not authentic. So the alchemical process that is required to transform these substances cannot take place, because the ingredients are ersatz. So that's just something I thought might fit into this, too.

Participant: I have a question. To me it is quite clear that the whole process from the physicians to the prescription, to the pharmacist, to the laboratory, and even the ones who analyze the powder, and at the very end the patients themselves, it's all fake. It's fake, and it's all filled with falseness, and the essential thing in this process is the powder, which must be very important in one way or another. And I wonder, what is this falseness and this fake about this whole process, what it is related to?

Participant: Well, it seems to me that - I read the book a couple of years ago, and it took me like two years to read it. And I cannot say I remember much of it. But the attitude in some of the chapters of Gurdjieff was that what human being needs, is Work. And this is very hard to accomplish, to find. Now, we had a few good traditions as human beings, but it's not that those traditions could save us, or give us the effect that Work has, but maybe let's say they would make our life a bit easier. For instance, when he speaks about this Persian, I think he was, that, in his village, they were still keeping some good traditions, like, you know, washing your organs after you go to the bathroom. Now, I think that I understood it like this, at least - that what he's trying to say, is that this will not give you Work. It had something healthy in it, and we even lost those little things, those healthy things. So, my lecture on this powder is that - and please, if there are other opinions, I want to hear it - is not that this... the real thing. It's something that could help us a little bit, and we even lost that, they even took that out of our lives. We did, not they.

Terje Tonne: Is there anyone who have anything to this question of haughtiness and servility? What is that about? Has it something to do with lack of communication?

All & Everything Conference 2010

Participant: To me, it suggest different kinds of insincerity.

Terje Tonne: Hmm?

Participant: Opium was used to calm someone from cough, which is a violent reaction of the body. And also to calm crying of babies. And being natural, I feel - that being a natural product, although it has some bad sides, because it has inside it the law of Triamazikamno, somehow it's got also regenerative power. And although, somehow, it helps to calm the body, does some more things to the maybe soul, spirit. One side is that I react to the reaction of the body, I don't listen to the reaction, so I want to shut it down. And that's my fault - my first mistake. And the pharmacist take advantage of me, and they give me some nonsense, some bullshit, they give me what I want, in final end. I mean, finally I get what I want, what I ask for - I ask for shut it down, I get it. But I have the option to try to find the law, the law of three inside me, and try to use it. But I don't remember, ordinary, mostly, I don't remember to do that. Thank you.

Participant: Ultimately, the biggest deception, before the pharmacists, is the people themselves who go to buy the medicine, as you suggest, because they're looking outside of themselves for something which perhaps they're capable of - they don't need - but they're capable of manufacturing within themselves. So they're looking outwards instead of inwards. And the hint is the, as you mentioned, the North Pole. But, it seems to me there is another side, and that's my personal opinion, that human beings also have this element of playfulness. So it's not always looking for the inner truth, but it's also a joy in playing with material elements that we find around us, just like children play and experiment. And they make powders and they're trying to find the effects of powders, so - yes, there are these games that pharmacists play, and people get fooled because they want to be fooled. I'm not sure how serious the matter is, and if one is to take it to such an extent, because at the same time we have a playful nature which has to do with discovering the wonders of the world, and seeing the game for what it is - it's a game. So, it's a serious game, perhaps, but it's still a game.

Participant: Well, I think the story with the Dover powder is very little game, it's very serious matter. It reflects the surrogate character of this powder, of medicine's drugs that we use, of language that we use, and it refers to surrogate traditions that we find nowadays in plentitude - in world, in Internet. And, eventually it points to the terror situation of living a surrogate life, ersatz life, and of course everything depends on how serious we are about the purpose of our life, and of life on Earth. But, as very often in Gurdjieff's writings, this episode is another reminder, alarm clock, telling us that we have to be, and to learn to do. And to overcome this blindness and the sleep think.

Participant: I think the key word in this chapter is sincerity. I also read some Sufi work, and two very key factors in any personal development, they seem to stress, are humility and sincerity. And that cause me to ponder the meaning of sincerity. And the more you ponder sincerity, or in my view, the more I ponder sincerity, the more I realize how difficult it is to be sincere. We all write "sincerely" at the end of letters, but when you really ponder the meaning of the word - and it's one of these words, it's like "love", where you can't define it, it comes from... it's a felt, it's feeling, it's very difficult to define, it's not honesty. That's my view of this - this whole chapter is built around the concept of sincerity, and ultimately sincerity with ourselves. Are we cheating ourselves, are we fooling ourselves, or are we being sincere with ourselves in what we're trying to achieve and how we're trying to achieve it, and what purposes are we trying to achieve it for.

Participant: I think it is also about the complexity of the world, that he wanted to indicate. Because, in the previous chapters he was writing that the world becomes unnecessary complex, and goes the wrong way. And this is a good example, because if you remember, he first describes how they changed the ingredients in the Dover powder, and then he describes that there's a way to check, but then, this way is also false. Yeah, you. The civilization has set it up the way that the user, the consumer, he can go out and check the quality of the powder. But in reality, whatever complex this was, and this requires the chemist, the analyst, who gets his education, who gets a job at the laboratory - he does not check, he does not care, because there's a social structure in place that prevents him from spoiling relationships with this pharmacist. So, whatever complex - the society gets complex, but this does not prevent it - it gets only falser, in a sense. And we have to remember that this was the twenties and the thirties of the last century, and we can see that it has gotten worse.

We have now ten layers of checks and balances that do not work. Do you agree?

Terje Tonne: I think it's very important -

Participant in background: <inaudible>... said... <inaudible>

Participant: Yeah, because people do this automatically, without conscience -

Participant in background: <inaudible>... even inside ourselves... <inaudible>

Participant: The doctor wants to make money, so he replaces opium with quinine, and the chemist in the laboratory, he was sent to the university by his mother. And he probably just wants to keep his job, because he's good for nothing, he's not a real professional. And then, now we have lots of those checks, and we know that although the pharmaceutical companies make some good molecules, good medicine, they also sometimes conceal from the public the facts that harm this public. And all <inaudible>. Those of you who are from the United States, they certainly read more and know more about this.

Terje Tonne: If you look at all these characters that you mention as somebody in myself, in ourselves, then I think you make a very good point. Did you say that there were somebody who didn't care?

Participant: Well - it is a structure where nobody cares.

All & Everything Conference 2010

Terje Tonne: Yes. And I think that for me, the warning is that we have something in ourself that doesn't care. How do we deal with this information?

Participant: Yeah, well -

Terje Tonne: That is the challenge.

Participant: This is what I thought would be the outcome. You have to think that if society is structured the way that it will not take care of yourself, so you're the only who can do that. And it's not because somebody is wilfully doing something or not doing something. It's because it's set out this way. Everything is set out - like, yesterday, we were talking about education, and it's nobody's fault, it's just - it is made this way.

Participant: Yeah, I - there's a short paragraph here which puts it very beautifully, I think. And it's because our inability to - he says, the disappearance of the ableness to be. As a consequence, he says, these two properties consist in this: that they always behave toward each other, either, so to say, haughtily, or servilely. During the manifestation of both these properties, there are paralyzed in them all relations on which are called "equal terms". And without anybody whomsoever, thanks to which, not only the inner sincere, but also even the outer, ordinary, habitual relations have become established among them in such a way that already, it has become quite usual, particularly in recent times, that if someone belongs to a caste considerably higher than the caste of another, then in everything, and always in relation to this other, there arise in him impulses called there either haughtiness, or contempt, or patronage, or condescension, and so on. And if someone considers his own caste lower than that of another, then there will infallibly arise in him impulses which they call self-abasement, false humility, sycophancy, boot-licking, cringing and many other such specific impulses, the totality of which constantly corrodes in their presences what is called the awareness of one's own individuality, which ought to be present in them also.

So we don't have that awareness, we have no ableness to be, so - I mean I can see all sorts of stuff in myself when I'm not in a state of awareness, that I behave like that. And I think that's one of the marvellous things about this chapter, that I can see myself on every page.

Host: Does anybody want to say anything else now, or should we <inaudible>

Participant: Sorry to keep you, but I'd like to take this opportunity to step out of this circle a little bit, and I think, suggest a methodology for understanding this chapter, at a different level. I thought I would describe how I read *Beelzebub's Tales* - because Gurdjieff says that you must read it three times. First is just reading any ordinary book, which is what we do, and it's pretty horrible, very difficult to understand. The second time we read it out loud, and I found that when I did that, the easiest way to do it was to read between the commas. You reach a comma, you pause.

So it starts: "It was in the year 223 after the creation of the world."

"By objective time calculation."

"Or."

And so on. And I found that then it was actually a beautiful book, it flowed like music, like a piece of music, and you could hear Gurdjieff's music in it. And then, for this chapter, the number for this chapter, I found was eighteen, and we've mentioned the number eighteen. And the way I read, and I don't know whether you would want to try it - I then read it, I record it, and I read it between the commas, and at each comma I pause for eighteen seconds. And then I read the next section and pause for eighteen seconds. And so on. If you want to try this, to read it is actual torture. But when you play it back, or listen to someone reading in this way, it absolutely transforms this book. You can treat it as a sort of meditation exercise, because it's quite a long wait, eighteen seconds. But I found that for me, this method has transformed my understanding of this book. And this, I think, connects to the fact that the things that we mentioned earlier, how the psyche of man is divided, and I've come to believe that each division of the psyche works at a different speed, a different tempo.

And that for this chapter, it's destined for one particular part of our psyche, and the particular tempo of what Gurdjieff might call the swing of thought, is this eighteen seconds. I don't know whether anyone is interested in that, but I found it to be a very effective way of reading this book. It takes a heck of a long time - you get about four pages done in an hour. And it's not, I hasten to add, it's not eighteen seconds for each chapter. Each chapter has a different time on it. So I hope you don't mind me mentioning all that.

Terje Tonne: Oh yeah, go ahead.

Participant: I may be incorrect, but I believe that Gurdjieff quotes Endlessness at least twice, here's commandments. And if I'm correct, my memory says that the eighteenth commandment of Endlessness, is "Love everything that breathes."

Participant: The first commandment of Jesus.

Participant: The eighteenth commandment of Endlessness.

<laughter>

Participant: I think that's good enough to end our afternoon.

Terje Tonne: Yes.

End of Session

Seminar 2: Chapter 6, Meetings with Remarkable Men

Abram Yelov

Facilitator: Ian MacFarlane

Introduction

Good morning everybody. This morning we will start off with Chapter 6 of *Meetings with Remarkable Men*: Abram Yelov. This will go until coffee break. I put together a short introduction of some of the points that I thought were worth further looking into in this chapter, of course anyone can chip in with any thoughts, questions, observations that they have later. I thought these points to me were significant and possibly worth considering as part of our trying to dissect the meaning of this chapter. So, quickly, I will run through a few slides here and expand on my thoughts. I have about five points of things that I thought we could possibly look at, if we have time or interest. Working through the chapter the first thing I saw significant was that Gurdjieff mentioned the study of ancient texts as possible sources of at least some of the things he gives us in the Work. He mentioned something to the effect that after exhausting his efforts to find any truths among contemporary men, he started studying ancient texts. In this chapter Abram Yelov was an antiquarian bookseller who had access to all kinds of ancient manuscripts and had a very extensive knowledge of the authors, the books they wrote and where these books could be obtained. And also he had an interest in the esoteric ideas in many of the ancient texts. So, part of this chapter has to do with, or at least mentions that the two of them studied ancient texts together trying to find out esoteric truths.

Moving on to what I call role playing. There are some stories about that in this chapter having to do with the Italian statue maker who made plaster statues and sold them in the market. In connection with the role playing there is the idea of making money by underhanded means. Not entirely honest. A little further on in the chapter, Gurdjieff mentions the character of Abram Yelov and he mentions that Abram had eyes that were burning like two live coals. That reminded me of a picture will show you later.

At the end, he talks again about the study of languages. He again mentions this fact of 18 languages in this chapter; so there is a connection with the chapter we did yesterday from *Beelzebub's Tales*.

So quickly, the study of ancient texts as possible sources of the Work. I have dug out a few examples of ancient texts that I have discovered on the internet that quite possibly Gurdjieff may have read in some sort of original manuscript form, given the time and the place he was looking at this information. The first is a diagram from Raymond Lull who lived from 1232 to 1316. This is a step diagram from one of his manuscripts at that time. Going up the steps, it starts, it looks like rocks and fire, vegetation, animals, man, angels and God and then up possibly to the sun, the Absolute. It reminded me of the step diagram from Ouspensky's book. The Chain of Being.

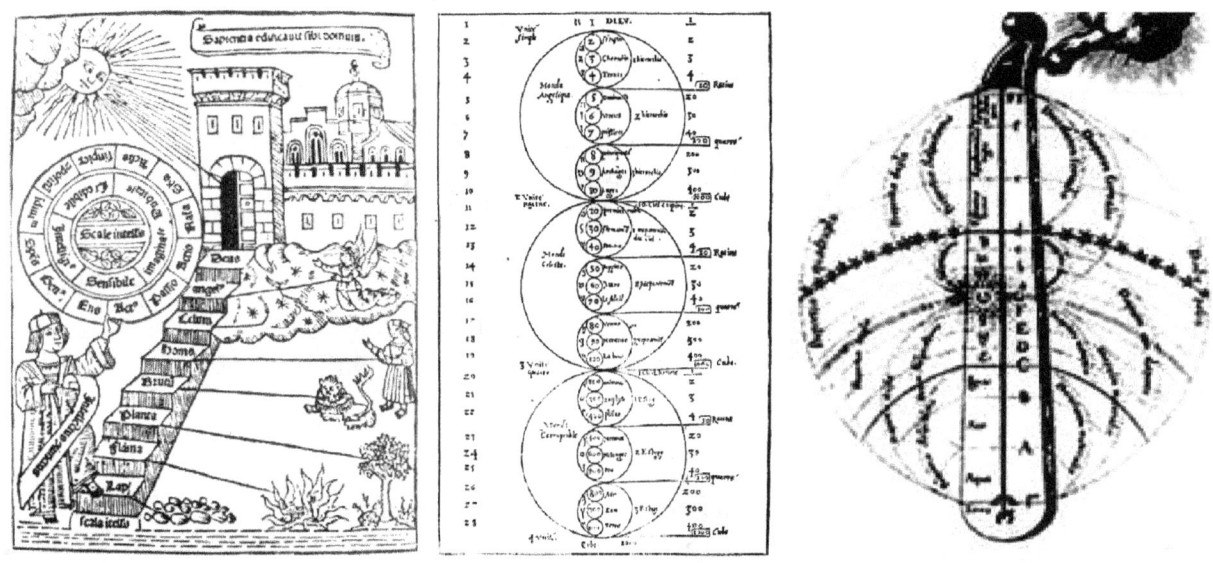

Raymond Lull Step Diagram   Harmony of the World   Fludd's Divine Monochord

And here's a similar diagram from 1550, or so, on the numerical relationships between three worlds. The Harmony of the World. This diagram again shows the nesting of the triads on different scales. Again somewhat reminiscent of the nesting of the enneagrams Dimitri showed us the other day.

Robert Fludd's famous divine monochord. Here we have the musical scale representing different levels of the Universe.

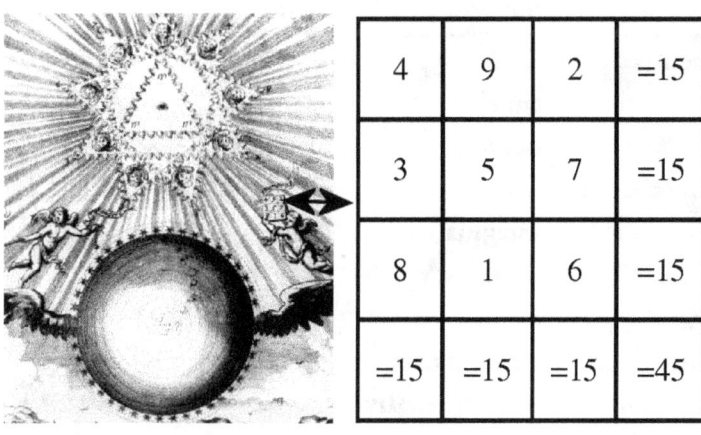
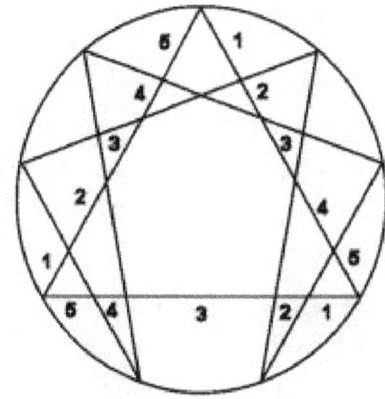

Kircher Enneagram   Magic Square of 15 / 45   Magic Triangle of 15/ 45

83

Again from 1600s, Gurdjieff may have seen things like this - Athanathus Kircher (1602-1680), here we have an enneagram. It is not the enneagram with the lines drawn exactly as we know it, but is a nine-pointed figure with a triad in the middle. A triangle. One interesting thing on this diagram is that you can see up here in the middle of the right side what is called a magic square. It is composed of the numbers 1 to 9 and if you add them up horizontally, vertically or diagonally, the numbers add up to 15. If you add all the numbers from 1 to 9 you get 45. I thought this interesting because why did he have this magic square of 15 in here with this enneagram? If you take the triangle in the (Gurdjieff) enneagram, it is crossed by the inner lines - thus, each side of the triangle has five segments - if you add up the numbers from 1-5 you get 15, if you add up the whole triangle, you get 45. So I'm not sure what significance this has for our study of the enneagram or *Beelzebub's Tales*, but maybe chapter 15 and chapter 45 might be worth looking at; you've all heard of squaring the circle well this is like triangulating the square or something because the numbers all add up. Although I am very sceptical myself of things that have to do with adding up numbers, like adding up the numbers in your name and that gives you something about your personality character. I am a little dubious of those kind of things. I thought this idea of 15 being involved with the enneagram.

And again another enneagram from Ramon Lull from his book Ars Brevis, in 1300. There are nine points in a circle but there are three circles on here and on each of these circles he had corresponding philosophical ideas and so on. He could move these three circles around so that he could have different ideas on each ring and as he moved the circles around he could juxtapose various ideas and derive philosophical arguments from it. It's a big thick book with all kinds of series of ideas broken up into nine points that he could put on his enneagram.

TABLE 6. THE ALPHABET OF THE *ARS BREVIS*.

	Fig. A	Fig. T	Questions and Rules†	Subjects	Virtues	Vices
B	goodness	difference	whether?	God	justice	avarice
C	greatness	concordance	what?	angel	prudence	gluttony
D	eternity*	contrariety	of what?	heaven	fortitude	lust
E	power	beginning	why?	man	temperance	pride
F	wisdom	middle	how much?	imaginative	faith	accidie
G	will	end	of what kind?	sensitive	hope	envy
H	virtue	majority	when?	vegetative	charity	ire
I	truth	equality	where?	elementative	patience	lying
K	glory	minority	how? and with what?	instrumentative	pity	inconstancy

And just shortly, here is a list - the Alphabet of the Ars Brevis - and it's down the one side its got abcdefghik, and these are some of the concepts that he would put on this enneagram and it's interesting to notice at the end we have the virtues and vices which is very reminiscent of the enneagram of the personality.

So I leave that to you to ponder on whether this has any significance in Gurdjieff's study or not; whether he was aware of this material.

In the role-playing side of things, Gurdjieff said that he played the role of a blockhead or someone who wasn't too smart when he went to work for the Italian statue maker. By playing this role of being someone who wasn't too smart, the Italian statue maker started trusting him and openly making his plaster mixtures and moulds and, so that Gurdjieff could find out his secrets of how he did this and once Gurdjieff had learned these secrets, then he went off and started his own business and undercut the Italian. So maybe we can look at how role playing is useful in this Work. That leads into he idea of making money by underhanded means, as he did trick the Italian guy into giving up his secrets and then he went out and made money himself selling, as he called it in the book, I forget the word he used, but, cheap chintzy statues that people would put in their houses as trinkets. He didn't seem to put a very high opinion of the value on these statues, and he talked about making money boxes and so on.

And this could maybe be related to the idea of finding esoteric knowledge using so-called underhanded means. For instance, Gurdjieff played the role to steal the secrets of making the plaster statues. There's also the story of him selling the American canaries. They would catch sparrows and die them various colours to make them look like something they weren't. And he would sell people fake canaries. There's the story of the map of pre-sand Egypt that he surreptitiously obtained. And there is also the interview that someone had with him and when they asked him where he got the Work, he said, "Well maybe I stole it".

So this idea of deception in the Work has come up quite often and I thought that might be an interesting thing to look into in this chapter. This of course raises the question of ethics in the Work. How much lying or misrepresentation in the name of the Work is acceptable.?

Eyes burning like two live coals was one of his descriptions of Abram Yelov. Here's a picture of Mr Gurdjieff with very striking eyes; many of you have seen this picture before. I just thought it was an interesting aside. And finally the study of different languages. We had a lot of discussion about that the other day. One could also think of the study of languages as the study of different paths or different ways of Working; different traditions. Gurdjieff certainly studied many different traditions in his early life; many of us here are continually studying other traditions or other languages, if one wants to speak about having a special language of the Work. Each tradition has its own language.

So that's again a summary of the points I made and now I will open up the floor to any comments and observations about this chapter that anyone would have.

All & Everything Conference 2010

Seminar Discussion

Participant 1: In addition to those examples what also struck me was the story of the tradition of the Aisors who were the stealers of crosses and the Armenians were the salted ones. I just want to get that correct in case there are any Armenians or Aisors in the room. As I read this it also resonated for me with the chapter from A&E we were discussing yesterday because there seemed to be interweaving contrasts between sincerity and deception. Some of this role playing didn't hurt anybody. To play on the religious feelings of sincere but simple people in manufacturing relics when one is supposedly a priest; to me that's very different than painting canaries for American tourists. The sincerity of Yelov in his relationships, even if he lost his temper he didn't hold a grudge. The rhythm of this, looking at the contrasts between one type of deception and another, the level of motivation, the quality of the heart and understanding behind that seemed to me to resonate with the chapter we had yesterday. I thought someone had put a lot of thought into pairing these two because they seemed to be companion pieces and pick up the themes we discussed yesterday.

Participant 2: In addition to these ways of making money there is the story about where he is shifting the typewriter with the carriage return button and he kept that for a long time so as to give the idea it was a lot of work and so on. But it was just pressing one button. These ways of making money to me seem to be connected with energy. Money is an energy and he is spending little energy to get some energy. Taking into account there is this much energy in each of the centres that we have available during our lifetime, the money we use is spent in order to get the organic body through this life paying bills and so on. It is an indication to not getting too involved in life. Not spending too much time to get hold of what we need for the planetary body. At the same time it is also an indication that we should spend our energy very carefully.

Participant 3: Something to be said about this idea about underhandedness; also the fact that none of these things were actually illegal. I think this is important because if one tries to draw a line saying that "is every action justified in the name of esoteric knowledge or whatever" the incidents of stealing murder and things like that, I think the line is drawn here in a much finer way. This is why I tend to subscribe with what Terje just said. Even the canaries - he did put in some effort, he didn't just take the canary and sell it as it was. His efforts should have been paid somehow. And calling it an American canary after all, when, you know, when American things are sold in a similar manner, just with a good wrapping. So I think there's a line he keeps well within legitimacy. He doesn't cross the line. The fact that he doesn't ever cross the line shows something I believe in the way he puts the matter. Yes he did break into the priests chest but what did he do he copied he didn't steal anything and that just went beyond some priests hesitation to use what he had. In a way that had no value for him whatsoever. for the priest.

Participant 21: I think that it can be agreed that at that time he was very much on the line of being legitimate of doing something illegal. I also remember in the *In Search of the Miraculous*, when Ouspensky came to him with questions about when will you tell us all the secrets, he told him maybe jokingly that he shouldn't wait, its up to you, you should be able to steal them if you have to at a certain point I remember that. I think that falls in line with what was said here. Further on in other chapters he dwells more on the business side and I think he was just a very talented person; he knew, and was pushing the lines a bit further in business using the lack of knowledge of other people; like as has been mentioned with the example of the carriage. The service industries do this daily; thousands of times with people when they take something that is easy to repair and they charge you who knows, and keep it for awhile, and tell you that the problem a lot more important than it really was. And its again in the structure of the society; everywhere in service they diagnose and then they cure and that's the same person. They are willing to diagnose the worst so they can get as much money as they can from the cure.

Participant 2: I start to think a little about the different sides of us; the different centers and so on. We have communication problems and sometimes it might be that we need underhand means to connect to different sides of ourselves.

Participant 5: Could you explain what underhanded means you use to connect with different.

Participant 2: I am not sure if I can explain that; but it seems that if I approach directly some part of myself I get into trouble. So I have to find a way besides that.

Participant 6: Yes I wanted to say that in that chapter when Gurdjieff is working for someone and pretending to be stupid and someone shows him a technique of how he works shows both the term, it doesn't take in this life - you don't have to be very bright to learn a skill so maybe he is implying a lot of people who apparently have the secrets or can do something, in a way they are a bit blockheads themselves, just know how to do one thing very well. It certainly wasn't illegal to do that and what he was learning was a technique. So I wouldn't call that stealing, that type of copying. What I would call stealing which I think is very important for me at least there's a difference between knowledge and information. Knowledge is freely available you can go onto the internet and type in a question in Google and you'll get millions of informative pages on that however when you're talking about knowledge which is not information, it has the signature of someone who has perhaps invented something of their own or is part of a lineage in which case it is important that one states the source where one got that information from. For instance if you are trying to look into the principles of how something works you might quote for instance Gurdjieff's ideas on how to conserve energy or do not express negative emotions. Gurdjieff said that as part of a teaching and if one was talking about that one refers to the source. By quoting the source one enables others to also go back to the ideas and do the research. It is important to always state the source because that way one can actually perpetuate knowledge; whereas what we see hear is examples of being a master in a market place which we all have to be in order to survive.

Participant 4: Seems to me that Mr Gurdjieff had a very active way of standing in front of life. In front of the difficulties that came in his search. The moment I read this book my question was, Am I like that? Could I have such an active way of standing in front of difficulties; would I have such a goal? Do I want to achieve something so bad that I can force a little the lines whatever. that means.

Participant 7: I was interested about what we said about underhand behaviour because I don't really understand this book at all but what little I do understand it seems to me that Gurdjieff is encouraging us to take the initiative; I think that's what you were alluding to. When Gurdjieff acts from underhand means he actually takes the initiative from himself. He himself initiates the actions rather than drifting with the rest of society; with the social mind, with the communal mind. He takes the initiative and that's the significance of the underhand actions of Gurdjieff. and he has acted upon it to his benefit.

Participant 4: I would like to return to the study of ancient texts as possible sources of work. The basis for this as I see it or the fundament for any real change has to come from something that is not me. in the sense of ordinary me. I cannot, so as to speak, fix my situation or repair my situation from the level of ordinary me so I need to get in the position where I am able to receive, this is the idea of the sources coming from outside. If you look at the triad of regeneration of form, matter and life as a neutralising factor it is completely different from the healing. So its not a question about repairing my machine or repairing my life, on an organic level, but it is a complete transformation or change that from the level of being an organic entity with the potential and then I can't use all the material that is implanted in me from the level of earth. The information has to come from a much higher level; this is what the ancient sources are referring to. Maybe try to put it at the peak point it would not be possible for me to really take this or be able to receive these sources if I had something in me that made me believe that I could do this myself. I have to be in the position where I can become an real antenna helpless, I must have something that recognises my helplessness and then I will be get in the position of becoming an antenna for these sources.

Participant 8: I think that one of the values that Yelov has is about respect of the religion of others. I think this ancient knowledge came to him from Aisors because here is the only place that Gurdjieff explains this. Its not a question of to whom a man prays but a question of his faith. Faith is conscience the foundation of which is made in childhood. If a man changes his religion he loses his conscience. Conscience is the most valuable thing in a man. I think this is something that came from the ancient knowledge.

Participant 4: In this paragraph referred to he separates religion from faith; faith is something we are born with as potential; it is there; when he speaks of childhood it is that purity by which we were born. There are different means of getting back to this source; its not a question about the door which you enter, which religion you use. It is beyond religion. He says he respects all religions but first of all I respect his conscience and since his conscience is sustained by his faith and his faith by his religion therefore I respect his religion. He doesn't respect as such, he respects religion as a means, as a tool, so he separates the two. And clearly says that the main thing is something that you are born with, that you have.

Participant 9: I would like to go back to something Dimitri, the Russian said about Gurdjieff urging Ouspensky to steal. The system the ideas; this brought to my mind a question. Did Gurdjieff actually have anything to be stolen? What would be his view to protect what he had? from people like Ouspensky. And then do we have anything that can be stolen. Are there people

Seminar 2

that want to steal it; and what would be the right attitude to have towards the things we have, that we consider worth stealing? Should we protect them and in what way?

Participant 10: I think this raises a very interesting point. Is truth a possession, do I own the truth? and do I sell it; and what does it mean if somebody steals the truth. Is it a property of certain groups of people. This raises all kinds of interesting questions. Why would I steal something that belongs to everybody universally. How much does truth cost. Can I steal an idea and profit by it?

Participant 11: I want to draw your attention to another aspect of this chapter, to the relationship between three people; Pogassian, Yelov and Gurdjieff. We see here three young men in Tbilisi Tiflis where I grew up. I can visualise these youngsters in their twenties, and the relationship between them, I would say they had very sincere, very close friendship. I even would go further and say they created a community or rather a brotherhood. We couldn't even think of them stealing something from each other. On the contrary the relationship are very warm, sincere and true. Then there is an outer world; the world outside. Don't forget they just entered the responsible stage of their lives. They are still close to the preparatory stage as they are young. The outer world is alien, its outside, is a source of energy, it gives means for living for sustaining themselves and also a world that can nourish their souls and help them in their spiritual quest. So on one side they find ancient texts and as we know from this book they find friends and sources of knowledge and sources of direct connection with higher levels of knowledge and with ancient tradition. T his is what the book is about. On the other hand this outer world has another lower aspect, here comes in stealing, underhanded means and sort of indifference.

Yes Gurdjieff made the tasteless statues. Sold them. Yelov helped him. The relationship between brotherhood of spiritual seekers and the complex outer is a problem that I wanted to draw your attention to. Thank you.
Participant 4: Thinking of stealing in light of inner psychology; there are some I's in us that are quite shameless. These I's we need to protect from stealing what we have. I have been warned about this speaking lightly about the work; speaking about ideas where circumstances are not supposed to do that because its on everyday level. These formatory parts don't realise that there are different levels. So I think one should protect the work oneself.; what one has worked for; from being robbed or taken down to the level of those I's. Really one should have nothing to do with this work. It is important for everyone in this work to realise there are I's in me that have nothing to do with this work and I must protect them from stealing. The motive for them to speak about the work is connected with ego. Bragging self-importance all that.

Speaker 8: What the words signal to my mind Is it wise? He should be careful when you try to focus your attention that maybe your thoughts or body action may steal your attention from you. Take it away. So I realized at this point what is brought here is us protecting our attention and focus from being stolen from what we have to do in order to survive in the outside world. So maybe this is not exactly ethical in the sense of the ethics as perceived in everyday life. But I suppose its very legitimate if you see it in the spiritual point of view. Where you have to do whatever it takes in order to protect your attention, your energy, as is said from being stolen from whatever is happening outside.

Participant 11: Well continuing with this line of thoughts a considerations I remembered several methods that I am using in Russia where I am working with a number of groups on the basis of Gurdjieffian and others ideas. and letters I remember that from time to time I ask my friends we don't have disciples and gurus; all my friends, my younger friends work with me and I with them, I asked them to go together to a market somewhere in the south of Russia and they receive notes with special tasks. Those tasks include begging money. So lets say five of us will go and ask for alms, for money. Others have tasks of standing in a crowded marketplace and preaching different religions. Christianity or Islam or Buddhism to passers by. There is a task of selling little pieces of paper. From notebooks we tear off several pieces of paper; the price the meaning of this paper is zero, but we try to sell these pieces of paper to salespeople and customers passing by for a certain price. When they ask us what the meaning of this paper; one of my friends said in the morning you fold the paper into two then into four and then you make a wish and then your day is filled with luck and success. There are other examples of what we do. Of the kind. This brings us back to our relationship with the outer world. The main purpose of these exercises that I give to my friends is to free themselves from the hypnosis of the everyday life; hypnosis of the outer world. I think this idea this project was inspired by Gurdjieff and by him painting birds, by stealing secrets of the production of bad taste statues, and from the whole style of his life. The outer world is not a human being. It is a mechanism. When dealing with this machine we have to leave out the morals we apply in our relations between us. We have to understand that we have to overcome our suggestibility. Our hypnosis: to be free when dealing with this world. Which is not easy. Thank you.

Participant 9: What Terje said about the I's in me who have nothing to do with the work reminded me what Jesus said the left side shouldn't know what the right side is doing. In this I see somehow my left side or personality wanting to steal the work and sometimes talking about the work from the left side, from the thief who wants to possess; doesn't have the right to do that but he still like to take it for himself.

Participant 12: I want to pursue this theme of alternating between looking outside and inside; and their correspondence. One thing that occurs to me now why I was so touched with the story with the Aisors as cross-stealer, looking inside myself, the simple primitive religious people of Russia who would believe in anything and were taken advantage of with these phony relics. As a you man there was a part of me which was burning and longing to prove to myself that there was something more than the reality that my outer senses, But I could also see that there was a part of me that was extremely gullible and wanted this so badly it was tempted to latch on to anything that had the aura of mystery. Something in my intellect put up a block here and produced a great deal of caution that prevented me, perhaps profitably one way and another from pursuing certain things for fear of being foolish or gullible for taking the risk. So I can see, in a sense, that there was, there is some "Aisors" in me using the Gurdjieff language the equivalent of cross-stealers, that would be quite willing to produce phony relics for this naive open part of myself. That's something I kept guard against for a long time.

For myself my own work following this line of thought, always finding a way to verify to my satisfaction that I have a real practical palpable experience that says something about these ideas has always been a driving aim for me. So with all these fascinating ideas and these wonderful diagrams, for myself I am always looking for the inner experience that may resonate with that. With being cautious not to create something because it would feel good to find a connection. I have to wait until it appears and then when it resonates then the idea or the metaphor or the symbol vibrates for me because its vibrating inside experientially. Since this work is about discovering our inner world it seems to me that is the aim of all of this, to explore outside, upside down, inside out, but always to look for what it wakes inside this universe that is me. Because otherwise it will be gullible it pick up phony relics, it will fool itself and both the victims and the thieves are inside of me. In different levels of underhandedness and cleverness I also feel it is very worthwhile to continue to look at this puzzling question about not to let the left hand to know what the right hand is doing. It is almost as if the parts that work, certainly for many years, have to keep themselves apart from, sort of at the North Pole, otherwise parts that are interested in life and the senses and quick fixes and quick ways of getting energy will distract them or steal from them or run them over. So they must be guarded against. Like sending the young saviour into Egypt so that it's not slaughtered by Herod, until it can be mature enough to be able to take care of itself in that inner world. I wondered too if it's useful to look at the typologies of Pogassian and Yelov and Gurdjieff. Perhaps as maybe man one two and three; or thinking centre, emotional centre, moving instinctive centre and their appropriate harmonious relationship with each other. And what can be accomplished when they find that appreciation and balance for the differences.

Participant 4: I want to follow the speaker about Outside and Inside. Once when Pentland was at George Cornelius place they discussed that the enneagram was got out in the market. And all the disadvantages about it. There was one of Georges students who complained to Pentland that now they even sell shoes that are printing in the snow the enneagram; and Pentland said, Yes, why not? I think that is the right attitude to have in regards stealing. One can easily I think get in a position where one wants to protect the work. And believe that this is a valuable I, one to protect the work from deteriorating in the outside world. If you take a closer look at it might be some kind of self importance; some negativity. I think it has to be like that whenever something valuable is launched, according to law somebody, some sources drawing on it, selling the enneagram, picking parts of this wonderful work and selling it in one way or another; it has to be like that. The only way we can protect this work from being stolen is to work on oneself in the actual moment; a moment just like this.

Participant 14: One thing that Dimitri asks is whether there is something to protect. It reminds me of a story of when descended on a Jewish mystical sect outside in the courtyard were the kids playing cards. Inside doing some ritual. So they broke into the holy of holies and they found an empty space. Just an empty space, which makes me ask what is the value? Is it work on oneself? I think just as beauty is in the eyes of the beholder one has to be true not to let others or society pollute one's right view of how things are. It is very easy to lie to oneself and pick up lies even at the subconscious level and start perceiving the world in a different, in a way that is not true. So on the one hand yes there is something there but its not tangible. Everybody can partake of it. How can you buy and sell something like that which is not separate from our own nature? On the other hand I do still insist there is a difference between knowledge and information. That knowledge has to do with, for instance with me, if you start picking off my nose and my hands my glasses at some point I will become unrecognisable. You will not be able to know me. So the boundaries that make up something are very important. That's why I believe that o teaching Mr Gurdjieff or any other teaching, it should be held and learned or given to others as a wholeness. Not take this part from here and this from there like a lot of new age groups do. They make a big soup and you don't know which part each comes from. I believe it is important to maintain the integrity of that as a sign of knowledge, of knowing who has signed.

Participant 15: About the idea of stealing and protection it reminds me of a saying from the Bible; "Don't throw the holy to the dogs". Of course we must use our discrimination to understand every time and moment what is holy and what is not. That we can transfer outside.

Participant 9: I want to say what is quite close to what Eleny just said; by no means do I want to diminish what Terje said before and what you said. Terje said the need to view this stealing as a process of diminishing the importance inside of me and letting I's of a lower nature take a hold of the work in me. I appreciate all these comments. I view them as being very much to the point. But there is also another dimension to it all. The work has to do with movements. With music and the copyrights to such activities, when we talk about the copyright of the music it's a real copyright of the score. When we talk about the copyright of movements it is the idea that there has been an effort for them not to leak and be used autonomously like Byron said a potpourri of information put together. The question is for me, there is copyrights to the score of the music, and movements have been-there's been an attempt to keep them safely and not disseminate them. So there's a first question right there is there anything else except the score of music and movements? Is there anything in the ideas of the verbal tradition that are secrets not to be revealed? Do we have a feeling about secrets being there and the pace by which these secrets are revealed form some part of the teaching or an aspect of the teaching? Or is everything in the books? In Gurdjieff's books, in Ouspensky's books and the books of other writers or is there something beyond just the presence? I am talking about information that is some sort of copyright. How are we to view this idea of copyright altogether? Whether it is for music or for the movements or for aspects of the ideas. What is the relationship, what is our responsibility to this copyright? How are we to deal with such matters? Or is it just as easy as saying that our work on ourselves the real moment of presence is the fence that separates the holy of holies with things left around for people to pick up indiscriminately? Do we have secrets? Yes I think we do.

Participant 16: What do you say?

Participant 9: Yes I think we do.

Participant 16: Can you say them?

Participant 9: I would be going into the secrets

Seminar 2

Participant 4: I think there are secrets; but those secrets cannot be put on paper. In this teaching it is clearly made a distinction between knowledge and understanding. One of the characters of the knowledge is that it can be conveyed, the understanding can not be conveyed. That is where the secrets are speaking for myself there are things that I have heard for years and years and years and suddenly I have an understanding of what it means. Of course it was completely different from any other ideas I had about it. I think there are secrets and they are very well protected. From me; inside me. I had to do some preparation. I had to use this knowledge; practice this knowledge and that is the key this work gives. Practice the knowledge and understanding will come. Without this practice there is no key into the room.

Participant 17: Part of me thinks its too late to have any secrets; that everything is out there anyway on the internet. and maybe it has to be balanced out. If I speak to somebody about work sometimes I can tell it goes in one ear and out the other. You can tell somebody the secrets of the universe and it goes in one ear and out the other. It explains this in real detail the chapter on form and sequence at the end of the book. where he talks about the reason of knowledge and the reason of understanding. He explains to Hassein that if he hadn't written the book in such a complicated way Hassein would just receive information which would go in one ear and out the other; but for the reason for understanding it would mean that Hassein would have to be logically confronted by with this information and he would have to struggle with it with all his might. He would have to ponder this teaching; the pondering takes part in a separate part of the brain. The result of that pondering would go into his subconscious and would be indelible. The implication being even though he died and not survived, that information gained by logical confrontation, would survive even his death. Gurdjieff is very aware of putting this information out in such a way that everybody would just read it and say "Oh yea I know about that" I think it has very profound implications.

Participant 9: I do want to bring some examples, some thoughts, possibly to satisfy Gabriel as well. We are talking about remembering the self. Or observing the self. That's a better example. We know that there are psychology groups that are talking about working observing the self. One could wonder where this idea came from. At the same time the fact is what they mean about observing the self is meaningless compared to what Gurdjieff meant when he said observe yourself. So somehow this information leaked on a level quite lower than it was meant to be; at the same time it wasn't quite going into one ear and out the other, it left something but on a lower level. Now in a group there's another example that one knows of sensing the body. Of course there is sensing in modern psychology as well and one might wonder if this came from it. But still even after four or five years in the group work where one is practising sensing the body, one might wonder what's so big about sensing the body?

The question is should he have been allowed to participate in a work that has this label sensing the body. Then in four years practicing this way, him coming up with a question, "So what, what's the big deal?" Again it's not just something getting into one ear and out the other. Its one creating a kind of unlawful reaction. Then we have the big example of the enneagram and the types. The ennea-types.

93

This is a ridicule of the enneagram. I am not saying that it doesn't have interesting aspects. All I am saying is it doesn't have anything to do with the way the law of three and the law of seven are supposed to convene into that symbol and all the knowledge that is supposed to be hidden there. Interesting way of talking about nine kinds of people. So again I think this is an historical phenomenon with the Gurdjieff work: that so many very great ideas have kind of walked away or taken away not quite entered one's head in one ear and out of the other and yet having robbed the teaching of the awe that the true dimension of these concepts of these ideas can create in man, even the idea of mechanicalness can be chewed like chewing gum so much that one can cease to understand the impact of this image. Again, it has been robbed of the awe it can create and it didn't just go from one ear and out the other, it did something on a lower level. Now one can easily say, at the rate things are going, in a few decades you will try to talk about the Gurdjieffian system and everybody will know it in quotation marks; everyone will know what it is to remember yourself, to observe yourself, what mechanicality means. Nobody will relate these things along with the enneagram to Gurdjieff. There will be common knowledge, robbed completely of its esoteric aspect. So we talk about copyrights, and copyrights means laws and lawyers and things like that. Lawyers cannot protect an idea from withering away and loosing its value. But we are in front of this phenomenon, a very real phenomenon; and if we could we might have to bring in lawyers and copyrights. Quite obviously many people do that with the scores and music. And the movements. They protect them with lawyers. So what I intended to bring about after Dimitri spoke of this exchange between Gurdjieff and Ouspensky, what I wanted to bring about is some sort of lawyer-like responsibility if there is any. I say lawyer-like because with an idea like observing yourself you cannot bring a lawyer to protect its copyright. You cannot do that. And yet you might feel it is the right moment to use it in a group or refrain from using it because you have a feeling it is not the right moment.

If you make a mistake maybe you have the responsibility to deceive people, that what they understood is wrong; completely; they missed the words, we didn't say observe, we used another word, we were talking about something else. When you see that they roam away from what is important in such an exchange. I think I am talking about a responsibility toward the teaching.

Ian MacFarlane: Anyway I think we have gone over our time we need to break now for coffee.

*** Coffee Break ***

Ian MacFarlane: This session was unscheduled; we have options; we can continue talking about Abram Yelov another topic from *Beelzebub's Tales*.

Participant 18: As to this mornings session when the subject of copyright and theft was discussed; of course an idea cannot be copyrighted; and nothing can be copyrighted until it is printed, published, written down or performed. Any of the ancient oral traditions, of great sagas are not copyright. They are out there for us to learn from or just enjoy. Another aspect was whether or not the theft of secrets of inner knowledge from any of the esoteric teachings could lessen the original. I think Eleny mentioned from the Gospel about casting pearls before swine. I would like to mention the one about the mustard tree. The mustard seed that falls on the path and is walked on and dies. Or the mustard seed that falls on rocky ground and there's no water is not nourished and it dies. But the mustard seed that falls into fertile ground grows into a mighty tree. So that if there are people who use some of the ideas that are sacred to us, in the wrong way, will not benefit from them. Whereas those who know how to use them will develop. I think the fear of any of these ideas becoming contaminated is maybe unnecessary. Its just a thought; does anyone think that any damage to the original can be done by some of the miss uses of them; for the wrong reasons; for commercial reasons; for egoism; for building up a circle around yourself. Can that really harm the original Work if it falls on rocky ground?

Participant 14: I am a teacher by profession. I have been teaching for many, many years; one thing I know is that pupils, children, will always tell the teacher make it simpler. Just like babies want their parents want their food cut into baby pieces, this work is not for babies. I don't believe in diluting teachings. I always say to myself and for others to keep it at the highest level; its up to the pupil to rise to the highest level. No matter even if they beg you to make it simpler and simpler. That way both those learning are elevated and the teaching is not diluted. So it doesn't change from wine into water. That's my personal

Participant 19: I would like to join you with esoteric knowledge; the meaning is hidden; not available to everyone because you need to be in a certain state of and to have a certain kind of approach and presentation for it to be valuable for you. If we take something valuable and make it accessible to everyone we devalue it. Anything which is of value is rare. Today we are in new age. We are on the internet. Everyone can have everything. We see inflation of spiritual teachers. Everyone knows a little bit and he is a spiritual teacher. I want to weave into it one further idea. Gurdjieff says in *In Search of the Miraculous* . How do you know you are in a unique esoteric school? By the fact that it has got new knowledge. It is coming from a different level of consciousness. He said this knowledge should be administered carefully. If you give all of it to everyone, its becoming not effective. Because everyone has got a little bit of knowledge and can do nothing with it. People who get it should be selected carefully so everyone will get a lot of knowledge thus it could be effective.

Participant 20: My view is that esoteric knowledge existed because it was necessary to keep it secret because of the social conditions and climate in which it evolved. We now live in a liberal age; *Beelzebub's Tales* was published 60 years ago and is available to anyone. All that Gurdjieff was teaching is in that book. I think there may come a time again where its necessary again for knowledge to be hidden. There is a saying "The subjective ways is becoming the objective ways" and "the objective ways is becoming the subjective ways". Knowledge emerges when the conditions are right. Socially it becomes available for those that can use it and later on it might have to hide itself again because of the social conditions changing.

Participant 14: I read a story recently about a group of people who were going on a secret expedition in Central America where Native Americans lived. They had a local guide and asked him do the old traditions survive? He said what do you mean? Do we still have the medicine man?

He answered them, the safest place to hide a secret is where everybody can see. He took them close by to a Christian Church very much like the church you could find in Mexico and big cities, but the tradition, original tradition was hidden in the ceremonies, e.g., they were changing the clothes of the virgin Mary at certain times, when there were festivals; They found many, many ways to keep their traditions disguised. This is the most effective way It's open for everybody who can see, who can find it, <audio unclear> … diluted, but shouldn't hide it either.

Participant 4: I have two questions, but first I want to read something from this book. Yelov had a very original view of mental work. He once said, "It's all the same. Our thoughts work day and night. Instead of allowing them to think about caps of invisibility of the riches of Aladdin, rather let them be occupied with something useful."

My first question is what does he mean by, "It's all the same."?

And second, "Are there practical examples taken from, e.g. today, how we practice this? How we practice putting the thoughts into something which is useful for ourselves.

Yes; that's what he's speaking of; isn't it? That it goes day and night; also here and now. Yelov had a very original view about mental work. He once said "It's all the same" Our thoughts work day and night. Instead of allowing them to think about caps of invisibility of the riches of Aladdin, rather let them be occupied with something useful.

Participant 9: Mme de Salzmann tried to give a specific answer to this specific question in the film *Meetings with Remarkable Men*. She had Yelov sit in the desert in one of those sheep chariots; formations of sheep were bound together by sticks of wood and Yelov was lying on them. He was learning Tibetan. From the way I remember the question that you just read and from the image that was projected in the film the idea I get is that there is a ceaseless flow of intellectual energy of thoughts; they take form, you cannot avoid having this flow of thoughts; they will take form by association to whatever pops into the reality of the person I am at that moment. Through Yelov they wanted to show that this energy could be directed consciously in the direction of learning a language. As a matter of fact it could be Tibetan, which was absolutely useless; there was no immediate need for Yelov to learn Tibetan. He had a little book or something like that and from this he was working. This is a way an effort is to answer this question in the film *Meetings with Remarkable Men*.

Participant 21: I was once witness to a very effective method that was given to the thought flow. This was in a Russian language school where they taught you to switch into the language you were learning very quickly after you started to learn it. Then you basically with the thought flow you had 24 hour practice. If you didn't know the word you should have looked it up. Then you constantly were thinking in a different language, a one you did not know half a year ago. I went through this myself when we took German. A very interesting thing happened. Nine months after we got into this practice I started dreaming in German and I was speaking perfectly in the dreams; I remember I was speaking like a native speaker at the level that in reality I could not speak; only a few years later. This technique was used purposely; they knew that this would work; they said switch to thinking in the language you are learning and keep other thoughts away. It turned out that its not very difficult, you can easily do that.

Participant 19: The Chinese have a saying, "I can't stop the birds from flying around my head, but I can prevent them from building a nest." This is one thing, these thoughts are constantly going around in my head but if I feed them with energy from my feelings then I am in serious trouble. I can't really stop thoughts because there's always one thought left that is stopping thoughts. But there's another way that's possible. Somebody asked Orage if after several lectures on how to work in these complicated systems etc is there not a simpler way than what you have just been telling us. He answered there is but I am not sure you are capable of doing it. He said if you say a mantra one hundred times a day then that has as much weight and creativity to it as any of the teachings that I have given you. He recited this mantra which if recited one hundred times a day one after the other can achieve the same objective as the teaching, the manta is more radiant than the sun, purer than the snow, subtler than ether, is the self, the self which lives in my heart, I am that self, that self am I. That's worth trying sometimes when all others are not working. You can't do it everyday but it can be a tool to bring something of a deeper nature to yourself.

Participant 14: When I think about quieting the mind of course there is meditations; supposedly they bring the mind from beta wave to alpha waves. From my experience inner work for many years, I came to the conclusion the way to quieten the mind quieten the thoughts its not by working on the thoughts but actually by quieting the emotions. Thoughts basically become excited when the emotions become heated; especially negative emotions of course. If we find technique of guided imagery/imagination to quieten and have peace in our emotions then almost immediately our thoughts become quiet as well. I know there are techniques especially in applied psychology they talk about working with the emotions through the mind. I believe that the emotions affect the mind much more than the mind affects the emotions. The way to get to the mind is through the emotions which I believe is the greatest problem a person has when he does inner work of reaching a higher level of consciousness. Not the mind-the emotions. They are totally untamed, we're totally identifying with their positive and negative aspects. I believe this is the great challenge.

Participant 19: I would say I agree entirely with you; that we live in the moon of our behaviour; and our moon is our solar plexus which has split off from our real heart and its the solar plexus where we all behave from; and its a very serious problem we have; but I agree if I can get in touch with that -if I go for a walk and pay attention to a certain part I have to find it on my right side (this is in *All and Everything*) that begins a separation between the centers and if I practice enough then the mind becomes completely empty and my feelings become completely empty; I am walking and I just exist at that moment. It doesn't last. If I allow something to come in I have lost it but its just a question of bringing it back. That's one of the ways I can stop and make myself positive.

All & Everything Conference 2010

Participant 4: What you said reminded me of the figure 2 in *In Search of the Miraculous* . There is this first section the body, the emotions and the intellect, and this huge amount of different I's. Underneath it is reversed. There is one I. Then is the head or the intellect and second to that underneath that, after that is the emotion and then the body. We are informed in this work it has to start with right thinking. When Nick was saying this wonderful mantra or poem I was reminded about this. To have three questions brought up in daytime but not to be answered. Advice I have been given is to not answer these questions and maybe they will be answered from your own essence; not words. The first was Who am I? The second Where am I? and the third What am I? Working with this means recognising that which wants to say something to them; that which wants to answer it. It has to be something in addition to that which immediately wants to say something about where I am what I am and so forth.

Participant 20: Talking about quietening thoughts I am entirely in disagreement with everyone. I never found in anything that Gurdjieff has written any sense of introspection, what I call introspection. I have found nothing about looking within. The way to quieten thoughts is that very gently direct your attention into your perception of the world outside; either hearing or visually to see yourself in a three dimensional world rather than simply a screen in front of you; by gently directing your attention on your perception of whatever form it is then your thoughts become secondary. Gradually there are small moments of absolute terror when your thoughts suddenly stop. It may take a while. Gradually these moments of terror you get used to them and then you get long moments of silence. I have found nothing in Gurdjieff that suggests to look within.

Participant 9: I would not normally say much about something which I disagree so thoroughly with. but I want to bring to points factually. One is when Beelzebub gives Hassein advice i.e. In the morning to make an effort to collect his inner parts and make them one. And the other one is where he says people who can make butter out of thin air-these are direct references to attention being drawn to the inside not the outside.

Participant 20: Sorry I disagree. I think you can collect your attention without looking within.

Participant 14: My experience is that both are absolutely correct. I will give you an example. I remember being very sick and worried because of inner turmoil with myself and sitting in my favourite chair and habitual posture, as soon as I had sat in that habitual posture it was the same merry-go-round. I was aware that outside of me life was still going on but that I was not partaking of that life. In a way was dying in a little shell I had created. The only way to, was to make a deliberate effort to place my attention outwards, so that I was interacting with the environment and receiving and giving out energy. So being aware of the breath and putting attention out I think is a sure way, for me, of waking up. On the other hand, another practice which I agree with what you say if the emotions are running awry you can't do anything so somehow that fire has to be cooled down. In Chinese thought there are fire and water meditations. You have the coolness, the ying female, the water and the fire, the masculine yang. You have to bring them into harmony. So I have found both help me.

Seminar 2

Participant 9: Sorry I don't understand what you mean both.

Participant 14: Both placing your attention out and in...<inaudible>

Participant 9: Well look. There is a difference between both at the same time and placing the attention to the outside, there's a difference there, right? If you're aware of breathing then part of the attention goes to the inside. Place your attention outside means you are not aware of the functions of the body. The minute that you are aware of some functions of the body part of the attention is to the inside. Its a balance of two directions or split attention. Or divided attention. When you are watching TV this is when your attention is outside. If you have a sensation of the breath, of the body, or you are even dimly aware of your emotions, or even dimly aware of the fact you're thinking, this means that part of the attention is directed towards the inside. So there's a difference between a divided attention that both occur and directed attention toward the outside when there is no cognition of what is happening inside.

Participant 20: My experience is as I have said by directing gently my attention on my perception I am very aware of what's happening inside me. But that awareness of what is happening inside me is quite different to what I have called introspection. I think introspection is a very negative and dangerous thing. If I try to look within, that is what I call introspection. When I look without, and focus on my awareness of the outer world, I then become aware at the same time; shall we call it a passive awareness, of what's happening within me. This is quite different from introspection which is looking inside actively.

Participant 4: Can I just add something to this. This work does not teach introspection but definitely urges us to look inside which is completely different to introspection. It is made very clear in the Oragean version Introspection is there defined as one I looking at another I through analysers. Analysing is not an awareness activity. Analysing is the function of the mental apparatus living its own life without awareness. That's why I have been warned of analysing. It is a clear distinction in the work what introspection is and what it is to look inside. It is two completely different things. Introspection operates on one level, looking inside you operate in a higher level in yourself, above the functioning of your thoughts. From there you can listen, see, use your senses.

Participant 19: Everything in the universe has a correspondence within me; as above, so below. So my head brain is what corresponds in sun absolute; and the sun absolute and he tells you in the chapter Purgatory. The beings that live in the sun absolute are the same beings that live there live in my head brain. But part of the head brain is reserved for objectivity; and objectivity in the work has absolutely no mistake about it, there is no analysis, there is no categorisation, and or any associations. there's no descriptions. So there's no thoughts or any associations. In addition to this there's what he calls impartiality. There's no liking or disliking. At that moment there's a certain element which is called_simultaneity which means there are no thoughts because most of our thoughts are of either past or the future, and going from the past to the future or reverse there's a moment of timelessness which means there are no thoughts. So objectivity has absolutely nothing to do with introspection. All introspection comes from thought so it cancels out any kind of introspection.

Participant 20: My experience of many of the conversations we've had here, my perception, is many are introspective and that's how I use the word. I judge things on my perception and try not to judge on theoretical considerations.

Participant 9: Let us clarify something; Introspection is like a specific thing that Vont introduced into psychology. The one that was criticised heavily by Husserl the philosopher as psychologism. They began by a theory that the mind is structured and functions in this or that way. They were verifying this because they were thinking about it. Observation of the self is quite different. It is something learned not in one day or one year. It is learned with constant practice over the years by participating in a group; discussing your experience with people who have been there before. That's the only real way of understanding what it means to observe yourself; which is one of the two pillars of the Gurdjieffian work; to observe yourself and to remember yourself. Okay? If you ever discussed with a psychologist, some years back, the idea of observing yourself, in all probability he would have rejected it. Now we are a little bit more modern. On the basis of it being introspection. This he would not understand what it means to observe oneself. The need for participation in the Gurdjieffian work, that Gurdjieff insisted so much about, that work cannot be done without participating in a group is exactly because this is one of the terms, to observe oneself, that need to be learned through practice. It cannot be proven to anybody who's not practised, that it even exists. It is difficult to understand it unless you have been in a group for I would say about four years to have a first understanding of what it means to observe oneself. The reason being its not one thing, it deepens. You have to understand the dynamics of it.

Participant 20: I disagree that self observation and self remembering are the foundations of the Gurdjieff work. Gurdjieff is initiating transformation from the ordinary man in the street into "normal men" and "normal women" who have quotation marks. Self observation is a property that the normal has but the ordinary man does not have. That the normal man can do, but the ordinary man cannot. Self remembering is a property of the normal man. But something that the ordinary man cannot do. A mistake has been made in the Gurdjieff work in believing that self remembering and self observation are the means by which this transformation is obtained. Based on reading *Beelzebub's Tales* that's not true. He says something different. I hope to be able to present that a little bit tomorrow. Thank you. My view on self remembering is different. Where does self knowledge arise? A good question. My take on this is self knowledge arises from remorse. Which is where one part sees and criticises another. The awakening; Gurdjieff says that reading *Beelzebub's Tales* he is placing in us the essence, into our sub conscious the essence of certain real notions which will then automatically of themselves, by themselves, completely mechanically transform us.

Participant 19: No, he says conscious mentation, what is conscious mentation?

Seminar 2

Participant 20: Conscious mentation is to gently direct my attention on my perceptions of the outside world and gradually quieten down my thoughts until I have an inner silence. I then have the opportunity to be silent if I wish.

Participant 19: Then you see my perceptions are all part of my five senses and my five senses are all completely subjective. But I am looking for objectivity. Objectivity comes from the other two senses, six and seven, which is consciousness and conscience.

Participant 20: I see that as theoretical. Gurdjieff is transforming us. He says man consists of two independent consciousnesses. Our ordinary consciousness and our subconscious and that the subconscious mind should predominate in the common presence of a man. By reading BTTG he gives us the mechanism by which this subconscious mind can predominate over the course of time; over the course of life and in the course of all the activities we choose to get involved with.

Participant 19: But it says in the chapter on form and sequence exactly the process which you've just described. Its qualified in the law of three. He's talking about what happens produces Zernofookalnian-friction so the book has to have, or you have to have the skill of how to introduce the reconciling principle. Why else do you read the book? Otherwise it remains just ordinary knowledge.

Participant 20: That's a theory.

Participant 19: Its not a theory; its in the book.
Participant 20: The important thing Gurdjieff says, the key difference between the conscious and subconscious mind is the conscious mind consists of elements put in to us from the outside. The development of the subconscious mind depends on our own efforts from within and no one else can make those efforts for us.

End of Session

The Autonomous Nervous System in Ideas of Gurdjieff and Modern Neurophysiology

Andreas Zarkadoulas and Anestis Christoforides

Abstract

This presentation includes a parallelism of Gurdjieff's ideas with the modern neurophysiology, mainly with regard to the autonomous nervous system. In *All and Everything - Beelzebub's Tales to His Grandson* Gurdjieff refers to the nerve ganglions of sympathetic nervous system, defining them as the centre of feeling. On the other hand, modern neurophysiology has proven that the autonomous nervous system has direct relation with what we call feeling.

In other points of his work, Gurdjieff considers that the biggest value for the Work with his system has the conscious contact with subconscious. He refers that the contact with subconscious is attained with the modification of blood circulation in the blood vessels. From the physiology we know that the change in the circulation of blood is subject to the autonomous nervous system.

From the parallelism of these opinions, it appears that Gurdjieff had acquaintance of subjects that became much later known in science, causing us to study his work with greater attention and in combination with modern scientific discoveries.

The Autonomous Nervous System in Ideas of Gurdjieff and Modern Neurophysiology

Whoever studies G. I. Gurdjieff's "*Beelzebub's Tales* to His Grandson" will soon wonder whether what he is reading is a fairytale and everything in there is pure fiction, or if there are certain truths behind this story. The use of terms of physiology and medicine by Gurdjieff became the motive for a comparative study of what is included in "All and Everything" in relation with modern science. This work was urged by Dimitri Peretzi. Dimitri has, for several years, occupied himself with the study of the balance between the sympathetic and parasympathetic systems.

One of the terms used by Gurdjieff in A & E is **brain nodes of the sympathetic nervous system** *[Beelzebub's Tales to His Grandson, Chapter 39, The Holy Planet "Purgatory", p.779-780]*

> ... it must be noticed that in the beginning these three-brained beings of the planet Earth who have taken your fancy, also had this third reconciling concentration,..., in the form of an independent brain localized in the region of their what is called 'breast.'

The Autonomous Nervous System in Ideas of Gurdjieff & Modern Neurophysiology

"But from the time when the process of their ordinary being-existence began particularly sharply to change for the worse, then Nature there, by certain causes flowing from the common-cosmic Trogoautoegocratic process, was compelled, without destroying the functioning itself of this brain of theirs, to change the system of its localization.

*..., she gradually dispersed the localization of this organ, ..., into small localizations over the whole of their common presence, but chiefly in the region of what is called the 'pit of the stomach.' The totality of these small localizations in this region they themselves at the present time call the solar plexus or the **'complex of the nodes of the sympathetic nervous system.'***

At another point Gurdjieff writes *[Beelzebub's Tales to His Grandson, Chapter 17, The Arch-absurd According to the Assertion of Beelzebub, Our Sun Neither Lights nor Heats, p.146-147]*

"This being-brain in the contemporary three-brained beings there is not localized in one common mass, as is proper to the presences of all the other three-brained beings of our Great Universe, but is localized in parts, ...

"But although, in its exterior form, this being-center of theirs has now variously placed concentrations, nevertheless all its separate functionings are correspondingly connected with each other, so that the sum total of these scattered parts can function exactly as in general it is proper for it to function.

*"They themselves call these separate localizations in their common presence **'nerve nodes.'***

*"It is interesting to notice that most of the separate parts of this being-brain are localized in them, just in that place of their planetary body where such a normal being-brain should be, namely, in the region of their breast, and the totality of these nerve-nodes in their breast, they call the **'Solar Plexus.'***

Also in his book *Life is real only then, when "I am", p.123* Gurdjieff mentions that:

*A man "feels" - when what are called the "initiative factors" issue from one of the dispersed localizations of his common presence which in contemporary science are called the **"sympathetic nerve nodes,"** the chief agglomeration of which is known by the name of **"solar plexus"** and the whole totality of which functioning, in the terminology long ago established by me, is called the **"feeling center"**; and he "senses"— when the basis of his "initiative factors" is the totality of what are called "the motor nerve nodes" of the spinal and partly of the head brain, which is called according to this terminology of mine the "moving center."*

In a few words Gurdjieff seems to consider the sympathetic nervous system essential, as far as emotion is concerned.

But, let's have a look, as simply as possible, at the nature of the sympathetic system, from a scientific point of view.

Our nervous system is divided in two: the Central and the Peripheral nervous system. The central nervous system is comprised of the brain and the spinal marrow and the peripheral nervous system is comprised of groups of nerve cells which are called nodes or ganglia and peripheral nerves that are outside the brain and the spinal marrow.

The peripheral nervous system is divided in two again: the body part and the autonomous part.

The body part provides the central nervous system with information about the position of the muscles and the limbs, and the external environment of the body, meaning that the body part of the peripheral nervous system is, in fact, the extension of the central nervous system inside the body.

The autonomous nervous system is the system that controls the bowel functions and is divided in three subsystems:

a) sympathetic system

b) parasympathetic system

c) bowels/intestinal system

We could say that the central nervous system regulates the body functions that are related to our will, while the autonomous nervous system regulates the body functions that are **not controlled** by our will.

For example, playing a musical instrument, digging the garden, writing a letter, are all matters of the central nervous system. While, having my heart beat fast before taking a test or making my hair stand on end when I feel terrified, are matters of the autonomous nervous system.

The sympathetic system is stimulated in conditions of fear, joy, sorrow, during muscular effort and generally in stress conditions. It is also stimulated by adrenaline.

The word Sympathetic comes from the Greek words: syn and pasho, meaning I suffer along with the others, I'm extroverted.

Sympathetic = extroverted

On the contrary, **the parasympathetic system** regulates the vital organs of the body in conditions of relaxation and tranquility, free from stimuli for intense activity; that is, it "applies the brakes" in the stimulation of the organism.

The Autonomous Nervous System in Ideas of Gurdjieff & Modern Neurophysiology

The term parasympathetic shows that it is completely different from the sympathetic and that it relates to the internal functions.

Parasympathetic = Esoteric system or introverted

The parasympathetic nervous system is activated during sleep and digestion.

Differences between the sympathetic and parasympathetic nervous systems

1. **Anatomical differences.** The centers of the sympathetic are found in the spinal marrow, while the centers of the parasympathetic are in the brain and the sacrum (base) of the spinal marrow. The pro ganglia fibers of the sympathetic are shorter in comparison to the fibers of the parasympathetic. **The ganglia of the sympathetic form stems,** while the ones of the parasympathetic do not. The met ganglia fibers of the sympathetic are short. The sympathetic is a lot more spread out than the parasympathetic.

2. **Differences in pharmacology.** Those two systems are stimulated by different medicines. The sympathetic is stimulated with adrenaline, while the parasympathetic is stimulated with acetylcholine.

The action of these two systems is complicated, for the purposes of this presentation though, we could say that, generally, **the stimulation of one or the other system affects us in opposite ways.**

The **sympathetic** system prepares the organism for action, that is, it stimulates all the body systems preparing it for intense activity.

The activation of the **parasympathetic** system produces the well known "hypnotic ecstasy", which is characterized by profound tranquility, serenity, partial or even full dissociation from external stimuli and partial or full focus on the inner world of the individual (Meditation).

It is as if the **sympathetic** system links us with **the outer world** and it is connected to our survival. In experiments where the sympathetic system was removed from animals it was found that they could neither act nor protect themselves. The information about the activity of the sympathetic nervous system seems to link with Gurdjieff's notion of **trogoautoegocrat.** On the other hand the parasympathetic nervous system which is related to focusing on the inner world of the individual seems to relate with Gurdjieff's notion of **autoegocrat.**

If we have a look at the evolution of the species we will see that the first organisms are one celled and they simply absorb food passively from the environment. Afterwards, as the organisms evolve, a mechanism is developed inside of them that allow them to recognize as food something in the world around them and act in a way that will secure this food. This new ability is related to the sympathetic nervous system.

We read in A&E: *[Beelzebub's Tales to His Grandson, Chapter 39, The Holy Planet "Purgatory", p.750 and 753]*

> "In order that you may more clearly understand how our ENDLESSNESS decided to attain immunity from the maleficent action of the merciless Heropass and of course how HE ultimately actualized it all, you must first of all know that before this, the Most Most Holy Sun Absolute was maintained and existed on the basis of the system called '**Autoegocrat**,' i.e., on that principle according to which the inner forces which maintained the existence of this cosmic concentration had an independent functioning, not depending on any forces proceeding from outside,...
>
> "And so, in consequence of the fact that for this new system of functioning of the forces which until then maintained the existence of the Most Most Holy Sun Absolute, there were required outside of the Sun Absolute corresponding sources in which such forces could arise and from which they could flow into the presence of the Most Most Holy Sun Absolute, our ALMIGHTY ENDLESSNESS was just then compelled to create our now existing Megalocosmos with all the cosmoses of different scales and relatively independent cosmic formations present in it, and from then on the system which maintained the existence of the Sun Absolute began to be called **Trogoautoegocrat**.

Let us now see how modern neurophysiology links the autonomous nervous system with emotion.

The scientific community has yet to reach a commonly acceptable definition of emotion. There is one definition in clinical psychology, a second in social psychology and a third in neurophysiology. There are even different definitions within each of these fields. Clinical psychology deals with the issue from the point of view of psychopathology dividing emotions to normal and abnormal ones. Social psychology is mainly interested in the emotional response of groups and societies and neuroscience deals with what goes on at the level of neurology, physiology, biochemistry etc.

The word "emotion" covers a wide range of phenomena, such as behavior, feelings and changes in the body state. This diversity of intended meanings has given rise to various theories and definitions concerning emotion among the scientific community.

From a historical perspective, early theories of emotion were mainly philosophical. However, in 1884, the James-Lange theory generated a controversy that has spread from the 19th century to the 21st century, proposing that one's perception of an event or object stimulates physiological reactions and behavioral responses, the occurrence of which are interpreted by the brain as a feeling. For example, we see a bear, become aroused, and then interpret that arousal as a feeling of fear.

There also exist cognitive theories of emotion that focus on the relation between cognitive schemas and emotion. Schachter (1959, 1964 and 1970) for example has a cognitive/physiological view of emotions, suggesting that emotional states are determined mainly by cognitive factors. This rather simply put theory suggest that emotional states are characterized by general arousal of the sympathetic nervous system and we interpret and classify these states from the situation we believe has brought them about and from our typical mode of perception. As far as behavioral theories of emotion are concerned, for the most part research has focused on what is directly observable and measurable. Those who have taken this approach usually regard emotion as a response, or a large class of responses, rather that as a state of the organism. In social theories, emotion is often conceptualized as a social phenomenon. For the most part, the stimuli for emotional reactions come from other people. Furthermore, in clinical psychology, by definition, emotion is implicated in all the affective disorders. In other words, clinical theories underline that if the emotions become so insistent as to be impossible to ignore, or so extreme as to interfere with normal life, then the result is the term "abnormal".

Since the James-Lange theory and mainly during the past four decades, research regarding emotion has focused on its physiology, aiming to investigate the substrates of emotion in the central nervous system (CNS), the peripheral nervous system and the endocrine system.

Although early physiological based theories on emotion were mostly inadequate and not well supported, they gave considerable evidence towards this direction. For instance, Fehr and Stern (1970) refer to "primary feelings" and 'immediate reflexes' that are seen as hypothalamic discharges that inhibit the cortex and excite the autonomous nervous system (ANS).

Similarly, the neuroscience approach is primarily concerned to account for emotions by explicating the physiological mechanisms on which they depend.

Rolls (1990) offer a theory of emotion, suggesting that emotion has particular functions that have obvious survival value. One of these functions is the elicitation of autonomous responses (e.g. a change in heart rate) and endocrine responses (e.g. the release of adrenaline) which prepare the body for action. The neural part of Rolls's theory of emotion, which he seems to view as basic, gives pride of place to the amygdalda, the orbitofrontal cortex and the hypothalamus.

It is more that obvious that latest scientific research regarding emotion is directed towards the structures and functions of the nervous system, and particularly those of the sympathetic nervous system. Typically of this, is a recent definition of emotion that is published in the Encyclopedia of Neuroscience (Springer, 2008) where emotions are defined as *"Physiological and behavioral responses to an important environmental object or event, typically mediated by the autonomous nervous system and subcortical brain structures. One's interpretation of emotional responses is often called a "feeling" and is typically considered separately from those responses"*.

The prevailing theories in neurophysiology, nowadays, accept that what we understand as emotion is, on one hand, an arousal in the body, and on the other, an intellectual explanation (in a few words, a label) for this arousal.

All & Everything Conference 2010

For the purposes of this presentation, the view of neurophysiology seems to be the most appropriate, considering that we compare it with Gurdjieff's writings where the ganglia of the sympathetic nervous system are mentioned, in the first place.

We read in the book: *Essentials of Neural Science and Behavior by Appleton and Lange-A Simon and Shuster Company"* of Eric R. Kandel, James H. Schwartz, Thomas M. Jessell, chapter 32.

> ### *The autonomous nervous system participates in emotional states*
>
> *Physiologic changes that accompany the emotional states are usually manifested with perspiration, dryness of mouth, tension in the stomach, accelerated breathing, rapid heart beat and muscle tension. These changes are caused by the autonomous nervous system.*
>
> *The sympathetic sector controls the reaction of fight or flight, while the parasympathetic sector controls the rest and digestion. In an emergency situation, the body may have to react in a sudden change of external or internal environment, like in battle, in the demands of a sport, in serious change of temperature or in loss of blood. In order to react with speed, as i.e. during a battle, the hypothalamus and the sympathetic nervous system cause increase of the sympathetic effect in the heart and in the gut, in the peripheral vessels and in the sweat glands. The enhanced blood flow, the change of body temperature and level of glucose of blood, allow rapid reactions in annoying exterior conditions. On the contrary the parasympathetic sector of the nervous system maintains the basic heart rate, the breathing and the metabolism under physiologic conditions.*
>
> *The main role in the control of operation of autonomous nervous system is played by the hypothalamus and the amygdala.*
>
> *The interaction of amygdala, hypothalamus, cerebral and autonomous nervous system, from one side, and amygdala, frontal and cerebral cortex, from the other, result in experiences that we describe as "sentimental".*

It is evident that there is a clear resemblance between Gurdjieff's ideas and the views of modern neurophysiology. Gurdjieff appears to have known about this matter, which became known to science at least fifty years later. Although the dominant role as far as our sentimental life is concerned, appears to be held by amygdala and secondly by the hypothalamus, the role of the autonomous nervous system and especially the sympathetic one, is also decisive.

Another medical issue that Gurdjieff mentions in "Beelzebub" is about blood circulation. He specifically says: *[Beelzebub's Tales to His Grandson, Chapter 32 Hypnotism p. 564-565]*

> *"The first fact is, that from the time when owing to their abnormal existence there began to be formed in them what is called the 'two-system-Zoostat,' that is, two independent*

*consciousnesses, then Great Nature began gradually to adapt Herself and finally adapted Herself to this, that after they arrive at a certain age, there begin to proceed in them two 'Inkliazanikshanas' of different what are called 'tempos,' that is, as they themselves would say, two **'blood circulations'** of different kind.*

"From this certain age mentioned, each one of these 'Inkliazanikshanas' of different tempo, that is to say each 'blood circulation,' begins to evoke in them the functioning of one of their mentioned consciousnesses; and vice versa, the intensive functioning of either consciousness begins to evoke in them the kind of blood circulation corresponding to it.

"The difference between these two independent kinds of blood circulation in their common presences is actualized by means of what is called 'tempo-Davlaksherian-circulation,' or, according to the expression there of what is called contemporary medicine, the 'difference-of-the-filling-of-the-blood-vessels'; that is to say, in the condition of the waking state, the 'center-of-gravity-of-the-blood-pressure' in their common presences obtains in one part of the general system of blood vessels, and in the condition of the passive state, in another part of the vessels.

And at another point: *[Beelzebub's Tales to His Grandson, Chapter 32 Hypnotism p. 568]*

*"And so, when thanks to a **change of tempo of their blood circulation** there is obtained a temporary suspension of the action of the localization of that false consciousness which has already become the 'autocratic ruler' of their common presences, thereby giving the sacred data of their **genuine consciousness** the possibility of unhindered blending with the total functioning of the planetary body during the period of their waking state, then indeed my boy, if the crystallization of data for engendering in that localization an idea of something opposite to that which has already arisen in them and somehow become fixed, is assisted in a corresponding manner, and if moreover the actions evoked by this idea are directed upon a disharmonized part of the planetary body, an accelerated change in it possible.*

So, here Gurdjieff refers to blood circulation and the relation its modification has with the two kinds of consciousness we possess, that is, the ordinary every day consciousness and the subconscious which he regards as our real consciousness. Gurdjieff uses the term subconscious saying: *[Beelzebub's Tales to His Grandson, Chapter 1, The Arousing of Thought, p. 24-25].*

*Now that you have become familiar with the story of our common countryman, the Transcaucasian Kurd, ..., I wish to bring to the knowledge of what is called your "pure waking consciousness" ... the essence of certain real notions may of themselves automatically, so to say, go from this "waking consciousness" - which most people in their ignorance mistake for the real consciousness, but which I affirm and experimentally prove is the fictitious one - into what you call the **subconscious**, which ought to be in my opinion the real human consciousness, and there by themselves mechanically bring about that* *transformation which should in general proceed in the entirety of a man and give him, from his own conscious mentation, the results he ought to have, which are proper to man and not merely to single- or double-brained animals.*

It is known that the term subconscious was used excessively by the psychoanalysts, who, the time that Gurdjieff wrote "Beelzebub", were in full swing; and as it is evident by the above extract, he uses it in the same context as modern psychology does.

We come again to physiology to see what changes blood circulation. *(Human Physiology, Arthur C. Guyton, MD)*

> *The nervous system controls the circulation of blood almost **exclusively through the autonomous nervous system**. The part of autonomous nervous system that has particular importance for the regulation of circulation is the sympathetic system. All the vessels apart from trichoids the pretrichoids constrictors and the postarterioles are neurally connected through the sympathetic nerves. The neural connections of small arteries and arterioles allow the sympathetic system, provided that it is stimulated, to increase resistance, altering thus the blood flow in the tissues. The neural connections of big vessels and particularly the veins allow the sympathetic system to alter their volume and thus the volume of the peripheral circulatory system.*

It is very clear that every change in blood circulation is linked to stimulations either of the sympathetic or the parasympathetic system and the question at this point arises: to what extend could we consciously affect the autonomous nervous system?

As we can see from the following extracts from the tales of Beelzebub the main issue of Work on the Self is the conscious participation of the subconscious in the consciousness of waking life and so **it stands to reason that this will be done through conscious influence on the autonomous nervous system.**

We read in Beelzebub *[Beelzebub's Tales to His Grandson, Chapter 26, The Legominism Concerning the Deliberations of the Very Saintly Ashiata Shiemash Under the Title of "The Terror-of-the-Situation", p. 359-360]*

> *"'During the period of my year of special observations on all of their manifestations and perceptions, I made it categorically clear to myself that although the factors for engendering in their presences the sacred being-impulses of Faith, Hope, and Love are already quite degenerated in the beings of this planet, nevertheless, the factor which ought to engender that being-impulse on which the whole psyche of beings of a three-brained system is in general based, and which impulse exists under the name of Objective-Conscience, is not yet atrophied in them, but remains in their presences almost in its primordial state.*

The Autonomous Nervous System in Ideas of Gurdjieff & Modern Neurophysiology

"'Thanks to the abnormally established conditions of external ordinary being-existence existing here, this factor has gradually penetrated and become embedded in that consciousness which is here called "**subconsciousness**," in consequence of which it takes no part whatever in the functioning of their ordinary consciousness.

"'Well, then, it was just then that I indubitably understood with all the separate ruminating parts representing the whole of my "I," that if **the functioning of that being-factor still surviving in their common presences were to participate in the general functioning of that consciousness of theirs in which they pass their daily, as they here say, "waking-existence,"** only then would it still be possible to save the contemporary three-brained beings here from the consequences of the properties of that organ which was intentionally implanted into their first ancestors.

"'My further meditations then confirmed for me that it would be possible to attain this only if their general being-existence were to flow for a long time under foreseeingly-corresponding conditions.

"'**When all the above-mentioned was completely transubstantiated in me, I decided to consecrate the whole of myself from that time on to the creation here of such conditions that the functioning of the "sacred-conscience" still surviving in their subconsciousness might gradually pass into the functioning of their ordinary consciousness.**

In a few words, what Gurdjieff says is that, on one hand, there are two different types of consciousness in human beings and that, on the other hand, the function of each one of them is regulated by the blood circulation, which, as we have seen, is a matter of the autonomous nervous system. Gurdjieff goes on to say that the aim of Ashiata Shiemash, which seems to be the aim of Work as well, is to enable the subconscious to gradually participate in our ordinary consciousness, which means that we should be able to consciously affect the autonomous nervous system so that we can change blood circulation and therefore consciousness.

The practice of Gurdjieff's work is the possession of the oral tradition of the **groups** and it remains to be seen whether the existing techniques actually prove what is said above; whether through Work meditation practices, that is, remembering the self and observing the self, changes in the stimulation of the autonomous nervous system are achieved.

Very recently a study was published at a prestigious medical journal which shows that through certain meditation techniques we can affect the autonomous nervous system.

__Central and autonomous nervous system interaction is altered by short-term meditation__, Yi-Yuan et al., Institute of Neuroinformatics and Laboratory for Body and Mind, Dalian University of Technology, Dalian 116024, China

> *However, the Integrative Body-Mind Training (IBMT - experiments in meditation) showed significantly better physiological reactions than simple relaxation control. These results reflected Autonomous Nervous System regulation with less effort, more relaxation of the body, and a calm state of mind during and after IBMT practice as compared to relaxation training…This result was consistent with previous findings of decreased sympathetic activity and increased parasympathetic activity during meditation.*

We will close this presentation with some of the many questions that are raised.

- **CAN WE CONSCIOUSLY AFFECT THE AUTONOMOUS NERVOUS SYSTEM (A. N. S.)?**

- **IS THE CONSCIOUS INFLUENCE ON THE A.N.S. SOME KIND OF INTERVENTION ON EMOTION?**

- **IS THE CHANGE OF "EGOS" RELATED TO THE CHANGE OF STIMULATION OF THE A. N. S.?**

- **IS THERE A CORRELATION BETWEEN "TROGO-AUTOEGOCRAT" AND SYMPATHETIC SYSTEM AND BETWEEN "AUTOEGOCRAT" AND PARASYMPATHETIC SYSTEM?**

© Copyright 2010 - Andreas Zarkadoulas - All Rights Reserved

The Autonomous Nervous System - Questions & Answers

(Thomae Komliki - translator)

Participant 1: Thank you very much. This is complicated stuff presented, but I tried to follow this and I tried to see it from the perspective of centers and it seems to correlate with what you are saying. The one system which is spoken about is the one which functions according to what it is supposed to function, that is the instinctive center; for example the intelligence in the intellectual part of the instinctive center is registering an impulse i.e. from the emotional part of the instinctive center. A practical example of this is when you put your hand on the top of a candle, then the registration is done in the emotional part of the instinctive center, sending this information up to the intellectual part of that center. That intelligence sends information down to the mechanical part of the moving center and that information is to withdraw your hand. That is done in order to prevent life from dying. Now this intelligent center, the intellectual part of the instinctive center can also be stimulated from the formatory apparatus, where you think of something which is connected to danger and because there is no consciousness of what is going on, the impulse is sent further to the emotional part of the emotional center and further to the instinctive center, which starts breathing rapidly, etc. etc. How I understand the necessity for creating an "I" who can be impartial to this imaginary affair, in order not to start all these instinctive reactions, when it is no need for them? Does this correspond with your presentation? Have I understood something of what you have said?

Andreas Zarkadoulas: In this presentation there has been an effort to compare what is written in Beelzebub and what is said by modern science. I consider your approach from the point of view of the centers very interesting but there is a problem how to find the equals between the division of the three centers in three sub-centers and what is said by neurophysiology. Personally I am very interested in this matter, but we are not yet in a position to state clearly that this is the emotional part of the emotional center and so on.

Participant 2: If I understand correctly, if I remember correctly, you said that the parasympathetic system takes care of activation of the physical body.

Andreas Zarkadoulas: Of the internal organs, that is the other way round.

Participant 3: Did you run any practical experiments showing that influencing the parasympathetic system would have results similar to those of meditation? Can you tell more about this?

Andreas Zarkadoulas: In this presentation we included an extract from an official research, one that was done by a University. Personally I have done experiments, but they are not published. I have personal experience, but it is not published, it is not official.

Questioner 3: Can you share it?

Andreas Zarkadoulas: Through meditation and the deeper we get in meditation we reach a point where the parasympathetic system starts functioning more and more intensely. It can even be measured by certain devices that measure the voltage of the skin and this can be translated into a degree of stimulation of the parasympathetic system.

Participant 4: I have a two-part question. Do I understand correctly, that the effect of the sympathetic nervous system is to constrict the blood vessels and the effect of the parasympathetic system is to relax? And the second question is: Is there research yet to look at the effect of the intentional creation of thought, an image of an emotional quality? We all know that the sympathetic and parasympathetic system response will be influenced by the emotional quality of a thought or an image. So is there research yet that demonstrates what we experience in ourselves in that regard? The definition that I saw on the screen of the activation of the sympathetic system is that of a response to some external stimulus and the interpretation.

Andreas Zarkadoulas: When a stimulus enters the body, the organism, it goes to a certain organ called thalamus, from that it goes through a faster way, through a short cut, to the amygdala, where this information is examined whether it has some degree of danger and if this is considered to be dangerous the amygdala sends to the hypothalamus a stimulus and then the hypothalamus motivates the sympathetic system, even before the neo-cortex has the time to understand what it happening. E.g. I can see a piece of wood, a stick that looks like a snake, and immediately the sympathetic system is stimulated, even before I realize that it is just a stick, because the snake is connected to fear. So the amygdala is an organ that controls whether the stimuli coming from outside are dangerous or not. But even so the stimulation proceeds, is being done through the autonomous nervous system.

Participant 4: But right now I can visualize a snake and I will experience sympathetic arousal. And I can now visualize a spiritual image and parasympathetic begins. So we know this, I think this is part of what our work is about, as Terje said to have a presence, an "I" that does not react to the emotional content of thought or an image. So is there yet a research that demonstrates the effect on the body of a voluntary mental imaging and thinking.

Andreas Zarkadoulas: I am not aware of such research. The value that these efforts have, to find the correlation between science and Gurdjieff's work, has great value for me, because they can help us further the Work on our self, without losing time, because Gurdjieff says that from the three ways that he has mentioned-the way of the fakir, the way of the monk and the way of the yogi-that the yogi is in the best position because he knows what it is that he has to do. If I know how to be able to affect the autonomous nervous system and stop the evolution of a negative emotion, like anger, in fact I have done, I have gone half the way of Work.

Participant 4: Thank you.

The Autonomous Nervous System - Questions & Answers

Participant 5: My question is, you seem to have related everything that has to do with the parasympathetic nervous system with meditation, so what is the relationship of meditation with Work?

Andreas Zarkadoulas: In this presentation it appears that I link the sympathetic nervous system with what Gurdjieff calls Trogoautoegograt and the parasympathetic with Autoegocrat. The situation appears to be that there has to be a balance between the outer world and the inner world, which means that we have different kinds of meditation. There is the meditation where I sit alone at home and everything happens inside me and a second kind of meditation is when I live my life in the outer world without identifying myself, so there is an issue of balance between the two worlds, the inner world and the outer world. So we could say that a kind of control over the sympathetic and the parasympathetic system gives us the ability to have a kind of balance between the two worlds. What we can do and it seems to have been proved by science is that we can stimulate the parasympathetic system so that we can be relaxed at any given moment, so is like applying the brakes to the sympathetic system, but it is not easy to bring about the same results through conscious efforts to the other system. But this is done any way through our contact with the outer world, which constantly offers stimuli. So this is exactly the point where I can control and have a degree of balance between the outside and the inside.

Participant 6: Have you done any research, or are you aware of any research, or maybe do you have an opinion in regards to consciously controlling the parasympathetic system, on using techniques of breath control, or pranayama, or other techniques such as yoga chanting to consciously altering the parasympathetic system.

Andreas Zarkadoulas: So what Ian said is actually true, but there it hasn't been a research signed or adopted by a University and in medicine unless there is a University supporting the research it cannot be acknowledged. All those people practicing yoga have this experience of their heart beat slowing down and this is the first sign of the parasympathetic system working.

Participant 7: However there are in cardiology clinics and hypertension clinics various techniques of this kind those are applied to the patients and have results, so they are doing it. I don't know if they have been published, but they are used.

Participant 8: My question is, you mentioned that, when the body receives sensation the information is related to the thalamus and then to the amygdala to see if there is something dangerous. If it can bypass, if it is not something which is dangerous, is allowed to pass through to the next filter. My question is that when we receive information from the outside world, through the eyes; we take the light and the brain filters the information to create an after image, of how we believe that this room is colored for instance. Is there a way of filtering that data mechanism out and be able to see things as they really are?

Andreas Zarkadoulas: By doing Gurdjieff's Work. Thank you.

There Is in our Life a Certain Very Great Purpose

Seymour B. Ginsburg

Abstract

At the end of *Beelzebub's Tales*, Gurdjieff tells us: "There is in our life a certain very great purpose and we must all serve this Great Common Purpose - in this lies the whole sense and predestination of our life." He goes on to say that a man or woman who is conscious, "acquires the possibility, simultaneously with serving the all-universal Actualizing, of applying part of his manifestations according to the providence of Great Nature for the purpose of acquiring for himself 'Imperishable Being'." (BT1226-7)

This gives rise to several questions:

(1) What is Gurdjieff's status to tell us that there is in our life a certain very great purpose, and is he connected to the esoteric conscious inner circle of humanity about which he spoke to Ouspensky and others?
(2) What is the certain very great purpose in our life to which we are all slaves?
(3) What makes it possible for us to acquire imperishable being while fulfilling the certain very great purpose in our life?
(4) What is the lot of those who fulfil the certain very great purpose in their life consciously and who thereby acquire imperishable being?

This paper addresses these questions and proposes answers in the context of theosophical teaching and Gurdjieff's role as a Bodhisattva, a member of the esoteric conscious inner circle of humanity along with others whom H.P. Blavatsky and J.G. Bennett have called "the Masters of Wisdom". In this respect the paper exposes the close link between Gurdjieff and these other Masters.

There Is in our Life a Certain Very Great Purpose

At the end of *Beelzebub's Tales to His Grandson,* Gurdjieff tells us: "There is in our life a certain very great purpose and we must all serve this Great Common Purpose - in this lies the whole sense and predestination of our life."[1] Gurdjieff goes on to explain that although everyone is equally a slave to this great purpose, the man or woman who has developed his own "I" is conscious, and "he acquires the possibility, simultaneously with serving the all-universal Actualizing, of applying part of his manifestations according to the providence of Great Nature for the purpose of acquiring

---

[1] Gurdjieff. G.I. *Beelzebub's Tales to His Grandson*. 1950. New York: Penguin-Compass, 1999. 1226-7.

for himself 'Imperishable Being'."[2] A word of warning is in order here: we have to be careful not to take the idea of imperishable being as a possibility for the personality which is false and is destroyed at death or soon thereafter. Gurdjieff tells us, "Essence is the truth in man, personality is the false."[3]

Gurdjieff's statements give rise to four questions:

(1) What is Gurdjieff's status and who is Gurdjieff really or what makes a Master?
(2) What is the certain very great purpose in our life to which we are all slaves?
(3) What makes it possible for us to acquire imperishable being while fulfilling the certain very great purpose in our life?
(4) What is the lot of those who fulfil the certain very great purpose in their life consciously and who acquire imperishable being?

To explore these questions, let's take a look at this situation from the standpoint of Endlessness, which these teachings tell us is who we really are. It is the open secret of the esoteric Christianity of Gurdjieff and of the inner teaching of Esoteric Christianity, Kabbalistic Judaism, Advaitic Hinduism, Esoteric Buddhism, Sufi Islam, and other real religions. Although it is an open secret, we cannot see it until we are ready to see it. Meanwhile, we play a role in our grim games in which we call ourselves Mr. or Ms. so-and-so. When we are ready to see it, we realize this artifice. But so long as we do not even doubt that we are a Mr. or Ms. so-and-so, there is little hope of our standing in Endlessness or essence, that is, in who we really are rather than in personality who we mistakenly believe ourselves to be. Nevertheless, it is in playing this personality role that there is realized the very great purpose in our life.

(1) What is Gurdjieff's status and who is Gurdjieff really or what makes a Master?

In the spring of 1978 in my personal quest for life's meaning, I came across Helena Blavatsky's writings (hereafter referred to by the initials she made famous, "H.P.B.") and joined the Theosophical Society. I eagerly attacked H.P.B.'s *magnum opus*, *The Secret Doctrine*, thinking that an understanding of her thought would provide a key to life's meaning. But I could not understand her 1400 page commentary on a mystical poem, possibly from a pre-Babylonian creation myth, that she called the *Stanzas of Dzyan*. Yet, I sensed something important in what she was attempting to say. In the effort to understand, I was led to two additional books of commentary on these stanzas, the first being *Man, the Measure of All Things* (1966), co-authored by Sri Madhava Ashish (1920-1997), a Scottish engineer who had come to India with the British military in World War II and subsequently turned Hindu monk, and his teacher, Sri Krishna Prem (1897-1965), another Englishman who had come to India in 1921 and who had also become a Hindu monk. This book describes the nature of the cosmos based upon the *Stanzas of Dzyan*. The second book, *Man, Son of Man*, authored by Ashish after Prem's passing, describes what man is

---

[2] Gurdjieff. 1227.
[3] Ouspensky, P.D. *In Search of the Miraculous*. London: Routledge & Kegan Paul, 1950. 162.

and the intentional effort required of him to fulfil the certain very great purpose in our lives about which Gurdjieff wrote. It was this book that caused me to meet Ashish in India, and these two books collectively are known as the *Man* books.

In that meeting Ashish advised me that when I returned home to America from India, I should begin to study the teachings of Gurdjieff. In a letter some ten years later he wrote: "The particular characteristic of the Theosophical Society is its direct inspiration by the Masters or Bodhisattvas. They fielded H.P.B. and stood behind her all her life. G [Gurdjieff] was one of them, which is why his teaching is in the same tradition.[4] (Letter Dec. 12, 1988). Ashish also told me to begin to pay attention to my dreams.

I decided to return to see Ashish the following spring, 1979, writing him to request this. Thus began our extensive correspondence in which I asked him all manner of questions concerning theosophy, Gurdjieff's teaching, how to approach the study of dreams, and the subject of Masters, the men whom H.P.B. called her teachers and who presumably transmitted psychically to her, the *Stanzas of Dzyan*. Many of Ashish's responses in his correspondence with me on these and other subjects were published in 2001 in the book, *In Search of the Unitive Vision*, a collection of more than one hundred of his letters. The newly published Quest Book, *The Masters Speak: An American Businessman Encounters Ashish and Gurdjieff* (Quest 2010) recounts that earlier version.

Sensing my confusion about the subject of Masters, Ashish suggested that if I were to return to India to see him, I should first visit another man, Sri Nisargadatta Maharaj who lived in Bombay, in order to help me understand just what makes a Master. This visit in 1979 to meet Nisargadatta and to again see Ashish would become the second in an annual pilgrimage that continued for nineteen years until Ashish's passing in 1997.

Of particular interest is Ashish's remark in a 1989 letter about Masters: "The Master is one with the Spirit. He exemplifies the final attainment. He is what is as yet only a partially realized potential in your own being. You can 'recognize' him only to the extent that you can feel the responses in your essence when like answers to like. G [Gurdjieff] is a Master."[5] (Letter, Jul. 7, 1989)

In another letter Ashish had this to say about Masters: "It may be a fact that some of the Masters derive their being from other worlds than this one. But too much attention given to this speculation can lead to the false view that they are so special as to have no relevance to the lives of ordinary mortals like us. In fact, so many of them have arisen from the ordinary mortals of this planet, and from so many different races and cultures on this planet, that they provide us with examples of what we should and can become here and now."[6] (Letter, Jan. 24, 1989)

---

[4] Ginsburg, *The Masters Speak*. 141.
[5] Ginsburg. *The Masters Speak*. 150.
[6] Ginsburg. *The Masters Speak*. 149.

There Is in our Life a Certain Very Great Purpose

One of the reasons Ashish sent me to meet Nisargadatta was because Nisargadatta was an example from his own life of what we should and can become here and now. Unlike Ashish and unlike Ashish's teacher, Sri Krishna Prem, both of whom lived ascetic lives in the remote Himalayas, Nisargadatta was an ordinary middle class Indian shopkeeper with a wife and four children, living in the midst of the craziness that is Mumbai (Bombay). In that sense his attainment is something to which any of us can aspire. Gurdjieff also tells us this. In *Beelzebub's Tales* he says, "each one of us must set for his chief aim to become in the process of our collective life a master."[7]

Gurdjieff described this circle of Masters, of which he was one, to P.D. Ouspensky, calling them the conscious inner circle of humanity. He said to Ouspensky, "The inner circle is called the 'esoteric'; this circle consists of people who have attained the highest development possible for man, each one of whom possesses individuality in the fullest degree, that is to say, an indivisible 'I,' all forms of consciousness possible for man, full control over these states of consciousness, the whole of knowledge possible for man, and a free and independent will."[8] He went on to explain that this esoteric circle is surrounded by a mesoteric inner circle of people and that circle is in turn surrounded by an exoteric inner circle. These three concentric circles represent different degrees of understanding but are all part of the conscious inner circle of humanity, as distinguished from an outer circle of mechanical humanity to which belong the vast majority of human beings.

Much errant nonsense has been published about Masters, attributing to them all sorts of supposedly miraculous powers to tantalize a gullible public. These powers, are not at all relevant to the teaching brought to us by these Masters, and whether any of them had such powers is highly problematic. But it is verifiable that certain seemingly unusual capacities can be developed in human beings. These include, among others, such talents as telepathy. But we love our myths whether they are accounts of Jesus raising someone from the dead or another Master flying magically from the hills of India to Mt. Kailash in Tibet each day for his morning meditation.[9]

Whatever the truth in our myths, they are the least important aspect of our inquiry. What is important for us to understand is that H.P.B.'s adept Masters were a succession of incarnated human beings as was Gurdjieff, rather than a cosmic hierarchy of supermen. The actual "miraculous" power that they did have in common was the ability to communicate with H.P.B. and others at a distance, a power known under various words such as "telepathy", of which there

---

[7] Gurdjieff. G.I. *Beelzebub's Tales to His Grandson*. 1950. New York: Penguin-Compass, 1999. 1236.

[8] Ouspensky. P.D. *In Search of the Miraculous*, London: Routledge & Kegan Paul, 1950. 310-312.

[9] Ginsburg. *The Masters Speak*, 283-284. "The famous Lahiri Mahasaya, the man you've read about in Yogananda's book, *Autobiography of a Yogi,* he claimed to have done his daily worship on Mt. Kailash. Yogananda did not mention the fact that the Mt. Kailash he refers to is in Ranikhet, whereas the reader immediately thinks of the Mt. Kailash up in Tibet. So Lahiri Mahasaya presumably, sort of magically went up to Tibet and back again every morning. It's one of these confusions." (Letter, Dec. 22, 1979)

are many verified accounts in human experience. P.D. Ouspensky, for example, wrote in amazement of Gurdjieff's telepathic powers, saying: "With this the miracle began ... It all started with my beginning to hear his thoughts."[10]

What we call "telepathy" is a natural function of our connectedness with each other at levels of the psyche, more interior than the turning thoughts of the lower mind as distinguished from higher mind. The Masters, at one with the Spirit, but having followed the Bodhisattva path of compassion toward their less evolved brethren, continue to guide humanity with telepathically transmitted wisdom both while incarnate and after leaving the physical body. We usually regard received wisdom as insight. Such insight often comes during silent meditation and through the symbolic language in which dreams speak to us. This is why Ashish placed such importance on our sitting quietly in meditation for long periods of time and on paying attention to our dreams and the symbolic language in which they speak.

H.P.B. was known to be highly psychic and she claimed to have psychically seen the *Stanzas of Dzyan*. About her reception of them, she wrote in an 1889 letter: "Knowledge comes in visions, first in dreams and in pictures presented to the inner eye during meditation. Thus have I been taught the whole system of evolution, the laws of being and all else that I know. ... And knowledge so obtained is so clear, so convincing, so indelible in the impression it makes upon the mind, that all other sources of information, all other methods of teaching with which we are familiar dwindle into insignificance in comparison with this."[11]

Although I did not understand it at the time, it was because Gurdjieff's teaching derives from the same source as H.P.B.'s teaching, that Ashish recommended it to me. That source is, in Gurdjieff's terms, the esoteric conscious inner circle of humanity. H.P.B. called that same source, the Masters of wisdom as did J.G. Bennett. H.P.B. herself never claimed to be part of the esoteric conscious inner circle of humanity, but she did claim to be the student of three teachers, counterparts of Gurdjieff, whom she called her Masters. These teachers are part of that esoteric conscious inner circle as is Gurdjieff.

Was Sri Madhava Ashish a member of the esoteric conscious inner circle of humanity, or was he at the level of understanding of the mesoteric or the exoteric inner circles? I cannot say, but I knew from the time of our initial meeting in 1978, that there was something special about him. Exactly what that something was, I could not then put my finger on. But there was about him a presence very different from other men.

Evidence of the connections between Gurdjieff and other members of the esoteric conscious inner circle of humanity who were H.P.B's teachers was presented in a paper given at *The 3rd*

---

[10] Ouspensky. *In Search of the Miraculous* . 262. See also 262-4.
[11] Blavatsky Collected Writings BCW XIII, 285. A fragment from the pen of H.P.B. in The Theosophist, Vol. XXXI, March, 1910, 685.

International Humanities Conference: All & Everything, 98.[12] Here is a summary of the evidence for these connections.

In the introduction to *The Secret Doctrine*, H.P.B. gives a prediction: "In Century the Twentieth some disciple more informed and far better fitted [than the current author H.P.B.] may be sent by the Masters of Wisdom ... [and] *The Secret Doctrine* is not a treatise, or a series of vague theories, but contains all that can be given out to the world in this [nineteenth] century."[13]

What was given out at the end of the nineteenth century were the first two volumes of *The Secret Doctrine* based on *The Stanzas of Dzyan*; the first volume entitled "Cosmogenesis" (the coming into being of the cosmos) and the second volume entitled "Anthropogenesis" (the coming into being of man). Both these volumes constitute an intellectual description of reality, but lack practical instruction for the intentional effort that man must make to acquire imperishable being. However, there is a further prediction given in *The Secret Doctrine* which goes on to say:

"These two volumes should form for the student a fitting prelude for Volumes III, and IV. Until the rubbish of the ages is cleared away from the minds of the Theosophists to whom these volumes are dedicated, it is impossible that the more practical teaching contained in the Third Volume should be understood."[14]

Just what is Gurdjieff's role in all this? H.P.B. answers this question in her *Secret Doctrine* commentary. She tells us that there are important parts of the teaching that she is not disclosing in these first two volumes. More is to be expected, especially as concerns the practical aspects of the teaching. H.P.B. tells us some interesting things about the predicted third and fourth volumes of *The Secret Doctrine* that will help us to connect them with Gurdjieff's teaching. She writes:
"In Volume III. of this work (the said volume and the IVth being almost ready) a brief history of all the great adepts known to the ancients and the moderns in their chronological order will be given, as also a bird's eye view of the Mysteries, their birth, growth, decay, and final death -- in Europe.[15]

"In that volume [III] a brief recapitulation will be made of all the principal adepts known to history, and the downfall of the mysteries will be described."[16]

---

[12] *The 3rd International Humanities Conference: All & Everything 98.* Ginsburg, Seymour B. "Gurdjieff, Blavatsky and the Masters of Wisdom" Loughton, UK: Planning Committee, All & Everything Conferences, 1998. 43-73.
[13] Blavatsky. S.D. I. xxxviii.
[14] Blavatsky. S.D. II. 797-8.
[15] Blavatsky. S.D.I. 437.
[16] Blavatsky. S.D.I. xl.

And what of Volume IV.? What will it contain? Once more H.P.B. tells us. She says, "Volume IV. will be almost entirely devoted to Occult teachings."[17] In respect to these occult teachings, consider the never completed *Third Series: Life is Real only then When I Am.*

In addition to these clues, we can select from any number of other statements made by H.P.B. as we look for indications of what more might be given. One such statement is her comment about oral transmission in relation to *The Secret Doctrine*. She writes: "that which is given in these volumes is selected from *oral*, as much as from written teachings."[18] Therefore, we shall want to consider what oral teaching has been given to us along with that which has been set down in writing.

But who is the disciple predicted by H.P.B., who will bring both the oral and written teachings in the twentieth century? The elders of the Theosophical Society in the first decade of the twentieth century, under the leadership of Annie Besant, were not unmindful of H.P.B.'s predictions. But they incorrectly chose J. Krishnamurti as the predicted teacher who would come in the twentieth century. Krishnamurti himself rejected this role in his arguably most important speech "Truth is a Pathless Land" given before thousands of theosophists in Holland in 1929.

Let us now look at Gurdjieff's position when he came public in Moscow beginning in 1912 and consider his actions over the next decades. Let us also assume that he is a Master, a member of the esoteric conscious inner circle of humanity, as Ashish recognized. Gurdjieff's connections with theosophy ran wide and deep, notwithstanding his negative views about naïve early theosophists and other occultists who did much fantasizing. Two of his closest students, P.D. Ouspensky and A.R. Orage, both of literary prominence in the first half of the 20th century, were well known speakers for the theosophical movement. Two lesser known figures in the theosophical movement of the 1920s, Maud Hoffman and Trevor Barker, became pupils of Gurdjieff when he visited London in 1922 and went with him to Fontainebleau to help prepare the *Prieure* to receive students.[19] Remarkably, all the while they were with Gurdjieff at Fontainebleau, these two pupils were working on the transcription, compilation and publication of *The Mahatma Letters*, a series of letters written by H.P.B.'s teachers, her Masters, to British officials in India in the late nineteenth century.[20] These Masters are the same group of teachers of whom Gurdjieff was one.

---

[17] Blavatsky. S.D.I. 437
[18] Blavatsky. S.D. I. xxxvii.
[19] Moore, James "A Footnote on Maud Hoffman and A.T. Barker." *Theosophical History*, Vol. 3, No. 3 (July 1990) 77-78.
[20] Maud Hoffman, an American Shakespearean actress residing in England with her close friend, the theosophist, Mabel Collins, became executrix of the estate of A. P. Sinnett and inherited the Mahatma letters which Sinnett had collected in India. She wrote a full page article for the New York Times, February 10, 1924, describing life at the Prieure under her teacher Gurdjieff. Hoffman appointed Trevor Barker, a British theosophist to edit the Mahatma letters for publication. Some of this work took place while Hoffman and Barker were pupils of Gurdjieff.

There Is in our Life a Certain Very Great Purpose

Let us assume that Gurdjieff wants to give the world indications that he is the teacher predicted in *The Secret Doctrine*, who will bring the practical teaching. How does he do it? Of course, he actually brings the practical teaching. That is his job. It is why he was sent in. The practical teaching is essentially oral, and he gives it out piecemeal to Ouspensky and others in the early Russian groups. Ouspensky recognizes this and writes "I realized very clearly that a great deal of time must pass before I could tell myself that I could outline the whole system correctly."[21] Eventually, Ouspensky does outline the system and writes it down as he understands it, however incompletely. This written account, *In Search of the Miraculous*, constitutes the most widely known and generally regarded authoritative exposition of the oral teaching imparted by Gurdjieff.

By the 1920s Gurdjieff is certainly aware of Krishnamurti's designation by the theosophists as the new world teacher. He can hardly stand in opposition to this. It would appear unseemly and he would be accused of self-serving. What does he do? Gurdjieff, after the auto accident in 1924, which determined that he would have to close his school, dedicates himself to writing. He writes the intentionally mythological *Beelzebub's Tales to his Grandson*, and writes into it a scenario that will fulfil *The Secret Doctrine* prediction. He does this by creating a great scientist who appears as a Saturnian bird, Gornahoor Harharkh, who helps Beelzebub to construct a telescope on the planet Mars, by which he is able to observe the happenings on Earth. In this way he is able to give "a bird's eye view of the Mysteries, their birth, growth, decay, and final death -- in Europe"; and he does this along with giving us "a brief history of all the great adepts known to the ancients and the moderns in their chronological order", just as had been predicted by H.P.B. in *The Secret Doctrine*.

Some students of Gurdjieff's teaching have recognized that *Beelzebub's Tales to His Grandson*, in spite of intentional obscuration, is largely Gurdjieff's autobiography, at least in his most recent incarnation as Gurdjieff and possibly in his many appearances in the past on this planet, in the role of teacher. Events in his "sixth descent" to the planet Earth which lead us into the twentieth century can definitely be linked to Gurdjieff's life here as we know it. Theosophical theory has it that a being sent in from above takes incarnation in a vehicle provided by ordinary human procreation. Beelzebub's statements that he "descended" onto earth, in describing each of his six visits, can be seen as his entering into incarnation for the purposes described in *Beelzebub's Tales to His Grandson*.

This is further confirmed in Beelzebub's description of the taking incarnation by the allegorical Ashiata Shiemash: "By the All Most Gracious Command of Our OMNI-LOVING COMMON FATHER ENDLESSNESS, our Cosmic Highest Most Very Saintly Individuals sometimes actualize within the presence of some terrestrial three-brained being, a 'definitized' conception of a sacred Individual in order that he, having become a terrestrial being with such a presence, may there on the spot 'orientate himself' and give to the process of their ordinary being-existence such a corresponding new direction, thanks to which the already crystallized consequences of the

---

[21] Ouspensky. 64.

properties of the organ Kundabuffer, as well as predispositions to such new crystallizations, might perhaps be removed from their presences."[22]

Gurdjieff may very well have been describing himself in the guise of Ashiata Shiemash into whose mouth he put the words: "To me, a trifling particle of the whole of the GREAT WHOLE, it was commanded from Above to be coated with the planetary body of a three-centered being of this planet and to assist all other such beings arising and existing upon it to free themselves from the consequences of the properties of that organ which, for great and important reasons, was actualized in the presences of their ancestors."[23]

Although Madhava Ashish told me to study Gurdjieff's teaching and he, himself, was a great fan of *Beelzebub's Tales to His Grandson*, in a letter, he made the following comment about what he called the *Man* books: "G's system [of cosmology] is tantalizing, but mythological in form. G did not intend to provide a rational framework. As he says at the beginning of the book [*Beelzebub's Tales to His Grandson*], he aims to destroy preconceived nations. Frankly, you will get a clearer approximation of the facts from the *Man* books [*Man, the Measure of All Things* and *Man, Son of Man*]. I think you will find G's ideas making more sense against the framework those books sketch."[24] (letter Feb. 26, 1993)

Ashish said this to me in 1993, about these two *Man* books that I came across in 1978 and which brought me to meet him. But it would be 2008, another fifteen years, before I picked up on his hint and began to re-examine the *Man* books, and especially *Man, Son of Man*. It is not because this book contains anything that cannot be dug out of *Beelzebub's Tales to His Grandson*, but Gurdjieff wrote it in mythological form just as H.P.B. wrote *The Secret Doctrine* in a confusing 19th century literary style. A more modern and straightforward explanation was needed, and this is what was given to us, in my view, by Gurdjieff and his cohorts of the esoteric conscious inner circle of humanity in the 1950s, a few years after Gurdjieff left incarnation. This explanation was telepathically transmitted through Prem and Ashish. In his book on dreams, *An Open Window: Dream as Everyman's Guide to the Spirit*, posthumously published in 2007, some ten years after his passing, Ashish described the receiving of the wisdom recorded in the *Man* books in the 1950s by him and Prem, in almost the same terms as H.P.B. used to describe her reception of this wisdom in the 1880s. The emphasis in both descriptions is upon the necessity of receiving wisdom through symbols in dream and in silent meditation where thought is stopped so that insight can be received. This is why silent meditation, known as "sitting" in Gurdjieff groups is so important, and this is why paying attention to symbols in dreams is equally important. About this, echoing H.P.B.'s description of how she received the *Stanzas of Dzyan* in meditation and dream, Ashish wrote:

---

[22] Gurdjieff. 347.
[23] Gurdjieff. 353.
[24] Ginsburg. 230.

There Is in our Life a Certain Very Great Purpose

"We [Prem and Ashish] went through a high period [in the 1950s] when a night without a dream was a wasted opportunity, a forgotten dream was a breach of trust. We hurried through our many chores to be free to pace up and down in the morning light, seeking meanings and their ramifications. Then as the mind began to come under control, little visions began to appear in meditation whose content was more direct, less concealed by symbols, than in ordinary dream. There was direct, personal instruction. And there were dreams which threw light on the Cosmogenesis and Anthropogenesis of the *Stanzas of Dzyan* on which we were attempting to write a commentary. Yet there was never direct dictation. One always had to struggle to understand what the symbols were saying, so that one was personally responsible for the form in which the general scheme was presented."[25]

In another letter Ashish said: "We [Prem and Ashish] wrote that the commentary has to stand on its own. Saying that inspiration and instruction was given by D. K. [Djwhal Khul, a theosophical Master] and others would add nothing to the validity of the work. We know to whom we owe it, but we are not going to make him answer for our misunderstandings and mistakes."[26] (letter Jan. 7, 1992)

There has been an unfortunate lack of interest in the study of dreams within the Gurdjieff community because of the misunderstanding of what Gurdjieff meant in a talk he gave in 1923 entitled "Energy - Sleep", published in *Views from the Real World.*[27] But even within the Gurdjieff literature one finds references to dream work by Gurdjieff students such as in the published writings of Margaret Anderson and Dr. Maurice Nicoll. And it is a little known fact that Gurdjieff worked with certain individual students helping them to understand their dreams.

In working with dreams, we need to learn the symbolic language in which our dreams speak to us. Often, but not always, these are messages from higher centers, really another term for the esoteric conscious inner circle of humanity, urging us to growth, maturity and wholeness. Who or what is the source of wisdom that communicates with us through insight given symbolically in meditation and dream? Can we imagine that it is really Gurdjieff himself when Gurdjieff appears in a dream, or that it is Jesus supplying the insight that sometimes comes in silent meditation, or that it is the Master Maurya who calls our attention to a passage in a book that answers a question? Ashish expressed it this way:

"Any one of those beings (if it has any meaning to speak of these being more than one essential being) can look out through the eyes of any existing form that has eyes. There is a series of masks, shaped in the familiar forms of Gurdjieff, Jesus, the Buddha, Maurya, etc., so that idiots like us can recognize them, through which the one power can communicate with us. Yet there is a sense

---

[25] Ashish, Sri Madhava. *An Open Window: Dream as Everyman's Guide to the Spirit*. New Delhi: Penguin, 2007. xvii.
[26] Ginsburg. 128.
[27] Gurdjieff. *Views from the Real World*. New York: Penguin, 1984, 115-20.

in which 'The Great Russian Bodhisattva' whom we last knew as Gurdjieff, at a certain level, is distinguishable from other bodhisattvas.[28] (letter Oct. 11, 1989)

<u>In sum, Gurdjieff's status is that he is a Master, a member of the esoteric conscious inner circle of humanity, as were H.P.B.'s teachers.</u>

(2) What is the very great purpose in our life to which we are all slaves?

To help us understand the certain very great purpose to which Gurdjieff refers, an allegorical Hindu children's story may help. It goes like this: All there is, in and beyond the universe is Brahman (or Endlessness or Self or God or whatever we wish to call it). There is nothing else. In spiritual philosophy this is known as unity or non-duality. But in our story Brahman is lonely because there is nothing else. So Brahman decides to divide itself into two parts so that it can know itself and play with itself. We can recognize this division of the unity into two parts calling them male and female, or positive and negative, and other similar terms. In this artificial division of one into two, an energy is released, a third part. It is Gurdjieff's third force. In ordinary Hinduism these three parts are given names as the three highest Hindu Gods, Brahma the creator, Shiva the destroyer, and Vishnu the preserver. This triad of Gods is known in Hinduism as the Trimurti, to which Gurdjieff refers.

Practitioners of Gurdjieff's teaching know from experience that what Gurdjieff brought was, as predicted by H.P.B, "the more practical teaching", the teaching about the intentional effort that we each must make. And it is through the practical teaching that Gurdjieff brought, the psychological self-awareness exercises and the physical self-awareness exercises, that we actually come to know ourself. We become aware of being conscious of ourself.

When Gurdjieff said that the words "know thyself ... which are generally ascribed to Socrates, actually lie at the basis of many systems and schools far more ancient than the Socratic"[29] he was not exaggerating. "Know thyself," he said, "is full of particularly deep meaning and is one of the symbols leading to the knowledge of truth."[30] The admonition, "Know Thyself" goes back long before the arising of *homo sapiens* vehicles on planet Earth. It goes back, in fact, to the manifestation of the universe as described in *The Secret Doctrine*. It is the admonition of and to Endlessness in its recurring voyage of self-discovery. On planet Earth that voyage is actualized in the three-brained *homo sapiens* beings, who are the vehicles through which Endlessness is able to know itself.

Among the most important statements in *Man, Son of Man* are the following five in which is revealed the answer to the question: What is this certain very great common purpose, in which lies the whole sense and predestination of our life? It is there stated:

---

[28] Ginsburg. 137.
[29] Ouspensky. 104.
[30] Ouspensky. 280.

(A) "The only unqualified Subject in the Cosmos is the One, which can never under any circumstances become an object of its own awareness."[31]

(B) "The primary creative impulse arising in absolute, undifferentiated Being can be described as a desire within Being to know itself, a desire which begins by producing a distinction between the subjective Knower and the desired object of knowledge, both separated and linked by the desirous act of knowing, and which ends by a multitude of knowing units being clothed in the objective garments of apparent form. There is, in other words, a purposeful striving within the unmanifest source of all things to make its inherent qualities apparent to itself—a necessary effort, because the diffused consciousness of Absolute Being cannot become aware of its own qualities until both a separation has been made between Knower and Known, and its qualities have been objectively represented."[32]

(C) "The urge to travel the path of spiritual endeavor springs from the Cosmic Being's urge towards its own fulfilment, an urge that is implanted in our hearts as it is implanted in the hearts of all creatures of the divine will. The inner goal towards which we are urged to turn is the goal of the cosmic cycle, and the purpose to gain that goal through man is the purpose of the whole process of evolution."[33]

(D) "When the Great Being once again sets out on His recurring voyage of self-discovery, then the bright jewel points of the perfected men [who are the esoteric conscious inner circle of humanity], re-clothe themselves in plastic form."[34]

(E) "The mystic's vision of the essential unity of all being is the supreme truth indeed, but even he is apt to forget that the bliss of union with the divine being is attainable only by virtue of our seeming separateness."[35]

C. G. Jung and psychologists of the Jungian school who have delved into the mystical side of Jung's teaching have well understood the need for this adventure in seeming separateness in psychological terms, writing: "In the early stages of ego development the opposites must be separated, and you might say that it is the task of the ego to get out of them. The young ego is obliged to separate from its environment and to define itself in terms of being different; … Separating the opposites is a task for the early part of life, and the union of the opposites is a task for the later part of life."[36]

Gurdjieff explains how the almost infinite diversity that we observe all about us fulfils the desire within Being to fully know itself. He tells us that it was actualized through the two great laws of world creation and world maintenance, the sacred Triamazikamno (the law of three forces) and the sacred Heptaparaparshinokh (the law of the octave). He tells us: "In the beginning, when nothing yet existed and when the whole of our Universe was empty endless space with the presence of

---

[31] Ashish, *Man, Son of Man*. 241.
[32] Ashish. *Man, Son of Man*. 5.
[33] Ashish. *Man, Son of Man*. 36.
[34] Ashish, *Man, Son of Man*. 303.
[35] Ashish. *Man, Son of Man*. 36.
[36] Edinger, Edward F. *The Mysterium Lectures: A Journey through C. G. Jung's Mysterium Coniunctionis*. Toronto: Inner City Books, 1995. 321.

only the prime-source cosmic substance 'Etherokrilno, our present Most Great and Most Most Holy Sun Absolute existed alone in all this empty space, and it was on this then sole cosmic concentration that our UNI-BEING CREATOR with HIS cherubim and seraphim had the place of HIS most glorious being. It was just during this same period of the flow of time that there came to our CREATOR ALL-MAINTAINER the forced need to create our present existing 'Megalocosmos,' i.e. our World."[37]

The need for the creation is so that Endlessness can know itself in almost infinite diversity. It is the certain very great purpose of our *homo sapiens* incarnation. This begins with the artificial division of the one subject into subject and object, or knower and known, or male and female. This division results in a release of energy. Because, as is explained in *Man, Son of Man*, the diffused consciousness of the absolute being of Endlessness cannot become aware of its own qualities until both a separation has been made between knower and known, and its qualities have been objectively represented, an artificial division by Endlessness is made into subject (masculine) and object (feminine). The release of energy resulting from this division is what Gurdjieff has called "the third force." It can be either attractive or repellent between the first and second forces. C.G. Jung recognized this from a psychological standpoint and in his *magnum opus*, the final and most mystical of his writings, *Mysterium Coniunctionis*, he wrote: "The factors which come together in the coniunctio [union] are conceived as opposites confronting one another in enmity or attracting one another in love."[38]

While the law of the three forces has been generally known throughout the history of mankind, the equally important law of the octave has for the most part been unknown, or if known, then often misunderstood. Gurdjieff explains this law to us in terms of time, because time is necessary for Endlessness to know itself in infinite diversity. Without time there would be no possibility of self-knowledge because of the instantaneous collapse of the artificial duality back into non-duality.

The manifestation, giving rise to the creation and materialization, and resulting from the sacred Triamazikamno or the law of three forces for the purpose of Endlessness's desire for self-knowledge, requires something more. The artificial division of the one into two (and effectively three) must instantaneously collapse back into one, meaning that there is no time and no possibility of self-knowledge, unless something further is done to prevent this instantaneous collapse. This something further is the changing of the Stopinders by Endlessness, in effect bringing into the process, the law of the octave - the sacred Heptaparaparshinokh, in which intentional irregularity has been inserted into what otherwise would be uniformity in the changing of rates of vibration throughout Endlessness. It is this irregularity intentionally inserted into the manifestation that gives rise to duration in which time allows the infinite variety through which Endlessness knows itself in infinite diversity. Duration in time allows the manifestation of our Megalocosmos created by the changing of the Stopinders and sustained by the reciprocal exchange of energies within the manifested universe. This reciprocal exchange prevents the diminishment of

---

[37] Gurdjieff. 748-9.
[38] Jung, C.G. *Mysterium Coniunctionis*. Princeton: Bollingen. 1965. 3.

duration and consequently prevents the diminishment of the almost infinite variety of experience by which Endlessness comes to know itself. The necessity for the creation is expressed in *Beelzebub's Tales to His Grandson:*

"Our present Most Great and Most Most Holy Sun Absolute [which] existed alone in all this empty space, and it was on this then sole cosmic concentration that our UNI-BEING CREATOR with HIS cherubim and seraphim had the place of HIS most glorious Being."[39] This is a description of reality before the creation of "our present existing 'Megalocosmos,' i.e., our World."[40] We then learn that "our ENDLESSNESS was forced to create the whole World which now exists at the present time."[41] The reason given for this is, "that our CREATOR OMNIPOTENT once ascertained that this same Sun Absolute, on which HE dwelt with HIS cherubim and seraphim was, although almost imperceptibly yet nevertheless gradually, diminishing in volume. … our OMNIPOTENT CREATOR for the first time made it clear that the cause of this gradual diminishing of the volume of the Sun Absolute was merely the Heropass, that is, the flow of Time itself,"[42] and thus "to attain immunity from the maleficent action of the of the merciless Heropass (time), HE ultimately actualized it all."[43]

The outward journey, the descent of spirit into matter for the purpose of experience, and the inward journey, the path of return, has often been described as a parabola. The descending arc of the parabola is the descent of spirit into the almost infinite diversity of matter however artificial. The return ascending arc is the ascent of matter, which is objectively unreal, back to spirit, the only objective reality, but now with the benefit of experience in Endlessness's desire to know itself.

The following "Diagram of Endlessness in the Form of Man" is intended to help clear up confusion because there are two series of seven orders of being, not one. The parabola in the seven circles on the left side represents inner man. About inner man, Gurdjieff says: "Your contemporary favorites very often use a notion taken by them from somewhere, I do not know whether instinctively, emotionally, or automatically, and expressed by them in the following words: 'We are the images of God.' These unfortunates do not even suspect that of everything known to most of them concerning cosmic truths, this expression of theirs is the only true one of them all. And indeed, each of them is the image of God, not of that 'God' which they have in their bobtailed picturing, but of the real God by which word we sometimes still call our common Megalocosmos."[44]

---

[39] Gurdjieff. 748-9.
[40] Gurdjieff. 749.
[41] Gurdjieff. 748.
[42] Gurdjieff. 749.
[43] Gurdjieff. 750.
[44] Gurdjieff. 775.

Man, more importantly, belongs to the non-materialized state than to the materialized *homo sapiens* vehicle. He is shown on the left side of the diagram as inner man, the Adam Kadmon of Gnosticism and Kabbalah. The seven orders of being represented by the seven circles on the right side of the diagram represent biological evolution providing vehicles for the ingression of consciousness. In *Man, Son of Man* we are told: "The descending order of creative powers meets the ascending order of physical forms at the junction between the desire level [the bottom circle of the parabola on the left] and the physical level [the fourth circle from the bottom of the series on the right]."[45] In terms of the biological evolution of a suitable vehicle, that junction takes place in the *hominid* vehicle, the precursor of the *homo sapiens*. Note also that the diagram is divided into three parts: (A) The unmanifest transcendent which is Endlessness "when nothing yet existed";[46] (C) The materialization where "the descending order of human characteristics meets the physical order of animal evolution";[47] and (B) What is called in *Man, Son of Man*, "the watery mid-region." In *Man, Son of Man*, it is said: "We have begun by plunging directly into a discussion on the strange, shifting, uneasy 'waters' of the Matrix - the mid-region of magical effects, ghosts, astral bodies, [the body Kesdjan] and other occult phenomena. Let us meet the question squarely. Those who reject this strange, magical area of experience as 'old wives tales' and 'superstitious nonsense' are rejecting the key to the secret of life along with it."[48]

"It is extremely difficult to give an adequate description of this deceptive middle-region of the universe. ... It has neither the relatively stable definition of the sensible universe, nor the intellectual clarity of the unmanifest Transcendent. So difficult is its nature to grasp that nearly all academic scientists prefer to ignore its presence, and so treacherous are its paths that most spiritual teachers seek to decry its importance. Yet we live constantly in its 'watery' atmosphere, our life and our very existence depend upon it, and every physical form in the universe has arisen through its mediacy, for it is the subtle, impressionable link between mental concept and physical form. In effect, it is the same energy-filled space out of which this universe has grown and in which it stands, but only at this outermost edge of the manifestation do those energies reach a sufficient intensity to become visible to us."[49] This mid-region is the region of connection, the region that explains telepathic communication such as that demonstrated by Gurdjieff and recounted by Ouspensky. It is also the region of body-Kesdjan existence after the first sacred Rascooarno (physical death) and the time at which the being-body-Kesdjan temporarily existent in this after death state "must decompose, irrespective of whether the higher being-part existing within it, had by that time attained the requisite degree of Reason."[50]

---

[45] Ashish, *Man, Son of Man*. 194.
[46] Gurdjieff. 748.
[47] Ashish. *Man, Son of Man*. 143.
[48] Ashish. *Man, Son of Man*. 85.
[49] Ashish. *Man, Son of Man*. 86.
[50] Gurdjieff. 766.

There Is in our Life a Certain Very Great Purpose

Diagram of Endlessness in the Form of Man
In Three Parts; and Two Series of Septenaries

(A) the Unmanifest Transcendent: "when nothing yet existed."[51]
(B) the Watery mid-region: "the body Kesdjan, together with the 'third-being-body … rise … to that sphere."[52]
(C) the Materialization: "the descending order of human characteristics meets the physical order of animal evolution."[53]

(A) The Unmanifest Transcendent, the Divine Unity from which all proceeds and whither all returns. (SD I,1)[54]

(B) The Watery mid-region between the sensible universe and the unmanifest transcendent. The mid-region of magical effects, ghosts, the body Kesdjan, and other occult phenomena. "Those who reject this strange, magical area of experience are rejecting the key to life along with it, for without [it], there could be no womb of becoming and no human birth."[55]

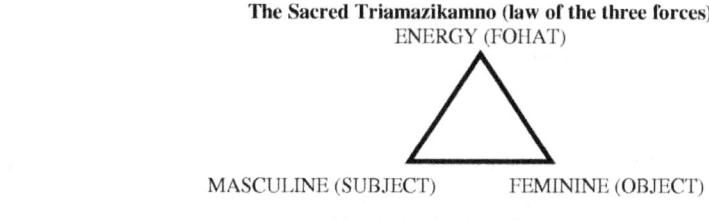

The Sacred Triamazikamno (law of the three forces)
ENERGY (FOHAT)

MASCULINE (SUBJECT)   FEMININE (OBJECT)

Parabola of Being of Inner Man   **Physical Vehicle: *Homo Sapiens***

Man most importantly comes from this watery mid-region and to this region he returns.[56]

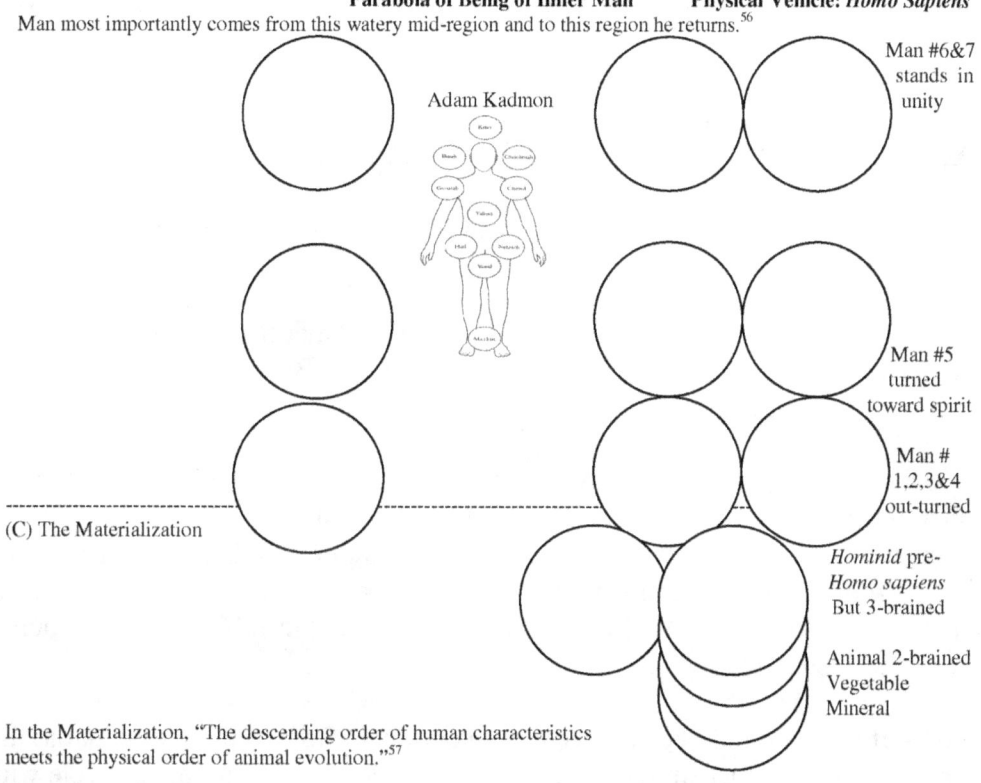

Adam Kadmon

Man #6&7 stands in unity

Man #5 turned toward spirit

Man # 1,2,3&4 out-turned

(C) The Materialization

Hominid pre-*Homo sapiens* But 3-brained

Animal 2-brained
Vegetable
Mineral

In the Materialization, "The descending order of human characteristics meets the physical order of animal evolution."[57]

---

[51] Gurdjieff. 748.
[52] Gurdjieff. 765.
[53] Ashish. *Man, Son of Man*. 143.
[54] Blavatsky. S.D. I. 1.
[55] Ashish, *Man, Son of Man*. 85.
[56] Gurdjieff. See pp. 765-8.
[57] Ashish, *Man, Son of Man*. 143.

Simply phrased, we are Endlessness as is everything in existence. The idea is expressed poetically in the Hymn to our Endlessness appearing at the end of *Beelzebub's Tales to His Grandson* [in part]:

"Thou Abundantly LOVING CAUSE of All That Exists,
Thou Unique VANQUISHER Of The Merciless Heropass, …
Extol Thee MAKER-CREATOR
Thou, The Beginning of All Ends,
Thou, Proceeding from Infinity,
Thou, Having The End Of All Things Within Thyself,
Thou, Our ENDLESS ENDLESSNESS."[58]

Notice that Endlessness in the hymn is "the beginning of all ends", and has "the end of all things within itself." This is a statement of non-duality. This non-dualistic view of mankind means that man is Endlessness and that Endlessness is man, not only in principle but in full knowledge of the fact.

<u>In sum, our very great purpose as Endlessness, incarnated in the *homo sapiens* vehicle, is to fulfil the desire within being to know itself fully and therefore in almost infinite diversity.</u>

(3) What makes it possible for us to acquire imperishable being while fulfilling the very great purpose in our life?

It is only in the three-brained *homo sapiens* vehicle on this planet that we, that is, Endlessness has the ability to know itself, to be aware of itself, on planet Earth. But this cannot happen without our intentional effort. We are told in *Man, Son of Man*:

"Unlike our arrival at manhood, we are subject to no inescapable compulsion to grow. Against our will we can neither be thrust upwards from below nor pulled upwards from above. Having achieved an instrument of its own will [*homo sapiens*], it is through that instrument that the divine Will achieves its purpose. It is as if the divine Will cannot compel itself by itself, and we, who are essentially moments in or of that Will must give ourselves to the fulfilment of its purpose if that purpose is to be fulfilled."[59]

"The perfection of man can only be achieved by intentional effort of the individual to discover his essential unity with the macrocosmic Man and so to complete the evolutionary cycle which begins with unexpressed potentials of life and ends with manifest vehicles through which the divine awareness achieves knowledge both of its essential unity and of its manifold nature."[60]

---

[58] Gurdjieff. 1174.
[59] Ashish. *Man, Son of Man*. 284.
[60] Ashish. *Man, Son of Man*. 302-3.

There Is in our Life a Certain Very Great Purpose

The intentional effort referred to requires what Gurdjieff has called "conscious labor and intentional suffering" throughout *Beelzebub's Tales to His Grandson*. Ashish was explicit in listing aspects of the intentional effort that is required. Foremost among these is Gurdjieff's admonition to "remember ourselves always and everywhere". It is this method, sometimes called "self witnessing" that moves us away from identification with the personality and toward our real nature that is the Self or Endlessness. But there are additional tools of which we can make use. In a 1989 letter Ashish listed these:

"1. Keep up the self-remembering exercises all the time.
2. Give your mind food for thought which stimulates your aim. [i.e. read spiritual writings]
3. Increase the periods and frequencies of meditation.
4. Record dreams and visions and work on their meanings.
5. Try to get inner sanction for even simple daily actions. The point is that the whole of your life has to be integrated around the center, and not just the spiritual bit of it.
6. Open yourself to the psychic contents of events, from perceiving the flow of life in plants to noting synchronicities. [These synchronicities when paid attention to, will provide overwhelming personal verification of what Gurdjieff has called, the real world.]
7. There is a connection between self-remembering and meditation. Keeping yourself centered at all times makes it easier to get into meditation at special times. This sort of effort is directed to a transpersonal goal. If you are dedicated to the way of the Masters (i.e. not to selfish liberation, but to helping others), then the Masters personify the goal. So your efforts take you directly towards them."[61] (letter May 25, 1989).

An important additional tool about which Ashish wrote separately and which Gurdjieff also explains is that the perfection of man, the three-brained being, requires a very fine energy, and is made possible because Great Nature has allowed to develop and remain in man, a certain "particle" through which imperishable being is acquired. Students of Gurdjieff's teaching, studying the enneagramatic refining of energies within the human body will understand how the refining of the three incoming foods produces the finest energy. It is this energy (hydrogen si 12) that can be used for procreation, for inner transformation, or for both.

Frank Pinder, a man who C.S. Nott tells us was very close to Gurdjieff, expressed it this way: "We are among [Great Nature's] experiments. But the Everlasting has left us a remnant of which she [Great Nature] could not deprive us. ... This has to do with Gurdjieff's "particle" in *Beelzebub's Tales to His Grandson*; but this particle or remnant, is powerless to evolve by specific gravity when the proper being-effort is not directed towards it. Here, Dame Nature ... has been compelled by higher powers to keep and make available to us certain organs otherwise than exclusively for her own use."[62]

---

[61] Ginsburg, *The Masters Speak.* 151-2.
[62] Nott, C.S. *Teachings of Gurdjieff*. New York: Penguin-Arkana, 1961. 226-7.

These organs, referred to by Pinder, as quoted by Nott, are the organs producing sexual energy refined from the processing of foods in our organism, but employed for inner transformation and otherwise than exclusively for procreation, when that energy is turned inward. Gurdjieff further explains this, and the loss of this knowledge in *Beelzebub's Tales to His Grandson*. (see pp. 781-4)[63]

On the employment of sexual energy for transmutation and other than for procreation, Sri Madhava Ashish wrote: "We all know something of the connection between sexual restraint and the 'production of substances necessary for the Work' or 'building the Kesdjan (astral) body'. We all know that in order to attain to the vision of the unity (Nirvana, or anything else one likes to call it) the 'outflows' have to be withdrawn, and that since all outflowing interests are derivatives of eros, withdrawal of the major erotic interest, sexual interest, is a major step in the process. Most of us are now aware that to interpret these requirements in terms of celibacy is mere literalness, and that a balance has to be found such that the fires of the external passions can themselves be harnessed to serve our self-transcending aim; a difficult, dangerous doctrine, in which it is only to easy to deceive ourselves … The compulsions must be extinguished, not the fires themselves. Mahatmas cannot be classified according to their sexuality. There have been men, like Ramana Maharshi, who, so far as we know, never had any sort of sexual life. But Nisargadatta was married and had children. Gurdjieff was married and had children."[64] (letter Jul. 6, 1979)

Gurdjieff developed the theme of the use of sexual energy for transmutation in the oral teaching given to Ouspensky: "For certain types a long and complete sexual abstinence is necessary for transmutation to begin; this means in other words that without a long and complete sexual abstinence transmutation will not begin. But once it has begun abstinence is no longer necessary. In other cases, that is, with other types, transmutation can begin in a normal sexual life - and on the contrary, can begin sooner and proceed better with a very great outward expenditure of sexual energy. In the third case the beginning of transmutation does not require abstinence, but having begun. Transmutation takes the whole of sexual energy and puts an end to normal sexual life or the outward expenditure of sexual energy."[65]

Like Ashish, Gurdjieff goes on to give warning, saying: "Speaking in general, there are only two correct ways of expending sexual energy - normal sexual life and transmutation. All inventions in this sphere are very dangerous."[66]

What makes it possible for us to acquire imperishable being while fulfilling the certain very great purpose in our life, are these tools including the use of sexual energy or libido for transmutation, and this is a capacity reserved for three-brained beings, the *homo sapiens*, and not for one and two-brained beings. Libido may or may not be associated with the discharge of bodily fluids in

---

[63] Gurdjieff. See, for example, 781-4.
[64] Ginsburg. 276-7.
[65] Ouspensky. 256.
[66] Ouspensky. 257.

either male or female, but rather with the importance of the turning inward of this very high and fine energy associated with intentional effort or earnestness including conscious labor and intentional suffering. The turning inward of this energy opens up channels in the psyche that allows access to what has been here called the watery mid-region of the astral or kesdjan domain. "[This energy] has to be seen as the divine Eros itself, even if its concentration does occur through the body. ... With this caution, there is nothing against invoking the power to heighten the sense of aspiration in meditation."[67] (letter Dec. 12, 1988)

<u>In sum, the use of these tools, as explained to us by Gurdjieff and other Masters makes it possible for us to acquire imperishable being while fulfilling the very great purpose in our life.</u>

(4) What is the lot of those who fulfil the very great purpose in their life consciously and who acquire imperishable being? As Ashish explains it:

"Behind the whole cosmos, behind the whole structure of manifest worlds and unmanifest principles, behind, supporting and surrounding, is the One Darkness, the origin, cause, purpose and destination of all existence. The Breath is its Breath, the Breath that in Greek was spoken of as *Pneuma,* in Latin as *Spiritus,* in Hebrew as *Ruach,* in Arabic as *Ruha,* in Sanskrit as *Atman.*[68] "The Divine Unity [is that] from which all proceeds and whither all returns."[69] (SD I, 1)

"Few men of our planet have at any time achieved the actual experience of this essential unity. Yet that he is able to achieve such experience is the key to man's significance in relation to the whole range of manifest and transcendent being, for of all the forms evolved by the divine outpouring, in man alone the bright mirror of Mind relates the field of content to the focus of consciousness in the act of understanding. From this act both the Self of Man and the universal Self accumulate their store of experience. Then, when the long process of evolution comes to fruition, the Man-Plant flowers, the cycle of the evolution is complete, man is God and God is man, not only in principle but in full knowledge of the fact."[70]

"Our task is therefore to refind that inner unity in which subject and object, man and woman, are once more fused in the blissful mingling of complementary natures. And to do this we have to sift every sensation, emotion, and thought, always reserving the more subtle or inner component of its content, until we come to know that sensations are the caresses of the cosmic Woman in whose embrace we live. Each one of us, indeed, is man and woman in one. Driven out from the paradisal androgyneity of the supreme bliss by the fiery wrath of the creative outrush, we have once again to bring our two halves together."[71]

---

[67] Ginsburg. 227-8,
[68] Ashish. *Man, Son of Man.* 38-9.
[69] Blavatsky. S.D. I. 1.
[70] Ashish. *Man, Son of Man.* 37.
[71] Ashish. *Man, Son of Man.* 213.

All & Everything Conference 2010

We are told in *Man, Son of Man*, that 'Imperishable Being' can be acquired simultaneously with serving the certain great common purpose of Endlessness to know itself which we all must serve: "He who blends his individual being with the Great Being enters into the bliss of the divine Source and as an individual ceases to exist. …

[In sum] The only certain survival of individuality occurs in the cases of those of us who reach the perfection of human evolution and are dedicated both to the preservation of the essential Wisdom and to the service of the Essential Being of the Cosmos."[72]

Conclusion

At the outset it was suggested that we look at our situation from the standpoint of Endlessness, who in fact we are, but playing the role of Mr. or Ms. so-and-so. Here is Sri Krishna Prem, Madhava Ashish's teacher, in full knowledge that he is Endlessness, speaking as Endlessness to advise the personality:

"Memory remains in me alone, the memory of lives too numerous to count. That memory is yours, if, during life, you learn to enter me. If not, I keep it for you till we meet again once more. Your brain is new, and in it will be stored those memories alone in which it has a part, so that you start 'once more on your adventure brave and new', unburdened by a load of memories too great for you to bear. Yet the stored wisdom of your past is always with you, for it remains in me who am in you. If you will listen for my voice within your heart, that voice will guide you so that in the maze of life your course will be shaped by a wisdom springing from you know not where, a wisdom that is not your own, but mine, and yet which is your Self, for you are me. … In all things seek for me who am your friend, your life, your very Self. He who finds me sees light within the darkness, life in the midst of death, joy in the heart of sorrow, rest on the wheel of change, love in the midst of hate. … As for the Path by which I may be found, I speak: it is for you to seize my meaning."[73]

Bibliography

Ashish, Sri Madhava. *An Open Window: Dream as Everyman's Guide to the Spirit*. New Delhi: Penguin, 2007.

Ashish, Sri Madhava. *Man, Son of Man*. Wheaton, IL. Theosophical Publishing House, 1969.

Blavatsky, H.P. *The Secret Doctrine*. 1888. Los Angeles: The Theosophy Company, 1974.

---

[72] Ashish. *Man, Son of Man*. 336-7.
[73] Prem, Sri Krishna. *Initiation into Yoga*. Wheaton, IL Quest-Theosophical Publishing House, 1976. 88.

There Is in our Life a Certain Very Great Purpose

Edinger, Edward F. *The Mysterium Lectures: A Journey through C. G. Jung's Mysterium Coniunctionis*. Toronto: Inner City Books, 1995.

Ginsburg, Seymour B. *In Search of the Unitive Vision*. Boca Raton, FL: New Paradigm Books, 2001.

Gurdjieff, G.I. *Beelzebub's Tales to His Grandson*. 1950. New York: Penguin-Compass, 1999.

Gurdjieff, G.I. *The Third Series: Life Is Real Only Then, When "I Am."* New York: Triangle Editions, 1975.

Gurdjieff, G.I. *Views from the Real World*. 1973. New York: Penguin, 1984.

Jung, C.G. *Mysterium Coniunctionis*. Princeton: Bollingen. 1965.

Nott, C.S. *Teachings of Gurdjieff*. New York: Penguin-Arkana, 1961.

Nicoll, Maurice. *Psychological Commentaries on the Teaching of Gurdjieff and Ouspensky*. London: Robinson & Watkins. 1952.

Ouspensky, P.D. *In Search of the Miraculous*. London: Routledge & Kegan Paul, 1950.

Prem, Sri Krishna. *Initiation into Yoga*. Wheaton, IL Quest-Theosophical Publishing House, 1976.

Prem, Sri Krishna & Ashish, Sri Madhava. *Man, the Measure of All Things*. Wheaton, IL. Theosophical Publishing House, 1969, 1966.

The Mahatma Letters to A.P. Sinnett. Transcribed, Compiled and with an Introduction by A. T. Barker. Adyar, India: Theosophical Publishing House, 1962.

The 3rd International Humanities Conference: All & Everything 98. Ginsburg, Seymour B. "Gurdjieff, Blavatsky and the Masters of Wisdom" Loughton, UK: Planning Committee, All & Everything Conferences, 1998.

© Copyright 2010 - Seymour B. Ginsburg - All Rights Reserved

There Is in our Life a Certain Very Great Purpose - Questions & Answers

Sy Ginsburg: I want to thank Nick Bryce for reading my paper so beautifully. He read it much better than I could have done had I been with you in person. But I am glad to be with you through the technological marvel of the Internet and Skype, and if anyone has any questions, I will be glad to try to answer them.

Participant 1: My teacher has said that siddhis or powers can be developed after a relatively short amount of practice. These powers can be very dangerous because power tends to corrupt. To have powers which you didn't have before can be a dangerous thing because your being has not been developed sufficiently to exercise them with due restraint. I just wonder if you could comment a little bit on that telepathy.

Sy Ginsburg: It is certainly true, and I would agree with your teacher that *siddhis* or powers, to the extent that they are real. And we always have to ask that question because there is so much bunk amongst people claiming such *siddhis*, although there are occasions where some of these powers are actually available. An example of this problem occurred on my first visit to India in 1978. Actually, I did not go there to see Madhava Ashish. I had a letter from him, replying to my letter of two months earlier, and it arrived in the mail just an hour before I was being picked up by a limo to go to the Miami, Florida airport, on my first trip to India. I had at that time decided to go to India with a small group of theosophists from South Florida who were going to see Sathya Sai Baba, the most well known guru in India. He is so well known because of the *siddhis* or powers presumably at his disposal.

Now Sai Baba, to the extent that these powers are real, and I am making that qualification, has used them to attract people. He has said on more than one occasion, "I do these things to give them what they want, a demonstration of these powers, so that they will want what I want to give them which has nothing to do with these sorts of powers but which tantalize the public." Blavatsky herself said, "Any fool can do these things. What do I care if people are curious about them to the glory of my Masters." So, yes they can be dangerous, and although a lot of them are not real, if they can be used to attract people to the inner search, they have value.

In connection with the paper, the main *siddhi* spoken about and which can be verified by all of us, is telepathy. This power is exactly what Ouspensky recognized in Gurdjieff and which is recounted in *In Search of the Miraculous* .

Participant 2: Can you tell me if the Theosophical Society in London is a place that someone can attend?

There Is in our Life a Certain Very Great Purpose - Questions & Answers

Sy Ginsburg: Yes, it's just off Portman Square in London. I've been there. It was some years ago. Of historic interest is the fact that when Ouspensky came to London in 1921, he gave a series of talks. Some of these were before large gatherings at the Albert Hall, but many of them were at the Theosophical Society in their building on Portman Square. But in terms of spiritual organizations, for the most part theosophists would have nothing to do with Gurdjieff because he slams them, as you likely know, in *Beelzebub's Tales*. Conversely, Gurdjieffians, at least the group that I was involved with, did not want their members going outside the Gurdjieffian tradition. But I would encourage anyone to look into theosophy. Like all these things, there is a lot of unimportant stuff, But if one digs a little bit, as I have done, I think you will find important things there such as these books by Ashish and his mentor Sri Krishna Prem, *Man, the Measure of All Things*, and particularly, *Man, Son of Man*. I have a copy of it here. I don't know if you can see it on the screen. It looks like this (holds it up). It is a book published by the Theosophical Publishing House, and many of the quotations in this paper came out of Ashish's wisdom as recorded in this book. This book is the more personally applicable of the two because it comments on anthropogenesis, or man himself, as opposed to cosmogenesis, the larger cosmos, that is commented upon in the other book.

As Ashish said, as recounted in the paper, the wisdom that allowed him and Prem to write these two books came in silent meditation and in dream, not in any sort of textual way, and they came almost entirely in symbols and visions. He said that they had to struggle to derive the wisdom that enabled them to write these books. Similarly, that quotation from a letter Madame Blavatsky wrote in 1889 published the year after she wrote *The Secret Doctrine* said almost the same thing. Theosophists, in general, are open to psychic phenomena so there is no restriction on investigations into that. Part of the thesis here, is that there is this large "watery mid-region" between the unmanifest transcendent and the materialized universe. Ashish says that we, man, more importantly belongs to this mid-region. You might say, it is our inner life or inner man, rather than our *homo sapiens* body-brain. So, I would encourage anyone to go to the Theosophical Society, and anyone can go there.

I can also add one little bit of personal information. Back in 1978 when I first got interested in these ideas, I was travelling a lot for business, and I visited the Theosophical Society when I happened to be in London. I was still trying to find some books that would help me understand Blavatsky, and at the Theosophical Society I was referred to a book written by Harry Benjamin, an introductory book on theosophy. It turned out that he had passed away but his wife, Elsie Benjamin, lived down in Hove (near Brighton). She was still living and would teach students. I became one. It turned out that Harry Benjamin, who wrote that introductory book, *Everyone's Guide to Theosophy*, and Elsie Benjamin, had been in a Gurdjieff group. It was a Nicoll based group led by Beryl Pogson. I was able to find this out by visiting her, and Harry had also written a little introductory Gurdjieff book called *Basic Self Knowledge: based on the Gurdjieff System of Development with Reference to the writings of Krishnamurti*. So these things, in my view, are very much connected, and there is no harm at all, and actually it would be very useful, if people with a theosophical interest and people with a Gurdjieffian interest are able to bring these two strands, of what Ashish calls the same tradition, together.

All & Everything Conference 2010

Participant 3: You touched upon this area of celibacy in sexuality. It reminded me about this diagram in *The Oragean Version*. There is this dotted line from the intellectual center to the sexual center which is outside the diagram and leads from the intellectual center to higher centers. I think it is a very important issue you are raising. The energy that we have naturally and we work for, has to be carefully taken care of. And these sexual forces are very powerful things, and again it reminds me of the necessity to have something in me, where I can watch what is going on in the apparatus. Can you say something more about any methods besides that?

Sy Ginsburg: In *In Search of the Miraculous*, I believe there are three or four pages where Ouspensky quotes Gurdjieff as explaining what Gurdjieff said about the sexual energy. It's very ambiguous. As I recall, for some people abstinence is necessary, for others it is not necessary. It varies all over the place. This is a sensitive subject, but whatever I put in the paper has been published. So, there is nothing that cannot be disclosed. The important thing to understand is that the fires of the external passions, in Ashish's terms, have to be harnessed to open up these inner channels to serve our self-transcending aim. But taking it literally in terms of celibacy is incorrect, and it has been quite accurately pointed out that many of these Masters have been active sexually. Certainly Gurdjieff was one of them. But Gurdjieff also said, as pointed out in the Ouspensky book, that this is a very dangerous area so one needs to be cautious. Nevertheless, it is one of the tools, an important tool, in that list of tools enumerated by Ashish. So, being students of Gurdjieff's teaching, we need to be aware of it and it needs to be looked into.

Participant 4: My question has to do with what you said about the Masters. I would like you to elaborate on two points. I would like to hear more about what is your definition of being a Master and what it is about Gurdjieff that makes him a Master, and the second thing is about the inner circle of Masters that sort of communicate between them. What do you know about that, what can you tell us about that?

Sy Ginsburg: Years ago I did a lot of speculative investigating. For example, Bennett tells us that there is a very famous saying of Gurdjieff that "we have to bury the dog deeper." You probably remember that from when Gurdjieff was rewriting chapters of the *Tales* to make it more difficult to read. Bennett speculated that the "dog" referred to the dog star Sirius, which is a binary star system. It's well known that Sirius is the brightest object in the sky with the exception of the sun, the moon and the planets. There is this theosophical speculation that somehow these Masters, these cosmic supermen have their lodge, their great lodge, somewhere within the star system Sirius. I believe that this is all fantasy.

As I quoted Ashish in the paper, it may very well be that some of these Masters are the result of experiences in prior universes. That is another question because how can we understand a prior universe if time is a function of space-time in this universe, the only universe we know. It is something to consider. However, as Ashish is quoted in the paper, he also pointed out that too much attention paid to this sort of speculation about cosmic supermen can lead us to the false view that they are so special as to have no relevance to the lives of ordinary mortals like us. There have been so many masters that have arisen from ordinary mortals of this planet, and from so many different races and cultures on this planet, that they provide us with examples of what we should and can become here and now. So, there is no reason for us to go into these wild speculations. Gurdjieff says explicitly, and you'll find it in the chapter "From the Author" in *Beelzebub Tales*, that each one of us must set for his chief aim to become a Master. It's our job to become a Master. What does that mean? It means that through the practical teachings we have been given, we need to make intentional effort to move our focus from the personality who we mistakenly believe we are, to essence or Endlessness, who we really are. Gurdjieff also says, essence is the truth, personality is the false. So, that is our work.

As I mentioned, Ashish sent me to meet Sri Nisargadatta on my second trip to India when I had decided to return to see him the following year, 1979. Unlike Ashish and his teacher, Sri Krishna Prem both of whom lived ascetic lives in the Himalayas, Nisargadatta was an ordinary middle class Indian shopkeeper living in Mumbai (Bombay) with a wife and children.

There is something about these people, these Masters, that is different. But it is easy to get hoodwinked because there are some very clever people with very strong personalities who will convince you to follow them. So, one does have to be careful. But there is a certain quality of being in these people that will resonate in each of us to the extent that our level of being can somehow experience that. Ashish himself never claimed to be a Master, and his teacher, Sri Krishna Prem would only consider himself to be a student-teacher.

As I looked at this question more closely, in *In Search of the Miraculous*, Gurdjieff describes three concentric circles of Masters. The one referred to in the paper is called the "esoteric conscious inner circle of humanity", and I suppose one would say that it is the highest level of Mastership, but he also says there is surrounding that, a "mesoteric or middle conscious inner circle of humanity" and surrounding that is an "exoteric conscious inner circle of humanity". But surrounding all of those is what he called the circle of mechanical humanity to which almost all three-brained beings on this planet belong. So our job, as I understand it, through whatever means suits our makeup, is to make intentional effort to sort of break into these inner circles. And that is to realize, for example, that I am not really Sy, I am only playing Sy. Each of us are only playing these roles but we get so immersed in them that we are convinced that we are the role. Mastership is something that, according to Gurdjieff should be our aim. A Master is one with the Spirit. That's what makes a Master. He/she has become free from the personality which is not objectively real.

So we work on it as best we can using all of these methods. The main one that Gurdjieff brought is constant self-remembering or self-witnessing because the more frequently and more deeply we do that, the further inwardly we stand and the further away we move from identification with the body-brain organism. And we use a number of these other things that through the ages people have found useful such as meditation, and examining dreams. Personally, I am convinced that most dream symbolism shows us identifications with personality aspects and these keep us honest as to identifications we assume we have gotten free of. But as we clear these away these identifications we begin to be shown reality more deeply.

Also, as we pay attention to synchronicities, we start to discover that synchronicities happen to all of us. These things are not accidental. But any synchronicity that I experience, and there have been many of them, are only second hand information to anyone else. But all of us will experience these synchronicities as we pay attention to them. Synchronicity is the word that Jung coined for these meaningful or connected coincidences. Because we are all connected at the deepest level, we are all Endlessness or essence.

The Two Chief Motors of our Existence: Food and Sex

Clare Mingins

Abstract

According to Gurdjieff, sex energy is the final result of the transformation of our ordinary food and drink. It is also the source of all higher energy and of Will, and is necessary to create a soul.

The ordinary person carries out incomplete absorption and transformation of active elements from the three being-foods. The small amount of energy produced is either automatically used up, wasted, or tainted. Ordinary human physiology is the physiology of abnormality. Orage pointed out that work on oneself produces fifty percent more mental energy and three times more emotional and sex energy than before.[1]

Here I look at various questions concerning the transformation of the three being-foods with reference to material in *Beelzebub's Tales* and Gurdjieff's oral teaching, and that of Bennett, Ouspensky and Orage. Information from the various sources often appears discrepant, perhaps intentionally so. Subjects considered include a composite food diagram, "food for real man," vegetarianism, "the most important part of the second-being food," evolution and involution of sex energy, half-beings, and others.

This paper is part of a broader piece of work looking at "Gurdjieff's Medicine."

The Two Chief Motors of our Existence - Food and Sex

Introduction

Gurdjieff's view of human beings, and indeed of all life, as apparatuses for transforming energy for higher purposes, and the interrelationship and interdependence of all things, necessitates great attention being given to the assimilation and transformation of the three being-foods, that is, food and drink, air and impressions. Yet the human being is a very peculiar apparatus, as Bennett said, "because he has the possibility to choose *how he will be used*."[2]

---

[1] *Oragean Version* p.157
[2] *Deeper Man* p.68

The digestive function and the sexual function, Gurdjieff said, are the two chief motors of our existence.[3] Food and sex do indeed form the chief engines and motivators of our automatic existence, but what significance do they have for our higher aspirations?

According to Gurdjieff, being-Exioëhary, or sex energy, is the inevitable final result of the transformation of our ordinary food and drink.[4] It is the final result of food transformation in ordinary life, but not, as Gurdjieff called it, a "completing result," as it only forms the last Stopinder[5] of this ascending food octave.[6] A completing process is one that passes through the last Stopinder of one octave into the Do of the higher octave, that is, the new cycle.[7] And, as we know,

> "....this same holy planet, which is called Purgatory, is for the whole of our Great Universe, as it were, the heart and place of concentration of all the completing results of the pulsation of everything that functions and exists in the Universe."[8]

Elizabeth Bennett also records that Gurdjieff told them that "When one came here [to his flat] to a meal, it was necessary to complete it, otherwise it all became artificial, and does you no good."[9]

In *Purgatory*, Gurdjieff said two apparently very different things: namely, that the first being-food can give almost nothing for the higher parts of our presence, but also that if the first being-food is taken with a certain kind of attitude, then in addition to serving the general Trogoautoegocratic process, substances derived from it may also be used for coating and perfecting the higher parts.[10] This emphasises the dependence that the normal digestion of the first being-food has on the digestion of the higher foods. It seems a certain attitude is vital for being able to absorb the maximum active elements from food.

First of all, I will look at the octaves of transformation of the three foods, as presented in various sources, and I will produce a kind of composite food diagram, to which I will also refer later. Then I will look at the subjects of active elements, "food for real man" and "the right food for man", "the most important part of the second being-food", fasting and vegetarianism, evolution of sex

---

[3] *Beelzebub's* Tales, 1950 p.944-945
[4] ibid. p.793
[5] Although the notes of the octave are generally thought of as the seven "deflections" or "centres of gravity" within it, and the term "Stopinder," is usually regarded as referring to everything between one note of the octave to the subsequent note (e.g. the first Stopinder being all substances between Do and Re), the two ideas are often combined by many, including Orage (e.g. *Oragean Version* p.156, though the term Stopinder is not used). This ambiguity also occurs in *Beelzebub's Tales* (1950 e.g. p.139 & p.750-751). I too follow this bad use of language!
[6] *Beelzebub's* Tales, 1950 p.791-792
[7] ibid.p.754
[8] ibid. p.745
[9] *Idiots* p.91
[10] *Beelzebub's Tales*, 1950 p.782 & p.784

The Two Chief Motors of our Existence: Food and Sex

energy and will, involution of sex energy and "food for the egoism", and finally, that strange idea of half-beings.

In that I am gradually trying to assimilate all this material, particularly from *Purgatory*, into the stuff of experience, there are still many places that only the intellect so far reaches. These places are the most subject to error, and I suspect that there are quite a few naïve intellectualisations contained in this paper that bark up the wrong tree. These subjects of course cannot be examined by the intellect alone. It is necessary to experience these different energies and processes in oneself, ponder upon them, and to transmute this understanding.

I am aware that my understanding and interpretation of some of these things is different to some very well-regarded people, past and present. This may simply be due to my naïveté and inexperience, or maybe not. There is even one area that I have to differ from Bennett, whom I very much respect. However, I am very willing to stand corrected.

I have a number of ongoing questions, and some of these are the following:

- What actually is an active element?
- What is this strange term that Gurdjieff sometimes uses in relation to food: "invertebrates"?
- What does "influenza" represent for Gurdjieff in regard to the second being-food?
- Why is the emotional state during a fast important?
- What is this lack of will in those who are vegetarian, if they mix with those who eat meat?
- What is the relation between will and Exioëhary?

The Octaves of Transformation of the Three Foods

As is well-known, Gurdjieff sometimes described the human being as a factory designed for the production of certain substances from the three being-foods.[11] However, in ordinary life it only ever produces enough to maintain its existence; it never has an output. A factory without an output is intolerable, and is really only fit to be scrapped. Gurdjieff, of course, taught how the factory could be made profitable, so it could fulfil the sense and aim of existence. Orage said that Doing is the final intended output of the factory.[12]

As a prelude to the subjects discussed later in this paper, I shall look at the process of transformation of active elements from the three being-foods, which will be more or less familiar to most of you, and on the way I shall mention various points that I have found interesting.

---

[11] e.g. *In Search of the Miraculous* p.179-81
[12] *Oragean Version* p.163

All & Everything Conference 2010

The following diagram is a composite one, using material from Orage, Ouspensky and the chapter *Purgatory* from *Beelzebub's Tales*. It shows the three storeys of the human factory - upper, middle and lower, representing the head, chest and lower part of the body. Each type of food of course has its own octave of transformation, but each is built on exactly the same principles.

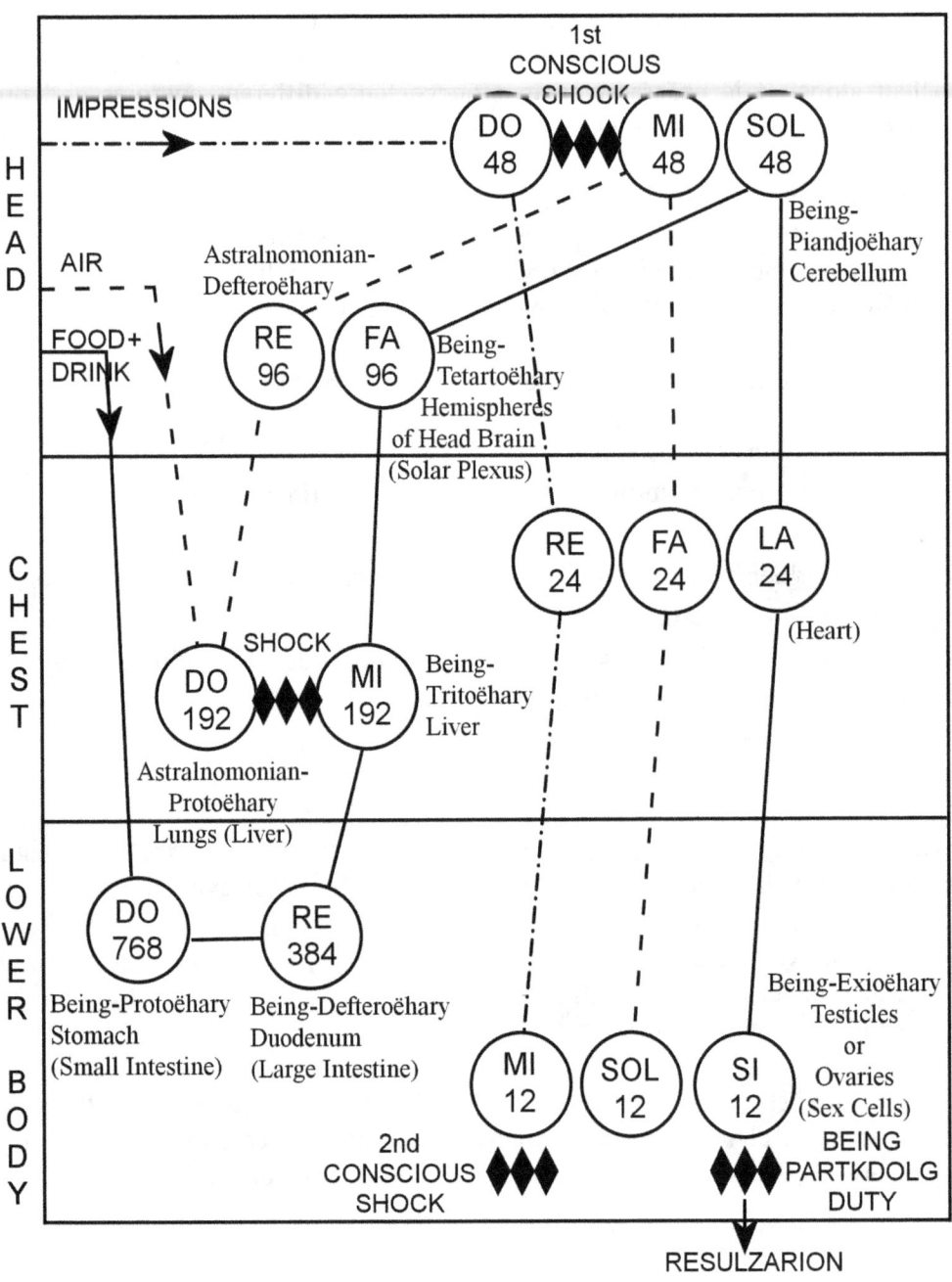

Fig.1 A Composite Food Diagram

The Two Chief Motors of our Existence: Food and Sex

There are a number of differences between the sources. At the very least, these seeming discrepancies between and within sources force one to struggle and to feel one's way around these ideas, enabling a more rounded approach. We should remember that the ideas are always presented in an incomplete and often not quite precise way for this very reason.

The words substance and energy are often used fairly interchangeably by some authors in this area, for example, Orage[13] and Bennett.[14] The latter often uses the word energy where Gurdjieff uses the word substances for the stages of food transformation.[15] In his earlier teaching, Gurdjieff would frequently use the word Hydrogen instead, with a particular vibration rate affixed. He also said, "Every function, every state, every thought, every emotion, requires a certain definite energy, a certain definite substance."[16] Bennett spoke of "....the material within which the energy is concentrated."[17] I shall also use the words energy and substance interchangeably, to the possible discomfort of those trained in physics.

The first food octave of transformation is also called in *Purgatory* the being-Heptaparaparshinokh.[18] Our ordinary food and drink enter at the mouth, which then undergoes various transformations through local processes of Harnelmiatznel. Eventually in the stomach it becomes what Gurdjieff calls being-Protoëhary.[19] Being-Protoëhary is a collection of substances, or "active elements," with the same density of vibrations, that forms Do of the first food octave. In Ouspensky, ordinary food is called Hydrogen 768, but Do 768 is also the first stage of the process of transformation in the organism.[20] In *Purgatory*, the term being-Protoëhary seems to be reserved for that transformation of food that is attained in the stomach.[21] Orage says that if the food enters as a liquid it skips the first stage,[22] that is, it is already at Re.

Being-Protoëhary then undergoes transmutation through local processes of Harnelmiatznel and eventually becomes being-Defteroëhary in the duodenum.[23] This is called being-Deuteroëhary in the Revised Edition of *Beelzebub's Tales*[24]; it is Re or hydrogen 384 in Ouspensky.[25]

---

[13] *The Gospel According to Orage* e.g. p.26 and p.74
[14] e.g. *Talks on Beelzebub's Tales* p.99
[15] e.g. *Sex and Spiritual development* p.46 cf *Beelzebub's Tales*, 1950 p.790 and p.791
[16] *In Search of the Miraculous* p.179
[17] *Deeper Man* p.33
[18] *Beelzebub's Tales*, 1950 e.g. p.787 & p.789
[19] ibid. p.786-787
[20] *In Search of the Miraculous* p.182
[21] *Beelzebub's Tales*, 1950 p.787
[22] *Gospel According to Orage* p.26
[23] *Beelzebub's Tales*, 1950 p.787
[24] *Beelzebub's Tales*, Revised Edition 2006 p.722
[25] *In Search of the Miraculous* p.183

Harnelmiatznel is of course the process by which every new thing is made: something higher joins with something lower, and together they produce something new which is in the middle.[26]

In the 1950 version of *Beelzebub's Tales* it says that between the stomach and the duodenum the being-Protoëhary passes over the whole of the intestinal tract undergoing this transformation to being-Defteroëhary.[27] This may put a slight strain on one's view of human biology! However, in the Revised Edition, the passing over of the whole of the intestinal tract is given to the stage between Re and Mi, the latter being Hydrogen 192 or being-Tritoëhary, which has its place of concentration in the liver.[28] That is, between the duodenum and the liver, being-Deuteroëhary passes over the whole of the intestinal tract and eventually becomes being-Tritoëhary in the liver. This, of course, is much easier to accord with conventional physiology, not that that should ever be a criterion in reading Gurdjieff's writings! It may be that apparent mistakes should be assumed intentional until proven otherwise by one's own authentic experience.

One of several differences between *Purgatory* and *The Oragean Version*, is that Orage has "small intestine" in place of the "stomach" in *Purgatory*, and "large intestine" in place of the "duodenum."[29] The passing of being-Protoëhary over the whole of the intestinal tract between "stomach" and "duodenum" in *Purgatory* of the 1950 version mentioned above would now make more anatomical sense if by the "duodenum" was actually meant the large intestine.

Now, having come to Mi, the food octave cannot proceed further without help coming from outside. This requirement for extraneous help at the Mi-Fa, and also Si-Do, intervals of every octave in order for transformation to continue is of course the whole point of the great Trogoautoegocratic principle of existence. Every completing process is dependent upon force entering from outside itself. Everything eats and is eaten.

The outside help for the Mi-Fa interval of the first food octave comes from the air octave. Air enters through the nose and undergoes transformation in the lungs into another type of Protoëhary, this time Astralnomonian-Protoëhary;[30] this is Do of the air octave, another Hydrogen 192, but Do 192. This Do 192 provides a shock at the barrier of the Mi-Fa interval of the first food octave, giving impetus to Being-Tritoëhary, Mi 192 of the food octave, to be able to continue its transformation to Fa 96.[31]

In *The Oragean Version*, the Do of the air octave is located in the liver rather than in the lungs as in *Purgatory*.[32] Indeed, Orage wrote in a letter to Jessie Dwight, "....just as the transformation of

---

[26] *Beelzebub's Tales*, 1950 p.751
[27] ibid.p.787
[28] *Beelzebub's Tales*, Revised Edition 2006 p.721
[29] *Oragean Version* p.157
[30] *Beelzebub's Tales*, 1950 p.788
[31] *In Search of the Miraculous* p.184
[32] *Oragean Version* p.157

food begins only in the stomach, so the transformation of air begins only in the liver. The liver is the air's stomach."[33] In *Purgatory*, the air Do, or astralnomonian-Protoëhary, indeed mixes with being-Tritoëhary which is present in the liver, at the mechano-coinciding Mdnel-In, and then itself goes on to be transformed into Re, or astralnomonian-Defteroëhary.[34] Similarly to the first being-food, in *Purgatory*, Astralnomonian-Protoëhary refers to the first transformation in the lungs,[35] whereas in *In Search of the Miraculous* Do 192 seems to be air itself.[36]

So Protoëhary, Defteroëhary and Tritoëhary form the first three Stopinders of food transformation. In the first food octave, Orage referred to them as solid, liquid and gas in his table on the levels of materiality in the octaves of digestion.[37] These substances have not yet reached the blood beyond the liver: this occurs at the next stage. Bennett says, "The food is not spiritual nourishment until it has reached our blood and then only when it begins to be blended with the air that we breathe."[38]

Mi 192 of the food octave, or being-Tritoëhary, undergoes transformation to being-Tetartoëhary,[39] or Fa 96, the first of the psychic energies. Being-Tetartoëhary is concentrated in the two hemispheres of the head brain in *Purgatory*, and this is why I have placed this stage in the upper storey of the composite diagram. However, in *The Oragean Version*, Fa of the first food octave is placed in the solar plexus in the middle storey.[40] And in *In Search of the Miraculous*, Fa 96 is also in the middle storey, though no description is given there as to where it is concentrated.[41]

Ouspensky records Gurdjieff as saying that Hydrogen 96 of the first food octave, which is being-Tetartoëhary, "is the matter of animal magnetism, of emanations from the human body....hormones, vitamins and so on...."[42] Gurdjieff also says, in *Beelzebub's Tales*, that being-Hanbledzoin, the blood of the Kesdjan body, is also called animal magnetism, and that Hanbledzoin arises "from all intentionally made being-efforts."[43] However, Gurdjieff also says that magnetism "consists not only of one substance but of several."[44] Perhaps it is more useful to regard only the intentionally arisen part of Tetartoëhary as the matter of magnetism.

---

[33] *Gurdjieff and Orage* p.127
[34] *Beelzebub's Tales*, 1950 p.789
[35] ibid.p.788-789 cf *In Search of the Miraculous* p.186
[36] *In Search of the Miraculous* p.184
[37] *Oragean Version* p.169
[38] *Intimations* p.20
[39] *Beelzebub's Tales*, 1950 p.789
[40] *Oragean Version* p.157
[41] *In Search of the Miraculous* p.184
[42] ibid.p.175
[43] *Beelzebub's Tales*, 1950 p.568 & p.1200
[44] *Views from the Real World* p.99

Bennett points out that Gurdjieff uses the term Hanbledzoin in many different ways.[45] Bennett calls Hanbledzoin "the truly human substance"[46] and the "action of the human essence."[47] However, he describes Tetartoëhary as an energy of "inventiveness and ingenuity."[48] and of "associations and emotions."[49] Given these latter descriptions, perhaps Tetartoëhary is concentrated in both the solar plexus and the hemispheres of the head brain, and so it maybe could straddle the upper two storeys in the food diagram.

Being-Tetartoëhary, or Fa 96, in the first food octave, undergoes transformation through the local processes of Harnelmiatznel until it becomes being-Piandjoëhary, or Sol 48, in the Sianoorinam or cerebellum,[50] which Orage also calls the higher intellectual centre and the seat of individuality.[51] In the Revised Edition of *Beelzebub's Tales* this is called being-Pentoëhary,[52] which also emphasises its character of being at the fifth step of the process, or Sol. In *The Oragean Version*, C. Daly King says, mistakenly, that in *Beelzebub's Tales* Gurdjieff locates the food Sol - air Mi in the cerebrum rather than the cerebellum as Orage describes.[53] However, in *Purgatory* the food Sol, that is, being-Piandjoëhary, is clearly described as having its central place of concentration in the cerebellum,[54] as in Orage's teaching. Bennett describes this as the energy of imagination and visualisation.[55]

Re 96, in the air octave, is transmuted to Mi 48, where ordinarily it comes to a stop.[56] Do 48, the beginning of the impressions octave, is usually not transformed at all.[57] Orage colourfully described our usual process of taking in impressions as like taking food into the mouth and just letting it sit there while drooling, expecting it to be digested in this way.[58]

In *Purgatory*, between being-Piandjoëhary, Sol 48, and being-Exioëhary, sex energy, Si 12, Gurdjieff does not name or describe a specific stage for La 24, other than to say that being-Piandjoëhary passes "in a particular way through the nerve nodes of spine and breast....and this particular way....is called 'Trnlva.'"[59] In *The Oragean Version*, La of the food octave is placed in

---

[45] *Talks on Beelzebub's Tales* p.68
[46] *Sunday Talks* p.33
[47] *Talks on Beelzebub's Tales* p. 69
[48] *Intimations* p.51
[49] *Sex and Spiritual Development* p.27
[50] *Beelzebub's Tales,* 1950 p.790-791
[51] *Gospel According to Orage*, p.20 & p.23
[52] *Beelzebub's Tales,* Revised Edition, 2006 p.724
[53] *Oragean Version* p.160
[54] *Beelzebub's Tales* 1950 p.790
[55] *Intimations* p.50 & *Sex and Spiritual Development* p.27
[56] *In Search of the Miraculous* p.186
[57] ibid.p.187
[58] *Gospel According to Orage* p.73
[59] *Beelzebub's Tales* 1950 p.791

what he calls the heart, or the higher emotional centre.[60] And Orage calls this La "emotion" in his table of levels of materiality[61] (Fig.2). However, this is not emotion as we ordinarily experience it.

Ordinary Food			**Air**		**Impressions**	
					Si	
					La	
			Si	"nectar"	Sol	"nectar"
			La	"ambrosia"	Fa	"ambrosia"
Si	Being-Exioëhary	sex	Sol	sex	Mi	sex
La		emotion	Fa	emotion	Re	emotion
Sol	Being-Piandjoëhary	thought	Mi	thought	Do	thought
Fa	Being-Tetartoëhary	magnetism	Re	magnetism		
Mi	Being-Tritoëhary	gas	Do	gas		
Re	Being-Defteroëhary	liquid				
Do	Being-Protoëhary	solid				

Fig. 2 Orage's full table of digestion octaves[62]

It may be worth noting that what are named the higher emotional centre and the higher intellectual centre are the opposite way around in the Orage and Ouspensky versions of Gurdjieff's teaching. With Orage the higher emotional is placed at a higher level after the higher intellectual centre,[63] and vice versa in *In Search of the Miraculous*.[64]

In Orage's "fish" diagram, Fig.3, we can see the normal connections between centres, among other things. In Orage's version of Gurdjieff's teaching, he places what he calls the heart, or higher emotional centre, in the middle storey between the sex cells in the lower storey and the cerebellum in the upper storey. The terms lower, middle and upper here of course have no relation to the degree of development of finer energies. The sex cells in Orage's "fish diagram" are contained in the lower storey, and yet are called the highest centre, centre 6.[65]

Si 12, or the sex energy derived from ordinary food, as the seventh and usually final stage of the digestion of the first food, is clearly seen in the Orage and Ouspensky food diagrams.[66] It corresponds to the last Stopinder of the being-Heptaparaparshinokh in *Purgatory* and is called the "totality of the 'sum of the substances.'"[67] However, Bennett says it is "one gradation higher than

---

[60] *Gospel According to Orage* p.75
[61] *Oragean Version* p.157 & p.87
[62] Adapted from *Oragean Version* p.170
[63] e.g. *The Gospel According to Orage* p.23
[64] *In Search of the Miraculous* p.195
[65] *Gospel According to Orage* p.20
[66] e.g. *Oragean Version* p.157 & *In Search of the Miraculous* p.187
[67] *Beelzebub's Tales*, 1950 p.791-792

the 'piandjoëhary.'"[68] And it is sixth on the list of temporarily independent centre of gravity crystallizations present in Tetartocosmoses in *Purgatory*.[69] Resulzarion, the seventh on this list, implies a result, which, as a completing result, would be the new Do.

FRONT	Cerebrum (Thought)	Centre 3	Centre 4	Cerebellum (Individuality)	BACK
	Solar Plexus (Emotion)	Centre 2	Centre 5	Heart (Consciousness)	
	Sex Cells (Will)	Centre 6	Centre 1	Base / Spinal Column (Physical action)	

Fig.3 Orage's "Fish diagram"[70]

Bennett says that Resulzarion is "where the food has been transformed into a substance of the body *Kesdjan*,"[71] which means that he also must regard it as being in the octave of the new Do after transformation of the substances of the seventh Stopinder of the preceding octave.[72] This seems markedly at odds with his assertion mentioned above that Exioëhary is at the sixth Stopinder. In that Exioëhary comes directly before Resulzarion in the mentioned list in *Purgatory*, Bennett therefore must either consider there to be something missing in this list between Exioëhary and Resulzarion, or he must actually think that Exioëhary *is* at the seventh Stopinder, and that the sixth Stopinder is missing in this list. If the latter is the case, then perhaps Bennett was being deliberately misleading, and complicit with Gurdjieff's avoiding mentioning the equivalent of La 24 in his later teachings.

---

[68] *Sex and Spiritual Development* p.53
[69] *Beelzebub's Tales*, 1950 p.761
[70] Adapted from *The Gospel According to Orage* p.20
[71] *Talks on Beelzebub's Tales* p.57
[72] e.g. *Beelzebub's Tales*, 1950 p.791-792

The Two Chief Motors of our Existence: Food and Sex

So why is there this apparent discrepancy about the sixth Stopinder of the first food octave? Perhaps Gurdjieff thought this necessary because of our corrupt natures. I wonder whether the ambiguity is connected to the degeneration of the emotions and of the sacred impulses of faith, hope and love, and the fact that most of Gurdjieff's practical teaching did not lie in directly working with the emotions (except negative ones[73]), but rather initially with the body and the mind, and why love is sometimes seen as lacking in his teaching.[74] Until the corrupt heart is purified, it may be that there will arise wrong results from trying to work directly with positive emotions.

Bennett, spoke of how "Degeneration of the sexual energy occurs when it becomes food for the egoism,"[75] and "The wastage and degeneration of sex is mainly due to the power of imagination in us....associated with....'piandjoëhary.' "[76] Piandjoëhary is a very powerful thing, but also dangerous if used wrongly, and with which we must be very, very careful in order to avoid undesirable consequences.[77] According to Bennett, it is the energy of creative imagination and visualisation, and that which "enables us to see in a direct way."[78]

He said further that, the Tetartoëhary, is what blends with the sexual energy.[79] In this statement, that is, that Exioëhary blends with Tetartoëhary, the energy of associations and emotions (implying the Harnelmiatznel), rather than with Piandjoëhary, it again seems to be the strange ignoring of La 24. Perhaps Bennett is, rather, referring to the usual but abnormal situation of wrong connections between the sex centre and the lower emotional and intellectual centres,[80] or the sex centre working with energy that is not its own, for example, of mixing sex with sentiment, or with associative thought. He also warned against special efforts to use Piandjoëhary by those who had not attained a certain purity in themselves.[81] He says that of the many processes with which we must work, half are to do with increasing consciousness and half are to do with the purification from ourselves of undesirable elements.[82]

Now, in contrast, in *In Search of the Miraculous* Gurdjieff says, "The note sol 48 by uniting with 'carbon' 12 present in the organism passes into 'nitrogen' 24 - la 24."[83]
Orage says, "[The sexual] function is very closely associated with the emotional centres, its fragmentary connection with Centre #5 [higher emotional centre or heart] arousing genuine

---

[73] e.g. *Our Life with Mr. Gurdjieff* p.175, *In Search of the Miraculous* p.112
[74] e.g. *In Search of the Miraculous* p.165
[75] *Sex and Spiritual Development* p.26
[76] ibid.p.27
[77] *Beelzebub's Tales*, 1950 p.791
[78] *Sex and Spiritual Development* p.27
[79] ibid.p.27
[80] e.g. see *Gospel According to Orage* p.20
[81] *Intimations* p.51
[82] ibid.p.19
[83] *In Search of the Miraculous* p.185

love...."[84] In my view, if being-Exioëhary blends with unadulterated being-Piandjoëhary, in the Harnelmiatznel, it gives rise to La 24, or what Orage calls "genuine love."

So, up till now, the stages of evolutionary transformations of the three foods described have referred to the limit of what is achieved in the ordinary person who does not do any special work. Having arrived at Si 12, being-Exioëhary, we reach the intentionally-actualized Mdnel-In. This requires a special intentional action for these substances to reach the Do of a new octave of higher substances. Namely, they can only be transformed by being-Partkdolg-duty, or conscious labours and intentional suffering. This seems to refer to the same thing as the earlier term "second conscious shock."[85] If this does not occur, and being-Exioëhary is not utilised in normal sexual activity, it must necessarily involve or decompose back to lower substances, and in so doing, according to Gurdjieff, causes many diseases of both the organic body and the psyche.[86] The evolution and involution of being-Exioëhary is considered in a later section in this paper.

It is interesting to consider Orage's full table of digestion octaves (Fig.2) in which the various stages of transformation of the three foods are described as solid, liquid, gas, magnetism, mind, emotion, sex, ambrosia, nectar.[87] The two latter substances are those that occur at the next levels after sex, or Hydrogen 12, in the air and impressions octaves.

Ordinary Food			**Air**		**Impressions**	
					Si	
					La	
			Si	"nectar"	Sol	"nectar"
			La	"ambrosia"	Fa	"ambrosia"
Si	Being-Exioëhary	sex	Sol	sex	Mi	sex
La		emotion	Fa	emotion	Re	emotion
Sol	Being-Piandjoëhary	thought	Mi	thought	Do	thought
Fa	Being-Tetartoëhary	magnetism	Re	magnetism		
Mi	Being-Tritoëhary	gas	Do	gas		
Re	Being-Defteroëhary	liquid				
Do	Being-Protoëhary	solid				

Fig. 2 Orage's full table of digestion octaves

Active elements

---

[84] *Gospel According to Orage* p.24
[85] *In Search of the Miraculous* p.192-193 & *The Gospel According to Orage* p.85
[86] *Beelzebub's Tales*, 1950 p.793 and p.809-10
[87] *Oragean Version* p.170 etc

The Two Chief Motors of our Existence: Food and Sex

Gurdjieff often speaks of active elements and their importance. Indeed, the food octaves are about the transformation of active elements.

In their totality, active elements compose the fundamental cosmic octave, the common-cosmic Ansanbaluiazar.[88] One meaning of this seems very similar to Gurdjieff's earlier term, recorded for instance by Ouspensky, the ray of creation. Here is the whole scale, everything from *merde* to God. Active elements issue from everything and again enter into everything,[89] They are the substances that are exchanged in the Iraniranumange, and in so doing bring about the great Trogoautoegocratic process that is the reason why our Universe is growing and not diminishing, which latter it would surely be expected to do given the effects of Time alone. It seems to me that Gurdjieff sometimes used the term, or variations upon it, "the fundamental common-cosmic Heptaparaparshinokh," as an alternative name for the common cosmic Ansanbaluiazar.[90]

The lowest Do of the fundamental Sacred Heptaparaparshinokh is composed of the active elements called Ashagiprotoëhary.[91] And Ashagiprotoëhary for the planet Earth is concentrated in the centre of the Moon and Anulios. The highest in the scale is Theomertmalogos or Word-God, the emanation of the Most Most Holy Sun Absolute.[92] Or it can be seen another way: for instance, Bennett described the Ansanbaluiazar as "the transformation of energies," where there is a scale of energies that extends from the affirming Theomertmalogos at the highest limit and the denying Etherokrilno at the lowest, with the holy reconciling as "The whole working of the universe, particularly through life...."[93] He also said that between these ultimate holy affirming and holy denying sources are different gradations that may be spoken of in different ways:

> "....in terms of different worlds, different states of consciousness, different modes of being, different potentialities for playing a cosmic role and so on. This is not talking about different things, it is different ways of talking about the same thing."[94]

Although Okidanokh, the omnipresent active element, is not mentioned at all in the chapter *Purgatory*, nor in its companion chapter *Heptaparaparshinokh*, this substance that is crystallised from the Etherokrilno from the blending of the three holy forces of the emanations of the Sun Absolute, passes through all the Stopinders of the common-cosmic Ansanbaluiazar.[95]

The first food octave comes between the fourth and fifth deflections of the common-cosmic Ansanbaluiazar: that is, being-Protoëhary at Fa, and then if being-Exioëhary at the end of this first

---

[88] *Beelzebub's Tales*, 1950 p.785
[89] ibid. 761
[90] ibid. e.g. p.758, p.779, p.781 etc
[91] e.g. *Beelzebub's Tales*, 1950 p.781
[92] ibid. p.771 & p.760
[93] *Talks on Beelzebub's Tales* p.51 & p.68-70
[94] ibid. p.68
[95] *Beelzebub's Tales*, 1950 p.139

food octave is transformed through being-Partkdolg duty to higher substances, then these higher substances form the Do of a new octave, the beginning of which corresponds to Sol of this big octave, the fundamental common-cosmic Heptaparaparshinokh.[96] Here, of course, is also the painful Harnel-Aoot, far from the beginning and far from the goal, but from where the germ of something higher can arise.

In *Purgatory*, Beelzebub says that the subjective properties and proportions of vivifyingness of active elements depend first of all on the form of functioning of the fifth Stopinder during their actualisation, and secondly whether they arose according to conscious intention or merely automatically.[97]

The first form of functioning of the fifth Stopinder, is where there are many extraneously-caused-vibrations, and so its functioning gives only external results. The second form of functioning is where there are no extraneously-caused-vibrations, and all the results of the process remain within that cosmic concentration. And the usual case is to have a mixture of these two conditions.[98] This Harnel-Aoot is the point at which egoism can destroy everything.

Gurdjieff spoke of the importance of having fresh food so that the active elements are still present; or of preserving food in the right way. If this is not done, and the active elements are not all retained, then this was a cause of the spoiling of the stomach.[99] He stressed the importance of the proper mixing of foods,[100] and his remarks on where active elements are concentrated in particular foods[101] as well as the way to increase the active elements present in some cases, are also very interesting.[102]

The ability to extract the active elements from the three foods is another key aspect. This is why conscious eating is so important. And when one sits down to eat a meal, one is partaking of all three being-foods. Eating with other people, which for Gurdjieff was a sacrament,[103] provides a richer source of the third food than eating alone. And prayers before meals, and knowing and reflecting on what the food is and where it has come from all play a vital part in what Orage called active digestion.[104]

---

[96] ibid. p.787 & p.792
[97] ibid. p.785
[98] ibid. p.754-5
[99] ibid. p.946
[100] e.g. *Ladies of the Rope* p.122
[101] e.g. *Beelzebub's Tales*, 1950 p.952, *Undiscovered Country* p.142
[102] e.g. *Ladies of the Rope* p.124
[103] *Idiots in Paris* p.46
[104] *Gospel According to Orage* p.73-74

The Two Chief Motors of our Existence: Food and Sex

In *In Search of the Miraculous*, Gurdjieff talks about how one person might extract many more active elements from air than another.[105] In a similar vein, he also said that by examining someone's excrement he could also tell what kind of person they were! If active elements are not absorbed they simply pass out through the organism again.

Certain foods Gurdjieff spoke of as being special. For example, divine starch. He said,

> "Necessary eat potato, he have starch....Starch is very important, one of seven divine things for man. Without it he could not even breathe....Starch gives everything - body heat, material, even God thing."[106]

In *Beelzebub's Tales*, he calls wheat "this divine grain" and that "the most important product for the first being-food...[was] called 'prosphora' which they themselves name 'bread,' "[107] and that this had sacred significance.[108] He also said that "Onion....perfect food for man. Have everything he need."[109]

Active elements, Beelzebub says, are "appointed by Great Nature for renewing in the common presences of beings what they have expended in worthily serving her."[110] This seems to imply that if these substances are not worthily expended through conscious work, that the necessary active elements may not be absorbed to renew them. This has implications for, among other things, the aging process. Active elements are required not only for the production of higher substances, but also for the maintenance of the "coarse planetary body."

Gurdjieff said that the law of Heptaparaparshinokh was everywhere the same: the active elements contained in the food for dinner and those in the food of impressions in the after-dinner music came from the same unified scale, although of different octaves.[111] He also said that active elements make everything.[112] They are how one makes honey from *merde* and butter from air. He spoke of the giving of names in ancient Egypt and said,

> "One man there was called Holy *Merde* and from such name he swaggered - because meaning was he had fulfilled such transformation with honor, used all active elements according to law."[113]

---

[105] *In Search of the Miraculous* p.188-189
[106] *Ladies of the Rope* p.122-123
[107] *Beelzebub's Tales*, 1950 p.951
[108] ibid. p.965
[109] *Episodes with Gurdjieff* p.28
[110] *Beelzebub's Tales*, 1950 p.952
[111] *Ladies of the Rope* p.116
[112] ibid. p.111
[113] ibid. p.117

He also said that they "can change even tail in man."[114]

"Food for real man" and "the right food for man"

A strange term sometimes present in discussions on food is "invertebrates." Gurdjieff's descriptions of invertebrates in lectures and his comments about them in conversation seem very different to our ordinary conceptions, and to how the term is used in contemporary biology. Even Bennett's descriptions of invertebrates and their place seem to have a very different taste to those of Gurdjieff's.[115]

Invertebrates are placed between plants and vertebrates in "the Diagram of Everything Living" in *In Search of the Miraculous*.[116] And in *The Oragean Version* also, a diagram of "the Organic Kingdom" places invertebrate life at the Mi-Fa interval between vegetable and vertebrate life.[117]

Gurdjieff said, "....man feeds on invertebrates," and,

> "According to the diagram of food man feeds on 'hydrogen' 768; according to this diagram [of Everything Living] on 'hydrogen' 96 [invertebrates]. Why? What does it mean? Both the one is right and the other is right."[118]

Hydrogen 96, as being-Tetartoëhary, is the beginning of the psychic energies. It could also be thought that invertebrates comprise a class of active elements, and are present as "higher Hydrogens" in the food we eat. If this is the case, then only certain people will be able to extract some of these higher Hydrogens, which may also have a bearing on Gurdjieff's phrase "food for real man." It seems that certain special foods are only possible to be utilised fully by a man not in quotation marks.

Kathryn Hulme mentions a dessert they had,

> "....some kind of strange oranges dark and ancient-looking with rough pebbled skins. 'This is food for Man,' he said to Jane, '*real* Man, not man in quotation marks....here, if you are a real Man, you can have all the time. Here is the quintessence of all the good that exists....'"[119]

Elizabeth Bennett relates,

---

[114] ibid. p.111
[115] e.g. *Gurdjieff: Making a New World* p.288
[116] *In Search of the Miraculous* p.323
[117] *Oragean Version* p.80
[118] *In Search of the Miraculous* p.322
[119] *Undiscovered Country* p.148

"He told about how the Chinese bury eggs for 25 years before eating them, and the story about the Roquefort cheese running away, and how, after the first mouthful, 'if wish repeat', it was necessary to be quick, or the cheese would have run away. Then he said quite seriously that this was a good thing; invertebrates make the right food for man."[120]

It is perhaps notable that Gurdjieff said that invertebrates *make* the right food for man. Perhaps the "invertebrates" are what also help ordinary food to be digested and transformed into substances that may be utilised and transmuted by human beings. If we think of invertebrates in a much wider sense than that given by modern biology, and look in general at non-vertebrate life outside the plant kingdom, then by far the largest proportion of organisms are unicellular. As to running away, a characteristic of animal as opposed to plant life is of course locomotion. Maybe Gurdjieff's "invertebrates" have more possibilities of movement, in terms of energy, than the plant food that they transform.

If "invertebrates" are micro-organisms, then bacteria, moulds and yeasts certainly play a vital role in the transformation of certain foods before they are eaten by people, for example, yoghurt, bread, alcohol, cheese. In addition, many foods often benefit from a certain degree of "fermentation." Rina Hands mentions an interesting episode connected with a "most delicious looking....sort of toad-in-the-hole" with "beautiful red caviar," and which did not appear on the table until a few days later, having been put in a hay-box, and according to her was then "rather worse for wear."[121] Gurdjieff's salad was also reputedly often left a few days, covered, on the veranda to "cook."

In *Beelzebub's Tales*, invertebrates are not mentioned as such. However, it may be that a similar idea using an alternative term is used. A possible candidate might be the word "worms." Beelzebub says, "....are not these worms also beings through whom cosmic substances are also transformed?"[122]

Vegetarianism and Fasting

Gurdjieff said that to be a vegetarian was an honourable thing, and that by rights human beings ought to be vegetarian.[123] [124] However, for a number of reasons this was not always a wise thing to do. In *Beelzebub's Tales*, the great philosopher Hertoonano asserts that if those who are vegetarian live amongst those who eat meat then the formation of "will power" ceases, and their psychic state grows worse, even though their body may become more healthy. This is the greatest of evils. He

---

[120] *Idiots in Paris* p.51
[121] *Diary of Madame Egout pour Sweet* p.45
[122] *Beelzebub's* Tales, 1950 p.952
[123] Vegetarian here means someone who eats only fruits and vegetables, or a vegan, i.e. only food without *eknokh*.
[124] *Diary of Madame Egout pour Sweet* p.70

says, "Thus, a good result for people who abstain from meat can be obtained exclusively only if they live always in complete isolation."[125]

Gurdjieff also says in an early talk, "If breathe same air must eat same food."[126] Again, here is the dependence of the first food octave on the digestion of the higher foods, and also the implication that meat-eaters preferentially extract active elements from the air compared with vegetarians. This vegetarianism and will-lessness may be connected, therefore, with a decrease in the formation of sex energy. However, if everyone is vegetarian, this does not happen.

Because the harm caused, particularly to the psyche, by the substance *eknokh* contained in animal products, varied at different times of the year, Hertoonano advised abstaining from these only at particular times. For a habitual meat-eater, this can be seen as a partial fasting.

Gurdjieff sometimes directed fasts for his pupils. But no one was forced to do this. Gladys Alexander wrote of the fasts undertaken at the Prieuré: "Mr. Gurdjieff explained that [the fast] must only be undertaken voluntarily and without fear."[127] The word "voluntarily" has again the connection with will. Gurdjieff said, "Fasting is only for the mind." One could perhaps say "Fasting is only for the will," though not in the ordinary sense, but in the sense of the production of a higher energy, or the creation of the true mind.

It is interesting to look at the food octaves in relation to fasting, and to ponder on what may happen when the first octave is, as it were, "missing" or at least diminished, for a time (though water is usually allowed), or if animal products are absent. With partial or complete fasting, there are either different proportions of, not as many, or there are no, active elements that require transformation from being-Protoëhary.

However, Gurdjieff said that, "Profit gained from fasting begins only after twelve days,"[128] which is probably beyond the aspiration of most people. It seems that it required twelve days for the substances derived from the first food to be used up, and for the real work on the higher octaves to begin. A preliminary enema was required for the fasting to be of any benefit,[129] and vigorous physical work was undertaken, in order that the strong digestive juices that continue to be secreted would be used up and not cause harm to the organism; Gurdjieff said, "....it is necessary to expend as much energy as possible. Then fasting can be beneficial."[130]

---

[125] *Beelzebub's Tales*, 1950 p.1020 & p.1019
[126] Talk, Aug 9, 1924
[127] *Gurdjieff: Making a New World* p.146
[128] *Fasting, breathing* – Prieuré 27th Jan 1923
[129] *Gurdjieff: Making a New World* p.146
[130] *In Search of the Miraculous* p.358

The Two Chief Motors of our Existence: Food and Sex

Although fasting can certainly be seen to provide certain health benefits for the body, if performed in the right way, this was not the point of it for Gurdjieff. The shock to the system and the change in metabolism it was designed to produce were for the sake of the increased intensity of transformation of air and impressions, for the benefit of the higher parts.

Gurdjieff spoke on the one hand of the importance of normal breathing in fasting,[131] and on the other, of the necessity of fasting with aim and intention and with consciousness, and that it may be a means of cleansing if certain conscious measures are taken.[132] Without these things, fasting is worthless. Purifying the system is no doubt less significant for the body than for the internal psychic energies. This may also have a bearing on the harm that is caused to the psyche by the substance *eknokh*, that is, that meat-eaters experience a worsening of their chief feature in regard to positiveness and morality in consequence of *eknokh*.[133]

The emotional state during the fast seems also extremely important. As in the quotation before, there must be no fear. C.S. Nott also spoke of the fasting from negative emotion and "the abstention from useless unwilled manifestations."[134] Olga and Thomas de Hartmann, who were devoted to each other, had to live apart during a particular fast, causing them to make a great emotional effort.[135] And in a Palm Sunday talk, Gurdjieff asked his pupils to learn by heart the words, prayer, passion, repentance, confession, communion, forgiveness, suffering, tranquillity, death, life.[136] Some, at least, of the subjects in this list could be seen as part of the "conscious measures" one should take while fasting.

Bennett pointed out that an individual fasting alone is very prone to produce a notion of inner superiority. This can spoil everything. He pointed out that when fasting is carried out by an entire community, as in Islam, this danger is avoided.[137] And Gurdjieff spoke of the importance of the presence of other people when fasting.[138]

And it is interesting to ponder on the double meaning of Gurdjieff's once saying to his Rope group, "If we do *not* eat now, then our animals will make revolution!"[139]

---

[131] *Fasting, breathing* – Prieuré 27th Jan 1923
[132] Talk, Palm Sunday, 1923
[133] *Beelzebub's Tales*, 1950 p.1019
[134] *Teachings of Gurdjieff* p.72
[135] *Our Life with Mr. Gurdjieff* p.67-68
[136] Talk, Palm Sunday, 1923
[137] *Witness* p.79-80
[138] *Constantinople Notes* p.31 & *Fasting, breathing* - Prieuré 27th Jan 1923
[139] *Undiscovered Country* p.135

All & Everything Conference 2010

The most important part of the second being-food

According to Gurdjieff, we no longer assimilate and transform the substances contained in air normally.[140] This, like all our other problems, is because of our abnormal existence; and we take in the second being-food automatically rather than intentionally.[141] The fundamental elements of this food arise both from the transformation of elements of the planets of our solar system, and also from the sun itself.[142] We are able to assimilate these only in so far as we have corresponding data, or substrata, in ourselves for this.[143] It is from our own transformation of these active elements that we may form Hanbledzoin.[144] And Hanbledzoin is what connects our thoughts and our emotions.[145]

Our emotional life depends on what we can extract from air. Likewise, how we breathe is affected by our emotional state. Orage says,

> "....the rhythm of the lungs, feeding upon air, depends upon the emotional center, which in turn depends upon the images presented to it by the brain. In this way the three centers are linked up."[146]

He also talks of how only by assimilating the "vitamins" of air are higher emotions possible, and that this can only come about through the breathing associated with a certain attitude.[147] This sounds very similar to the "certain kind of attitude" when taking the first being-food, mentioned earlier,[148] that enables even elements from ordinary food to be used for the higher parts. And attitude, for Orage, is a psychological posture.[149]

Gurdjieff spoke of an exercise that should become a habit, that produces an attitude enabling right breathing and thus the assimilation of the good part of air, which comes from the prime source. He said, "....you should try to realize your own significance and the significance of those around you," and, "....always try to sense this significance....whenever your attention rests on anyone," and that this could be done through acquiring "....data always to realize the inevitability of their death, and your own death...."[150]

---

[140] *Beelzebub's Tales*, 1950 p.572
[141] ibid.p.808
[142] ibid.p.781
[143] ibid.p.571
[144] *Beelzebub's Tales*, 1950 p.569-570
[145] ibid.p.1200
[146] Blanche Grant notes 1931, p.38
[147] ibid. p.8
[148] p.2 of this paper
[149] Blanche Grant notes, 1931 p.8
[150] *Teachings of Gurdjieff* p.114-115

The Two Chief Motors of our Existence: Food and Sex

And in *Purgatory*, Beelzebub says that the ability to ponder on the sense of existence arising from the transmutation of understanding of the two fundamental sacred laws, especially Heptaparaparshinokh, enables one to correctly evaluate the essential significance of one's own presence.[151]

Gurdjieff talks about certain cosmic crystallizations present in the air we breathe that are, for the normal person, substances for use in self-perfection.[152] Indeed, he calls them the most important part of the composition of the second being-food. However, in ordinary contemporary people, instead of this, they cause a disease with a definite harmful action. This he said was because in our abnormal existence, and in the absence of substrata corresponding to the requirements of the lawful process of Djartklom, we do not assimilate and transform these crystallizations into higher substances any more.[153]

He gives as examples of names given to this disease, " 'grippe,' 'influenza,' 'Spanish influenza,' 'dengue,' and others."[154] That is, various kinds of viruses, with the potential to cause epidemics, with prostration, an inability to function even in ordinary life, and sometimes death. Spanish influenza is mentioned again, equally enigmatically, as occurring in modern times during Chirnooanovo, that is, when the centre of gravity of the planet is displaced:

> "....during 'Chirnooanovo'....instead of this remorse of conscience, there usually arise there....epidemics....'Black Death,' 'cholera,' 'Spanish influenza,' and so on."[155]

Here, bacterial illnesses are also mentioned, that is "Black Death" and "cholera," but which have an equally devastating effect on people.

One could think of an epidemic of suggestibility or mass psychosis causing corresponding incapacity to perform ordinary basic functions and duties. Or the similar contagiousness of the identifying with negative emotions.

The kind of air, or the quality of the air, seems very important for its capacity to nourish. It is the presence of other people or animals that can enable a fasting person not to lose weight, according to Gurdjieff.[156] It seems that the emanations of others can serve as food. Gurdjieff said that the assimilation of the most important part of the air is dependent on our inner state, which depends mostly on the form of our mutual relationship.[157] Usually we react to the emanations of others and send out our own emanations, which means that we are not in a position to receive and digest

---

[151] *Beelzebub's Tales*, 1950 p.755-756
[152] ibid.p.571
[153] ibid.p.571
[154] ibid. p.572
[155] ibid. p.959-960
[156] *Fasting, breathing*, Prieuré, 27th Jan.1923
[157] *Beelzebub's Tales*, 1950 p.571

them. We suffer in vain by having, for example, "anger, jealousy and resentment towards others,"[158] and thus are, like an old goat, "a movable source of horrible emanations."[159]

If these "viruses" are to do with the indigestion of our own and others' emanations, then conversely if we are able to digest these emanations, perhaps from the realisation of the inevitability of death, then we can transform the "sufferings in vain" into material for coating the higher parts. There is also the association with remorse, mentioned a short while ago, where Beelzebub implies that without remorse, when the centre of gravity of the planet is displaced, this disease of "influenza" and the like occurs. And we are reminded of the harmfulness of egoism, for oneself as well as for others.

We know, of course, that everything that Gurdjieff said, but especially everything in *Beelzebub's Tales*, has more than one single meaning. Orage said that everything in this book has three meanings and seven aspects,[160] which implies that there are twenty one different, definite and equally valid interpretations for every full statement. It is very easy to latch on to one interpretation that attracts us, to the exclusion of others.

For example, in our search for depth of meaning, we can easily overlook an important literal aspect. It is possible that Gurdjieff also regarded at least certain viruses and bacteria as literally having a role in our self-development. It may be worth bearing in mind Gurdjieff's other remarks in regard to antibiotics, for example, "penicillin is poison for the psyche."[161] Bennett certainly took this literally and seriously. And the "substrata" mentioned before could have a relation with elements of our immune system, for example, antibodies. If this is so, then a high quality in our relationships with others, and remorse for being distracted from our aim, could be seen as the best way to approach an influenza pandemic!

Orage spoke of the difference between our usual respiration and the possibility of changing it to aspiration. He said,

> "Aspiration is hope plus effort....it is because of this double nature of aspiration that it was symbolized in ancient times by the two wings of the eagle on the ox. One wing was hope, the other effort."[162]

And he said that when respiration was changed to aspiration, then we could assimilate and digest not only substances in air from the moon, earth and other planets, but also from the sun and

---

[158] *Teachings of Gurdjieff* p.114
[159] Meeting 26, Paris, 25th May 1944
[160] *Teachings of Gurdjieff* p.178
[161] *Witness* p.197
[162] Blanche Grant notes, 1931 p.9

galaxy.[163] Through assimilating these higher substances, the aspirant may eventually be initiated into "the Brotherhood of the Originators of making butter from air."[164]

Evolution and involution of sex energy

This question of sex, said Gurdjieff, "is a question which plays the most important role in the life of everyone,"[165] and, "Happy he who understands the function of the Exioëhary for the transformation of his being. Unhappy he who uses them in a unilateral manner."[166] He also said that Exioëhary is our most sacred possession, and should serve for the coating and perfecting of our highest parts.[167]

The development of will, or a permanent I, a key idea in Gurdjieff's teaching, is dependent on the transformation of Exioëhary. Orage said that the potential of the sex centre "is the ability to do."[168] Bennett saw the Omnipresent Okidanokh as the Creative Will[169] and that through the splitting and striving to reblend of the three separated forces of Okidanokh comes the realisation of will. The Creative Energy in Bennett's scale of energies, which he says he learned the basis of through Gurdjieff, is connected with will.[170] Conversely, it is also interesting to note the association that Beelzebub points out between the spoiling of our digestive organs and the disease of "impotence."[171]

Bennett spoke of how the higher Creative Energy may blend with the lower Sensitive Energy, which is the energy of sensing and which may be accumulated through work, and how this releases Conscious Energy, which is on the level between the Creative and Sensitive Energies.[172] This, of course, is the Harnelmiatznel once again. He says, "it is by the sexual power that man has his most easy access to the creative energy." The transformation of Conscious Energy to liberate Creative Energy, however, is dependent on its blending with the Unitive Energy, which is the energy of cosmic love.[173]

So if this is its high purpose, why does Exioëhary so often end up in the sewer?

---

[163] ibid. p.42
[164] *Beelzebub's Tales*, 1950 p.38
[165] *Meetings with Remarkable Men* p.56
[166] Meeting 4, 8th April 1943
[167] *Beelzebub's Tales*, 1950 p.791-792
[168] *Gospel According to Orage* p.24
[169] e.g. *Gurdjieff: Making a New World* p.202
[170] *Deeper Man* p.88, p.48 & p.64-65
[171] *Beelzebub's Tales*, 1950 p.943
[172] *Deeper man* p.62
[173] *Sex and Spiritual Development* p.13 & p.47

In terms of transformation, what does not go up must come down. Thus, because people do not transform sex energy, that is, because it does not evolve further under the usual conditions, then when it is not used up in ordinary sexual activity, it simply involves back from whence it came. This, according to Gurdjieff, resulted in many illnesses and also shortened people's lives.[174] Sex energy can be transmuted to higher substances only with the ceaseless undertaking of being-Partkdolg-Duty.[175] And Gurdjieff said, through Beelzebub, that it is "....possible, by means of these substances Exioëhary formed in them, to perfect themselves....only if the second and third being foods are intentionally absorbed and consciously digested in one's presence...."[176]

Gurdjieff said that in regard to "The disharmony of this function [of sex]....the fundamental cause....is their negligence....in keeping their sex organs clean."[177] Although this has an important literal significance, it can also be thought of in terms of the psyche and of mentation. In addition, the sexual partner was also a kind of "water closet" who enabled the excretion of excess and involving Exioëhary. But each person had to have the right kind of water closet for them.[178]

Bennett said that normal sexual activity was necessary for its regulatory effect on the psychic energies in general, because it serves an excretory function for Exioëhary.[179] Those who neither use Exioëhary for procreation, nor excrete it in normal sexual activity, nor carry out being-Partkdolg-duty and transmute it to higher substances, Bennett said, are inevitably prone to fantasising.[180] Orage said, "Do not permit your brain-systems (mind) to be soiled. How does one soil one's mind? The two chief means are through phantasy and sentimentality....by the reinforcement of such data from within..."[181]

So, Exioëhary, although it is the source of all higher energy, can also cause a lot of problems if it is not used rightly. There are three right uses of Exioëhary: ordinary sexual activity, procreation, and its transmutation to higher substances. This latter may be with or without sexual abstinence, though it may be thought that with the latter there is more Hydrogen 12 available to be transmuted. Orage pointed out, however, that three times as much sex energy (i.e. H12) is produced when working on oneself.[182] Gurdjieff did sometimes advise abstinence.[183] However, it seems that he himself, even if he was continually fulfilling being-Partkdolg-duty, had a great need, at least at times, for the regulation of internal energies through ordinary sexual activity.[184]

---

[174] *Beelzebub's Tales*, 1950 p.793
[175] ibid.p.807
[176] ibid.p.808
[177] ibid. p.974
[178] *Meeting 4, 8th April 1943*
[179] e.g. *Sex and Spiritual Development* p.16
[180] ibid.p.24
[181] *Oragean Version* p.188
[182] ibid.p.157
[183] e.g. *In Search of the Miraculous* p.256
[184] e.g. *A Memoir with Recipes* p.34

The Two Chief Motors of our Existence: Food and Sex

Abstention without being-Partkdolg-duty produces a build-up of degradation products of Exioëhary. Exioëhary is tainted and becomes a poison when it involves, and it is wasted when ordinary sexual activity is carried out in the usual unconscious way, although even this latter serves an excretory, regulatory function.

"Venereal diseases," owing to involution of Exioëhary, are a frightening array, as described by Gurdjieff: a certain duality of the psyche - with external bigotry and internal cynicism[185] - lack of piety,[186] lack of faith,[187] lack of love for one's neighbour, fatness,[188] thinness,[189] shortening of life,[190] destroying the thirst for being,[191] deperfecting one's previously established essence-individuality,[192] paralysing the striving for evolution,[193] pimples,[194] runny noses,[195] an increase in the fixing of the consequences of the organ Kundabuffer,[196] an inability to mentate properly,[197] dispersal throughout the body of "poisonioonoskirian vibrations."[198]

And with the usual wrong connections between the sex centre and the lower centres, there occurs wrong use of sex energy, with other centres stealing the fine Hydrogen 12, causing excessive force in various activities, undue excitement, vehemence, etc.

The last few pages of *Purgatory* in *Beelzebub's Tales* are taken up with describing the processes occurring in "these contemporary abstaining monks." Just prior to this, Beelzebub indicates that he is going to provide an example to illuminate the meaning of the expressions, hen's laughter and castor oil that he has just used.

> "....it can truly be said that if these understandings and notions of your eccentrics about their questions of the beyond were heard by our hens, they would begin to laugh so hard that the same thing might happen to them from their laughter as happens there among your favorites from what is called castor oil."[199]

---

[185] *Beelzebub's Tales*, 1950 p.810
[186] ibid.p.981-982
[187] ibid.p.982
[188] ibid.p.809
[189] ibid.p.809
[190] ibid.p.793
[191] ibid.p.793-794
[192] ibid.p.793
[193] ibid.p.534
[194] e.g. *Beelzebub's Tales*, 1950 p.547
[195] *Beelzebub's Tales,* Revised edition, 2006 p.963
[196] *Beelzebub's Tales*, 1950 p.810
[197] ibid.p.737
[198] ibid.p.809
[199] ibid.p.805

Castor oil, being an ideal purgative to cleanse the body of impurities, is also referred to elsewhere in *Beelzebub's Tales* and other of Gurdjieff's teaching. In addition, Gurdjieff says that laughter pumps out and discards superfluous waste energy.[200] So, even if the chicken-brained laugh, as indeed we often do reading *Beelzebub's Tales*, then this cleanses the psyche of some of its poisons. In a similar way, one could say that sex acts like castor oil, in the ordinary way, promoting the excretion of harmful involutionary products of Exioëhary.

We should remember that there are two kinds of soul, both of which derive from Exioëhary. The one especially beloved of our Common Father Creator, is that which, after purification, has the possibility of uniting with the Prime Source of everything existing.[201] The other Bennett described as one meaning of Hasnamuss, from the Persian, "soul of shit."[202] We who try to work on ourselves are especially in danger of developing this latter, much more so than the ordinary person, if in so doing we fail to renounce our egoism.

Half-beings

In *Beelzebub's Tales*, it is said that because Ashagiprotoëhary, which comprises the substances at the lowest Do of the common-cosmic Ansanbaluiazar, is concentrated in the centres of our satellites, Moon and Anulios, rather than in the centre of our planet, we are made male and female, that is, Keschapmartnian rather than Polormedekhtic, or that we are "nearly half beings."[203]

Dean Borsch in *Meetings with Remarkable Men* said that each person is an incomplete type, and that only together with someone of corresponding type of the opposite sex does one become a complete type. To come under the influence of a non-corresponding type, due to the law of polarity and one's sexual needs, was largely to lose one's individuality and to be not responsible for one's manifestations.

> "That is why it is absolutely necessary for every person, in the process of his responsible life, to have beside him a person of the opposite sex of corresponding type for mutual completion in every respect."[204]

More is said on the necessity for corresponding types in conjugal pairs in *Beelzebub's Tales*, and how the Zirlikners, the physician-astrologers, of Karatas were experts in this area.[205] However, for contemporary people, conjugal pairs nearly always do not correspond in type.[206] According to Gurdjieff, said Bennett, "type is a combination of triads in the essence, and certain triads

---

[200] *In Search of the Miraculous* p.236
[201] *Beelzebub's Tales*, 1950 p.24 & p.800-801
[202] *Deeper Man* p.109
[203] *Beelzebub's Tales*, 1950 p.770-771, p.774 and p.781
[204] *Meetings with Remarkable Men* p.56
[205] *Beelzebub's Tales*, 1950 p.287
[206] ibid.p.289

compliment [sic] each other while others do not,"[207] and there is a certain "....essence pattern which makes a union a fruitful and stable one...."[208]

Bennett speaks of the possibility of one man and one woman together creating a single soul between them, almost as if this could not be done by either one of them alone.[209] As the soul is not part of our divided sexual nature, it can only be created through union. He also says that, "real marriage is a very, very rare event in human life," and marriage must also be deserved, because male and female energies will cancel each other out unless there is an independent third force.[210] Only with a reconciling factor can there be true union of a man and a woman, and thus union of will.

Whether or not we are or have been married, or have a partner, most of us are very far both from the creation of a soul and from real marriage. Yet if we are serious about Gurdjieff's teaching, we should be occupied only with this: making a soul.[211]

Although it might seem a tragedy that we are made and usually remain, at least for a long time, incomplete beings, yet the incomplete is as necessary as the complete. This is because the incomplete is always, whether consciously or unconsciously, searching for that which will make it complete. But this problem of lack, of something missing, is part of the very fabric of our life, and of our possibilities.

In its biggest sense, Bennett says,

> "....privation has been introduced into the cosmos so that **the creation can create itself**. If it were not aware of being separated from its Source there would be nothing to make it return to its Source. Hence, privation is the beginning of the creation." '[212]

This incompleteness of our nature, from which springs our sexuality, drives everything that we do, fuelled by the digestion of all the three foods. But the path divides into two. One way is to allow ourselves to be driven into egoism, separating ourselves still further from other people, splitting our psyche still more deeply, or satisfying our sexual urges simply for pleasure. The other way is the way toward union, which may begin with the essence-touching process of sexual contact, and evolve with another through union of Being, to union of Will, and to the creation of a soul from two disparate natures, with the reconciling force of the Work.

The opening that is produced toward the other in this process, enables also an opening toward all people and to the whole world. Bennett said, movingly,

---

[207] *Sex and Spiritual Development* p.20
[208] ibid. p.41
[209] *Gurdjieff: Making a New World* p.233
[210] *Sex and Spiritual Development* p.54 & p.31 and *Deeper Man* p.145
[211] *Ladies of the Rope* p.122
[212] *Talks on Beelzebub's Tales* p.67

"We are not separate, either from those who have gone before us or those who will come after us. The human race is one."

And, of course, his prayer for before meals begins, "All life is one....."[213]

From this creation of a single soul, to the uniting with humanity and all life, we may move towards our ultimate goal: to unite with the Source, to become a particle of the whole of the great whole,[214] to be a brain cell in the mind of God.[215]

© Copyright 2010 - Clare Mingins - All Rights Reserved

---

[213] oral tradition
[214] *Beelzebub's Tales*, 1950 p.353
[215] Orage: letter to Jessie, 27.11.1926, quoted in *Gurdjieff and Orage* p.131

The Two Chief Motors of our Existence: Food and Sex

Bibliography

Beekman-Taylor, Paul *Gurdjieff and Orage: Brothers in Elysium,* Weiser Books, 2001
Bennett, J.G. *Deeper Man,* Turnstone Press, 1985
Bennett, J.G. *Gurdjieff - Making a New World,* Turnstone books, 1976
Bennett, J.G. *Intimations: Talks with J.G. Bennett at Beshara,* Beshara Publications, 1975
Bennett, J.G. *Sunday Talks at Coombe Springs,* Bennett Books, 2004
Bennett, J.G. *Talks on Beelzebub's Tales,* Samuel Weiser Inc, 1993
Bennett, J.G. *The Relationship Between Sex and Spiritual Development,* Samuel Weiser Inc, 1981
Bennett, J.G. *Witness: The Story of a Search,* Bennett Books, 2007
Bennett, J.G. and E. *Idiots in Paris,* Coombe Springs Press, 1980
King, C. Daly *The Oragean Version,* Privately printed 1951
Ferapontov, M. *The Constantinople Notes of Mr. Ferapontov*
Grant, Blanche *Notes,* 1931
Gurdjieff, G.I. *Beelzebub's Tales to His Grandson,* 1950 version, Two Rivers Press, 1993
Gurdjieff, G.I. *Beelzebub's Tales to His Grandson,* Revised edition, Triangle Editions, 2006
Gurdjieff, G.I. *Meetings with Remarkable Men,* Arkana 1988
Gurdjieff, G.I. *Paris Wartime Meetings 1941-1946,* Library of Congress, Washington
Gurdjieff, G.I. various talks
Gurdjieff, G.I. *Views from the Real World,* Arkana, 1984
Gurdjieff-Everitt, L. *A Memoir with Recipes,* SLG Books, 1997
Hands, Rina *Diary of Madame Egout pour Sweet,* Two Rivers Press, 1991
Hartmann, T. and O. *Our Life with Mr. Gurdjieff,* Penguin books, 1992
Hulme, Kathryn *Undiscovered Country,* Little, Brown & Company, 1966
Nott, C.S. *Journey Through this World,* Samuel Weiser Inc, 1969
Nott, C.S. *Teachings of Gurdjieff,* Routledge & Kegan Paul, 1982
Orage, A.R. *The Gospel According to Orage,* Privately printed
Ouspensky, P.D. *In Search of the Miraculous,* Arkana, 1987
Patterson, W.P. *Ladies of the Rope,* Arete Communications, 1999
Wolfe, Edwin *Episodes with Gurdjieff,* RMSG Press, 2002

The Two Chief Motors of our Existence - Questions & Answers

Participant 1: I found it interesting to note that as you went through the diagram explaining all the various fractions of the food, that the descriptions given in Ouspensky's book, in the chapter on Purgatory, in the *Oragean Version*, and from Bennett - well there were various similarities, there were also places where there were many discrepancies in the descriptions. When these four people can't all agree on the exact layout of this diagram, how much harder it is for us to do this as well. And to relate that to this conference in a certain way, one of the reasons we have a conference is to come and discuss these types of discrepancies and see what we can learn from each other about these interpretations. So maybe you could say a bit more about why you think these discrepancies crept in to these various descriptions.

Clare Mingins: I suppose my view is that if they all spoke about more or less the same thing, then we would be able to slot it into a nice place in our formatory apparatus, and be quite happy with that. And it would just remain in our reason of knowing and not have any chance for helping us to transform our being. But the fact that these different versions are not quite the same is quite unsatisfactory for a certain part of me, and it doesn't satisfy either the formatory apparatus or something else. And these are such important subjects that we need to understand them, and so I think that the struggle in both trying to understand why there should be different versions and how to sense these different processes in oneself can enable one to move further and to increase one's level of being.

Participant 2: Thank you very much for this presentation, and I share your dissatisfaction as you just mentioned. I must admit that when you came up with first picture, something in me said, "No, no, not this again. I know all this." But as you were proceeding, you presented so many different aspects and, I would say, original views, especially when you are relating direct to the *Tales*, and you see this in connection direct with the *Tales*. Now my question is if you could say something about the "fish" diagram of *The Oragean Version*. In the upper part there is placed, if I remember this right, the higher intellectual centre. Can you say something about why the higher emotional centre is in the middle part, and that he puts the higher intellectual centre on the right there.

Clare Mingins: So, just to make it clear: Centre 4 which is the cerebellum he calls the higher intellectual centre, and Centre 5, which is not present in *Purgatory*, he calls the heart or higher emotional centre. It just happens to be the opposite way around to Gurdjieff's teaching in Ouspensky. But I think perhaps our association with the terms intellectual and emotional are perhaps wrong when it comes to these higher centres, because perhaps they each have more association with emotions and intellect themselves, than we normally think of the lower emotional and intellectual centre. I think they include a lot more than we can perhaps usually associate with these terms, intellectual and emotional. And perhaps they are not very satisfactory terms.

The Two Chief Motors of our Existence: Food and Sex - Questions & Answers

Participant 2: That diagram has puzzled me for a very, very long time, and I tried to find a solution to it but I couldn't, so I just took the opportunity to ask you now.

Participant 3: My question has to do with the food diagram. And it has to do with the end three notes, Mi Sol Si 12. I know what I want to ask but it is very difficult to formulate it, so I am sorry, you will have to bear with me. Maybe I'll have to make more than one effort. It's a question of localisation: where exactly would we consider them to be localised? That's one part of the question, one aspect of it. More specifically, we know that the lower part of the spine is full of sexual ganglia, of ganglia that control the sexual region. So it has to have something to do with sexual energy. And of course, we have the sexual organs that must have something to do with sexual energy, and the depositories of the sperm, and the ova, and all that, which must have something to do with the sexual energy. Is it possible to say a few things about the localisation of each, it's relationship with Mi Sol Si 12, and in general what would the difference be in working with sexual energy of the sensation one has of the lower part of spine with the direct sensation one has of the sexual organs?

Clare Mingins: I think I might just confine myself to the first question! I couldn't begin to answer the second part of the question. But I have to say I just look at these things in a very simple way, and Si 12 which is the ordinary sexual energy which we are accustomed to, is described by Gurdjieff in *Purgatory* as being concentrated in the testicles or ovaries, but for example, Mi 12 in Ouspensky - when one is able to remember oneself one forms Mi 12 -and the object, I think he said, of all religions, schools and that, was the transformation of Mi 12, and that Hydrogen 12 should be in every cell of the body. So perhaps it is not just concentrated in one particular part. That's as far as I can go.

Participant 4: I'm looking at the three foods there, and I've always felt that the foods are coming from outside and that the top one in my terminology would be perceptions. And I've always been puzzled as to why it's called impressions. Is that perhaps some sort of lawful inexactitude or is there some significance in that in your view?

Clare Mingins: Perhaps perceptions is as good a word. But, I don't know. Impressions is the one that Gurdjieff has chosen.

Participant 5: The aspect of this diagram that has always been most intriguing to me actually doesn't appear on this rendition. And that is that the air octave completes in a quality of La 6...

Clare Mingins: It's off the end!

Participant 5: ...up in the head. And looking at the table of vibrations, presumably that quality of vibration, that Hydrogen 6, is as far as the human being can go, and then there are two step ups. We are the second step down, whatever that means. So, this is a most extraordinarily interesting presentation, and I just want to point out there's an even bigger mystery, because somehow up in the head the quality of this highest energy beyond the creative sexual energy seems to appear when air is fully digested. Perhaps you have a comment?

Clare Mingins: Yes, I suppose I was just concentrating on the things that are easier to notice in oneself, because a lot of the higher transformation, for me anyway, is theoretical, and something to be aimed for. It's not there yet.

Participant 5: So this is absolutely nothing to say that this is as far as we can go in terms of our understanding of physiology.

Clare Mingins: I think so, yes. I think in *Purgatory* doesn't he say that Exioëhary is the final result of the transformation of each of the three being foods. So it would imply that Si of each octave of air, food and impressions, or Exioëhary of each octave is, theoretically anyway, possible. So that in Orage's table, the Si of each octave, being-Exioëhary, astralnomonian-Exioëhary and "impressions"-Exioëhary, theoretically anyway, is possible for a fully developed human being.

Participant 5: So that would be represented by ambrosia.

Clare Mingins: La 6 of the air octave would be ambrosia, according to Orage's terminology.

Participant 6: I'm thinking about these discrepancies and so on, and my thought is that we might not look at this as in absolute terms, but as sort of tools to help us think about some of these things. So in the end we should throw away the tables.

Clare Mingins: Maybe it's just a tool, I quite agree.

Participant 7: First of all I would like to thank you for a well-researched, well-presented food diagram. It so happens that just before coming here I was studying the chapter of *Purgatory*, and actually trying to place these three octaves on the enneagram. I haven't really finished or reached a conclusion, but I was wondering if you have tried to do something like that?

Clare Mingins: The simple answer is, no I haven't tried, but I'm sure it would be fascinating. I personally don't understand the enneagram at all. It is a complete mystery to me. So I am sure there are many experts here in the audience who could enlighten us.

Participant 8: I'm interested in, Orage calls it, nectar and ambrosia. But Gurdjieff calls it abrustdonis and helkdonis. So there's another stage after Exioëhary, and it's converted again into these terms he uses. Abrustdonis I think goes to the heart, and helkdonis goes to the head brain.

Clare Mingins: Thank you.

The Two Chief Motors of our Existence: Food and Sex - Questions & Answers

Participant 4: I wondered if some of the discrepancies might arise as might not the human organism change as it develops, so that there is a change in location of these different energies as a result?

Clare Mingins: That may be. Yes, I'm sure there are certain differences between people, different genders, different levels of being.

Participant 4: Between the developed man and the undeveloped man?

Clare Mingins: Yes. I think the various stages probably remain similar but the substances within each Stopinder vary according to the active elements that one is able to extract from each food according to one's being, I guess.

Participant 9: The discrepancies between these versions of Ouspensky and Orage can also serve to illustrate for us or warn us that despite the achievements of these characters, who we all regard very highly, it was still not impossible for them to make error. And it also serves to highlight the difficulties that we all face, and the alertness that we need to apply to every moment in this task that we're engaged in.

Clare Mingins: I'm sure you're right. I think it reminds us that we shouldn't take anyone's word for it, not even Orage, Bennett, or even Gurdjieff. That we have to see for ourselves.

Participant 9: Exactly.

Participant 10: In this diagram [Orage table of digestion octaves] where it says sex, what does it mean? Does it mean sexual energy, the action of sex? Because, I don't know anything, I know very little about these things. But just looking at it, maybe if you could explain it. It says solid, liquid, gas, which I can understand, do, re, mi. Then there is an interval. And you have a different order, which is magnetism, thoughts and emotion, which seem to be faculties operating. And what does it mean by sex?

Clare Mingins: Well, I suppose it's all the Hydrogen 12's, the Si Sol Mi 12 of each octave. I suppose it just refers to that very powerful energy which can be used in all sorts of ways. I mean, ordinary sexual activity, but also any creative work requires sex energy to be transformed. It's perhaps the most powerful thing we have. That's all I can really say.

Participant 11: I remember it said in the *Tales* that in the Karnak spaceship they had special times for absorbing the second being-food. And then a question, what's absorbing? And then after absorbing must be digestion. And digestion from djartklom, somehow. I think the idea of this is that somehow digestion, first splitting the one into three, and then so it's possible to be digested by the three bodies. The equivalent of the three first split somehow into the equivalent of the body, somehow. I don't know if I make sense.

All & Everything Conference 2010

Clare Mingins: I think it's too complicated a question for me! But if anyone in the audience would like to respond, I would be very happy.

Participant 5: As I'm watching my own fascination with this material and hearing this question, my understanding is that the sex energy that we're talking about is a quality of energy that has the capacity to create. It can at the physical level participate in creating another physical body, for something to incarnate into. But it creates images and ideas and conceptualisations. And I'd say the danger of that I heard you just speak about Clare is that we can get lost in these wonderful theoretical conceptualisations of others' creation and our participation with, when I think the question here is being directed at direct experience, djartklom. When I divide my attention, when I split into two, and I appear as the third element, there's a surge of energy. Something is released. There's the potential for new possibility of understanding in that moment. And our actual participation here other than creative conceptualising is to try and be present to our body, present to our breath, present to incoming impressions, and perhaps present to relevant associations, such as one of these formulations that might appear in a moment to illuminate something we're experiencing. But it probably would be a misuse of that creative energy for us to fall headfirst into these incredibly complex conceptualisations which I think are here to try and help us with our experience, not with falling into imagination.

Clare Mingins: Thank you.

Participant 6: What strikes me through all these diagrams is that sex is on an extremely high level. And what we ordinarily talk about as sex is not on this level. So, it makes me wonder, it's some mystery.

Clare Mingins: Yes. Going back to Orage's "fish" diagram: this is the sex centre which he calls the highest centre, and these are the normal connections. So Centre 1 which he calls physical action/spinal column (moving centre), should be connected to the emotional centre, which is connected to the intellectual centre, which is connected to the cerebellum or higher intellectual centre, which is connected to the heart, which is connected to the sex cells. But, ordinarily, the "fish" has gone wrong. So the sex centre which is the highest centre has connections to the lower emotional centre, connections to the lower intellectual centre, so it's mixed up with ordinary associative thought, with emotions, and with the moving centre, so daydreams and imagination, and it all goes wrong. Instead of when there are right connections, I think that's probably when it can become that very powerful thing which can be used to coat our higher parts.

Participant 1: When referring to the transformation of sexual energy, sometimes I'm a little mystified by this in the sense that we seem to be talking about, well we have this energy and we can either use it for procreation or for creating higher bodies. When one looks at what is involved in the sexual energy, on the physical level there is sperm and ova, and associated with that is the production of hormones, testosterone being one of the main ones, in both men and women it is necessary to fuel or generate the sex drive, and of course people can get injections of testosterone if they're having problems with sexual motivation, also people can have vasectomies as a birth control method which prevents the issuance of sperm in men, or various methods where women taking hormone pills and so on to stop the monthly cycle. And then there are other things like nitrous oxide is necessary to have an erection and engorgement of the organs. And of course the brain where some of these, testosterone and so on, would be processed and various centres of the brain to mediate and coordinate all the physical activity and the desire to engage in a sexual practice or a spiritual practice of transforming this energy. Of course the other neurotransmitters and hormones involved with pleasure and so on. When you talk about transforming sexual energy, are we talking about all of these at once, or are we zeroing in on one particular aspect? Which of these energies would one specifically be working on, or chemicals, or hormones, neurotransmitters?

Clare Mingins: I know that some people do try to marry up Western science, physiology, medicine, with Gurdjieff's teaching. And I'm sure that's very laudable and useful. But my approach tends to be very different because I prefer to use Gurdjieff's teaching as a tool to help me, I suppose, understand experiences. Not in any particularly chemical, medical type of way, which is my other life. And when I do try to compare them or marry them up, there is something that for me doesn't quite work and isn't useful, isn't practical. And perhaps modern medicine isn't yet advanced enough to do that properly. Perhaps in a hundred years time we'll be able to do that in a much more profitable way. So, I have a lot of respect for people who do try to combine the two. I mean, in this conference and other conferences there have been some very good talks.
And you were talking about all these other things like testosterone injections, the pill, vasectomy, which obviously do alter levels of the sexual energy, and nitric oxide, and Viagra, I'm sure you could be referring to. But these, although they have their purpose in ordinary life for people, I'm sure they do cause a disharmony in our inner functioning, and perhaps an increase in the risk of involution of Exioëhary, and all these "horrible diseases" that Gurdjieff throughout *Beelzebub's Tales* associates with the involution of Exioëhary.

Participant 3: Well, at last I find something I disagree with you, Clare, after all these years!

Clare Mingins: Great!

Participant 3: Because I consider myself like one of those people you said who are trying to combine Gurdjieff's ideas with science. It has nothing to do with an intellectual thing. That's the whole point. It has precisely to do with experience. That's the essence of combination. And I appreciate Ian's comment and question on that. I think it's a question we all have. Because we go on using with such freedom all these expressions. And what are they? We jump from do re mi fa sol la si's, to organs, to Protoëhary, Defteroëhary, and all that. Why are we doing this thing? I mean, we do it to express our sensation and then we should concentrate on that, or we should refer to organs or to anatomical parts and we are leaving loose ends in this way. I think once one gets involved in this game of mapping things from symbol to reality, from expressions on a diagram to experience, it's legitimate to ask such questions as Ian has. After all, experience is there to be influenced by will, so to speak. And it's interesting to know what exactly do I influence? Do we have a clear image of what it means to work with the sexual centre, for example? What does it mean? Do I have attention concentrated on a specific anatomical area? To suppress urges? All this is very vague. And it cannot stay like that if one wishes to work. It is impossible to verify any aspect of all these things unless he has an image of what he is doing. Now the image does not necessarily have to come through a diagram. I will accept that. There doesn't necessarily have to be a clarity of intellectual nature as to what one's doing. But certainly there has to be a clarity of experiential nature.

Clare Mingins: Yes

Participant 3: Because you feel inside urges and forces and influences and you need to know exactly where you need to apply your will. Otherwise there is no other way of applying first shock and second shock and all these things, that's the whole point of work, to know where to apply the shocks. So I think that there is a point in translating all these diagrams into experience, and all work done in the direction of mating, marrying as you said, the Gurdjieff ideas with science is precisely that: the effort to express the idea of influencing one's sensations, one's internal landscape, the sensation and feelings of one's internal landscape, influencing in the appropriate way, and the marrying process is a process of making sure that this thing is not is disaccord with scientific observations, or incomplete, they're not two completely different realms. Because if they are, and I'm terribly sorry that you're a doctor, if they are and if one leaves doctorship to be a working person and then assumes his doctoral identity after hours, this seems to be a very great dichotomy in one's life, which is against the gist of it all, I believe.

Clare Mingins: Well, I disagree. I have a great dichotomy in my life, yes, but I don't feel that at this stage it is for me appropriate to combine them.

Participant 3: But I believe we have to face the question at some time, that Ian posed, to tell you the truth.

Clare Mingins: Yes, but I also think at the time that Gurdjieff was writing and teaching, his ideas were not at all in accord with the current science of the day in many areas, and I think a lot of things have been discovered since then which in a way have validated some things that he had said. And I think the same is true today that there are things that probably don't tie up with each other in modern medicine and Gurdjieff's teaching that may in the future be more in accord. And so that was why I was saying that for me in a hundred years time maybe I would be able to do the job of looking at them both with more, for me, satisfaction.

Participant 3: Quite so, I agree with you. On the other hand, science always comes after experience. So the fact that Gurdjieff was talking from experience does not mean that he was not being scientific. And the fact is that he underlines the fact that what he's dealing with is science. Objective science is science, yes, it is not "not science."

Clare Mingins: But his science and our modern science are quite a different kettle of fish.

The Two Chief Motors of our Existence: Food and Sex - Questions & Answers

Participant 11: It has become more clear to me with what has been said that sexual energy, that what we say is generally sexual energy, to me is not the same as sexual drive or sexual urge. To me sexual drive and urge is sexual energy but is already on the way to the bathroom somehow.

Participant 12: Yes, I'm afraid I get confused with all this science and all the diagrams. And whilst I find some of them useful, most of them are an impediment to actually experiencing what's required of us. And I remember a teacher, who I won't name but who was a pupil of Gurdjieff from 1925 to the day he died, who was listening to a group talking about the table of hydrogens and he went absolutely crazy with him, and he said this is absolute nonsense. He said, when you make love to a beautiful woman you work on yourself and that's all that's required.

Participant 4: Many of us have a very bad diet, and many of us have breathing problems and breathe very bad air. Is there any suggestion in what you've researched that the quality of our food and the quality of the air we breathe might affect the quality of our sexual energy. So would that work for me?

Clare Mingins: I'm sure that the more one tries to improve the quality of the food that's taken in, the better. So that's fresh food, cooked in the right way; good air - I mean Gurdjieff described the quality of air as being dependent upon the presence of other people often, and emanations of other people being an important part of the second being-food; and impressions - I know that my impressions in a big city are very different to at home where I live in the countryside and perhaps there is quite a different food there, and I'm sure it all affects the energies of the different levels in these processes. And of course the vegetarian, eating no animal products whatsoever, and how Gurdjieff said that will is affected, if they mix with meat eaters - that will, or as I translate it, Exioëhary, the potential to form will, is reduced. So I think there are many things in what you say.

The Gurdjieff Tradition: To Be Continued

Arkady Rovner

Abstract

Gurdjieff's tradition, generally known as the Fourth Way, has come to a lengthy pending stage after almost one hundred years of its history. Today, when those who met G.I. Gurdjieff in person and who studied under his supervision are no longer among us, the tradition appears to be without a commonly recognized center of gravity. Various groups and individuals all over the world practice the Fourth Way as they see fit, thus taking full responsibility for their interpretation of Gurdjieff's teaching. Some of the adherents of the Fourth Way travel along the road of rediscovering for themselves such respectable ancient traditions such as Sufism, Advaita-Vedanta, and even Christianity as being the real sources of Gurdjieff's tradition. Still others have chosen the way of creation of new syncretic teachings based on the Fourth Way and other traditions. As a result of this discord, Gurdjieff's tradition has been gradually reduced in practice to the Gurdjieff Movements, an essential but by no means a central element of his teaching.

Thus we have the following questions before us, which require urgent answers. What are the most essential components and what is the core element of Gurdjieff's teaching? What could be the continuation or the new shape of the Fourth Way? What attracts the modern spiritual seeker to the Fourth Way and what no longer does? Finally, what type of a person is this seeker who is capable of understanding and following Gurdjieff's path in earnest?

The answers to these questions could be found by means of research, experiments and examination of Gurdjieff's writings, which encourage us to seek independent solutions for any arising problems. One must keep in mind that we are dealing with the problem of paramount importance, namely, with the future destiny of Gurdjieff's tradition.

The following quotation from Gurdjieff's early talks hits the point precisely: "…now we speak in a language which two hundred years hence will no longer be the same, and two hundred years ago the language was different." *Views from the Real World*, p. 211.

In his *Beelzebub's Tales,* chapter 30, Gurdjieff broadly elaborates on the subject of transmission of the Knowledge by enlightened members of the club of "Adherents-of-Legominism," tying this transmission with the Law of Sevenfoldness and other phenomena. The problem in question is dealt with numerous times throughout this book.

The author's sincere and strong objective lies in addressing those questions in his presentation.

The Gurdjieff Tradition: To Be Continued

What is the main objective of this presentation?

I would like to speak of the current state and the future destiny of Gurdjieff's tradition in the light of the ideas presented, primarily, in "*Beelzebub's Tales* to His Grandson," as well as in the other written works by and about the founder of this tradition. In the present day, the state of Gurdjieff's tradition requires a sober approach and responsible consideration more than ever before, in the light of the fact that was noted by Wim van Dullemen, a person well known for his devotion to the Gurdjieff Movements and music, who wrote: "the Gurdjieff Work is a difficult area to investigate because of the prevailing sense of secrecy, as well as the increasing isolation and lack of cooperation, if not hostility, between the lineages."[1]

Gurdjieff's tradition, generally known as the Fourth Way, after almost one hundred years of its history has come to a for a long time pending state of uncertainty about its future. Whereas the number of publications related to Gurdjieff and the Fourth Way is rapidly growing, especially those written in the genre of memoirs or as general overviews, very few people understand what is Gurdjieff's Work and even fewer people actually practice it. Today, when all of those who met G.I. Gurdjieff in person and who studied under his supervision are no longer among us, the tradition appears to be devoid of a commonly recognized center of gravity. Some of the former adherents of the Fourth Way have gone along the road of rediscovering for themselves such respectable ancient traditions as Sufism, Advaita-Vedanta, Shamanism, and even Christianity, considering them to be the main sources of Gurdjieff's tradition. Still others chose the way of creating new syncretic teachings on the basis of the Fourth Way and other traditions. In the present time various groups and individuals all over the world practice the Fourth Way as they see fit, thus taking full responsibility for their interpretation of Gurdjieff's teaching. As a result of that discord, Gurdjieff's tradition has been gradually reduced in practice to the Gurdjieff Movements, an essential but by no means a central element of his teaching. And the Movements themselves in many instances have become a product of the present-day global "Supermarket for Self-Development".

Thus we have to ask the following questions: What are the most essential components and what is the core element of Gurdjieff's teaching? What attracts the modern spiritual seeker to the Fourth Way and what no longer does? What could be the future of the Fourth Way?

The answers to these questions could be found by means of comprehension, research as well as examination of Gurdjieff's writings and the works of his disciples. Gurdjieff constantly spoke of Legominism as the main aspect of a spiritual tradition defining it in the Chapter 30 of "*Beelzebub's Tales*" as "transmission of true knowledge to distant generations through corresponding initiates."[2] The ideas concerning transmission of true knowledge have created a

---

[1] Wim van Dullemen, *The History of Gurdjieff Movements*, Newsletter 1/2002.
[2] G.I. Gurdjieff, *Beelzebub's Tales to His Grandson*, Penguin, Arkana 1999, p. 459

recurring theme in this all-embracing epic. Therefore, Gurdjieff's teaching must be looked upon in the light of the idea of Legominism as it was outlined in this book. Our first task is to find out the actual meaning of this concept.

What does Gurdjieff writes about Legominism in "*Beelzebub's Tales*"?

In the same chapter we read: "This word Legominism," replied Beelzebub, "is given to one of the means existing there of transmitting from generation to generation information about certain events of long-past ages, through just those three-brained beings who are thought worthy to be and who are called initiates."[3] The 'initiates', according to Gurdjieff, are those enlightened beings "who had acquired in their presences… objective data, which could be sensed by other beings."[4]

In Chapter 23 of *Beelzebub's Tales* entitled "The Fourth Sojourn of Beelzebub on the Planet Earth" Gurdjieff relates the story of "this learned society Akhaldan which arose then on the continent Atlantis and which was composed of three-brained beings of the Earth … 735 years before the second Transapalnian perturbation …[5] We learn that "It was founded on the initiative of a being there named Belcultassi, who was then able to bring the perfecting of his higher being part to the Being of a Saint 'Eternal Individual'; and this higher part of his now already dwells on the holy planet Purgatory."[6] A little later, many other beings that also had such a presence joined him. They founded the Society of Akhaldans, which was in Gurdjieff's words, "the first and perhaps last great terrestrial learned society."[7] The word 'akhaldan' thus expressed the following concept: "'the striving to become aware of the sense and aim of the Being of beings.'"[8] Still later, for the purposes of general character, they divided up into seven of independent groups, each group focusing on a particular field of knowledge such as geography, 'vibrations', mathematics, etc. However the very existence of this learned society was endangered by "the second transapalnian perturbation" and the members of that organization migrated to another continent and settled in the country that currently bears the name of Egypt.

Reading further into "*Beelzebub's Tales*" (Chapter 30, "Art") we learn that during Beelzebub's fifth trip to Earth he visited Babylon. Once, walking in on a certain street of that city, he saw a signboard announcing that a club for foreign learned beings, the Adherents-of-Legominism, had been newly opened. After joining this club and becoming its full member, Beelzebub attended a presentation by a Chaldean learned being named Aksharpanziar, who recommended two essential things: first, to preserve the old way of transmitting Legominism through a succession of enlightened beings, and then, to add to it another way, that of concealing elements of Legominism

---

[3] Ibid., p.349.
[4] Ibid., p.350
[5] Ibid., p.294
[6] Ibid., p.294
[7] Ibid., p.299
[8] Ibid., p.297

either in objects created by human beings or in their rituals, both artificially distorted for purpose of their safe preservation.

A very special place in this book by Gurdjieff was ascribed to a saintly being named Ashiata Shiemash. "The Very Saintly Ashiata Shiemash was the only Messenger sent from Above ... who succeeded by His holy labors in creating on that planet conditions in which the existence of its unfortunate beings somewhat resembled for a certain time the existence of the three-brained beings of the other planets of our great Universe ..."[9] We learn that Ashiata Shiemash helped human beings in many ways, and that he has delivered a Legominism called "The Terror of the Situation," the full text of which we find in Chapter 26. We also learn that this Legominism was inscribed on a marble-table and "at the present time this surviving tablet is the chief sacred relic of a small group of initiated beings there, called the 'Brotherhood-Olbogmek,' whose place of existence is situated in the middle of the continent Asia."[10]

In the following Chapter (27) Gurdjieff writes about two groups of enlightened beings, namely, the Tchaftantouri and the Heechtvori Brotherhoods, the name of the second signifying 'Only-he-will-be-called-and-will-become-the-Son-of-God-who-acquires-in-himself-Conscience.'[11]. Both Brotherhoods were guided by the great saint Ashiata Shiemash. Ashiata Shiemash has sent the 'great initiates' from these two brotherhoods with appropriate instructions to organize similar brotherhoods in other countries and towns on the continent of Asia. As a result of the care and guidance of Ashiata Shiemash "the question of conscience already began to predominate at that period ... particularly among those who existed on the continent Asia."[12]

Later, even the word 'initiates' has come to have two different meanings, Gurdjieff states and elaborates on the theme: "In one sense it is used for the same purpose as before, that is to say, those beings there are so named who became initiates thanks to their personal conscious labors and intentional sufferings; and thereby, as I have already told you, they acquire in themselves objective merits which can be sensed by other beings irrespective of brain-system, and which also evoke in others trust and respect. In the other sense, those beings call each other by this name who belong to those what are called there 'criminal gangs' which in the said period have greatly multiplied there and whose members have as their chief aim to 'steal' from those around them only 'essence-values.'"[13]

"Well then, my boy, Gurdjieff-Beelzebub concludes, speaking to his grandson, Hassein, Legominism is the name given to the successive transmission of information about long-past events which have occurred on the planet Earth from initiates to initiates of the first kind, that is,

---

[9] Ibid., p.348
[10] Ibid., p.349
[11] Ibid., p.368
[12] Ibid., p.374
[13] Ibid., p.350

from really meritorious beings who have themselves received their information from similar meritorious beings."[14]

Beelzebub turns his mind to the question why all the efforts of enlightened individuals and brotherhoods failed and why false 'initiates' could gain the upper hand in the "struggle of Magicians", and he explains that by referring to periodical catastrophes that destroy everything on Earth, to the fits of madness that make humans kill each other and to the hasnamussian tendency that gradually spreads all over the Earth.

Summing up what we have learned about Legominism from *"Beelzebub's Tales,"* we could state the following. Firstly, Legominism is the true knowledge that is transmitted from generation to generation by the genuine initiates. Secondly, Legominism either contains information about certain events of long-past ages or appears in the form of principles that are useful to those who strive towards acquiring for themselves their higher being-bodies. Thirdly, during periods of mass psychosis, social "perturbations" and spreading of the hasnamussian tendency, Legominism assumes converted forms by concealing its composite parts from misuse and irreparable distortion.

What else do we know about the origin of Gurdjieff's teaching?

We know from various sources, all of them referring to Gurdjieff's statements, that his teaching has been assembled from the information that he and his associates had acquired during their search for ancient knowledge. That knowledge had been neglected and forgotten in the course of time by the generations of human beings living in abnormal conditions, who due to those circumstances had lost their memories along with their higher being-bodies. The best known and most often quoted text on the subject is the passage from Chapter One of P.D. Ouspensky's classic book *In Search for the Miraculous* which goes as following: "But how did you study?" – "I was not alone. There were all kinds of specialists among us. Everyone studied on the lines of his particular subject. Afterwards, when we forgathered, we put together everything we had found."[15]

On another account, according to Gurdjieff's own writings, this knowledge had been obtained by Gurdjieff as the result of his profound introspections and years of intense experiment. Gurdjieff writes: "I arrived then, in the above-mentioned year, at the definite conclusion that it would be utterly impossible to find out what I was looking for among my contemporaries and therefore decided one day to abandon everything and to retire for a definite period into complete isolation, away from all manifestations of the outer world, and to endeavor by means of active reflections to attain to this myself or to think out some new ways for my fertile researches."[16] So he went to a secluded monastery in Central Asia, and after that dedicated a number of years to a thorough

---

[14] Ibid., p.350-351
[15] P.D. Ouspensky. *In Search of the Miraculous*. Fragments of an Unknown Teaching, a Harvest Book Harcourt, San Diego, New York, London 2001, p. 15.
[16] G.I. Gurdjieff, *Herald of Coming Good*. First Appeal to Contemporary Humanity, Paris 1933, p. 14.

research with the intention "to investigate from all sides, and to understand, the exact significance and purpose of the life of man"[17] and to "discover, at all costs, some manner or means for destroying in people the predilection for suggestibility which causes them to fall easily under the influence of 'mass hypnosis'."[18]

Although we see here two different assumptions concerning the origin of Gurdjieff's teaching, they appear to be essentially complementing one another. We have sufficient reason, based on our intuition and experience, to make the following affirmations: Gurdjieff's teaching was the result of his profound introspection, at the same time it was procured together with a group of his associates and obtained from a contact with a source of higher knowledge. Hence, Gurdjieff's tradition presents an example of Legominism or a manifestation of true knowledge containing veritable information about certain events of long-past ages and profound principles for those who strive towards acquiring their higher being-bodies for themselves. Since Gurdjieff's Legominism has been revealed during a period of social "perturbation," mass psychosis and a spread of the hasnamussian tendency, it is natural that Gurdjieff, who spent a significant part of his life searching for this knowledge, was concerned with transmitting it to his disciples and with the subsequent continuation of his line of transmission. At the same time he made sure that his Legominism assumed a masked form with its essential elements concealed, and thus protected from possible misuse, distortion or damage.

What was the subsequent destiny of Gurdjieff's Legominism?

In 1912, shortly before the beginning of WWI and the Russian revolution, Gurdjieff arrived to Moscow and began his Work with groups of his Russian followers. This marked the end of the legendary part of his history – from now on up to his death in 1949 Gurdjieff's life was documented in the utmost detail by his disciples.

The teaching revealed by Gurdjieff was sophisticated and composite, and he himself played the role of the center of gravity, which held all the components together. After Gurdjieff's decease, his teaching, being essentially left without a gravity center, split into the intellectual part, the individual Work, the group Work, the latter including the Movements, and music. These parts eventually became independent of each other, and presently they coexist in a complementary manner. Some people read Gurdjieff others practice Gurdjieff individually or in groups, still other dance and listen to Gurdjieff's music.

Already during Gurdjieff's lifetime several of his senior disciples, P.D. Ouspensky, A.R. Orage, J.G. Bennett and a few others, began the transmission of Gurdjieff's Legominism to their own followers. Later on, many of Gurdjieff's disciples, such as Pierre Elliott, Frank Lloyd Wright, Willem Nyland, John Pentland and others, have also made their own contributions, to the best of their abilities, to the further dissemination and development of this tradition. Some of them,

---

[17] G.I. Gurdjieff, *Life is real only then, when I am*, E.P. Dutton & C., N.Y. 1973, p.26.
[18] Ibid., p.27.

headed by M-me de Salzmann, organized the Gurdjieff Foundation, which became the official inheritor of Gurdjieff's legacy. For the sake of protecting the authenticity of transmission of the teaching, the Gurdjieff Foundation has surrounded itself with a wall of mystery, similar to that which was created several decades earlier in London by P.D. Ouspensky.

The Gurdjieff Foundation became the established center for Gurdjieff's Work in Europe and the US, acting diligently in its task of preserving Gurdjieff's heritage, publishing his writings, teaching his Movements, supporting performances of his music and tending to its adherents. We experience a considerable amount of gratitude to the Foundation for what it has done, albeit some disappointment in regard to its shortcomings. In the present time, the Gurdjieff Foundation has lost its central role of the leader of Gurdjieff's tradition. As the result of its defensive position in the modern world, a large amount of genuine interest awakened in people by Gurdjieff's striking personality and by his powerful ideas is being wasted. Instead of knocking patiently at the door of the Foundation, the reader of literature on the Fourth Way, or a person who has heard about Gurdjieff from a friend, would rather satisfy his or her spiritual need by joining a local group for the Movements, which would most likely be led by an instructor from the Rajneeshes, the Fellowship of Friends, the School of Psychoanthropology or, more likely, by an independent leader who himself studied with questionable instructors.

The Work of P.D. Ouspensky and J.G. Bennett had been carried out in an atmosphere of opposition between the "conservatives" and the "innovators". As far back as in 1956, John Bennett was complaining about the impossibility of cooperating with the "conservatives," having explained their position as that of an overly reverent attitude towards Gurdjieff and his teaching. The reason for this was, in his opinion, a lack among the "conservatives" of instructors endowed with the knowledge, certitude and gift of improvisation comparable with Gurdjieff's.

On the other hand, the approach of P.D. Ouspensky and J.G. Bennett suffered from an excess of rationalism and unproven assumptions, and their teaching strategies and techniques, when compared with that of their teacher revealed a great deal of ungrounded improvisation.

What is the present state of Gurdjieff's Legominism?

Presently in Europe, America, Asia and Australia against the background of the "Supermarket for Self-Development", we can see numerous groups and individuals practicing the Fourth Way at their own initiative. A certain part of those entities consist of either groups of Gurdjieff Movements or of groups of alleged Gurdjieff Work, often led by representatives of non-Gurdjieffian or dubious neo-Gurdjieffian orientations. Some groups have been established by the dropouts from the Gurdjieff Foundation, who were not satisfied with either the teaching methods used by instructors from the Foundation or with the instructors themselves. There also exist semi-Fourth Way groups that have chosen to have no leader, as well as Fourth Way web-sites not affiliated to any of the Gurdjieff trends, including the Gurdjieff Foundation.

The Gurdjieff Tradition: To Be Continued

The intellectual part of Gurdjieff's teaching is well represented in the Master's books, lectures and talks, as well as in the books about Gurdjieff and his ideas. It is the most appealing element of the teaching because of its profound content and striking form. However, during the course of time the form of the intellectual part of the teaching gradually began to look stiffer and more ponderous. The modern reader, who is accustomed to the fleeting style and quick and easy challenges in the works of Rajneesh and Castaneda, often finds Gurdjieff's style rather bulky and obscure. In addition, the doctrines created on the basis of Gurdjieff's teachings by his main interpreters, Ouspensky and Bennett, have turned over the years into kinds of rationalistic systems, which have lost the plasticity of living and developing ideas.

Even the language of the Fourth Way presently seems to be already out of date, and all those who use it, feel compelled to expand and modernize it by bringing new ideas and images into their discourse and, hence, to shatter the foundations of the teaching. The following quotation from Gurdjieff's early talks makes the point precisely: "…now we speak in a language which two hundred years hence will no longer be the same, and two hundred years ago the language was different."[19] One hundred years have sufficed to prove that the author of those words was right. The Gurdjieff Movements are presently a dominant self-sufficient phenomenon, and there have been numerous cases when only after a long time of practicing the Movements the participants begin to realize the significance and magnitude of their creator and of the other elements of his legacy.

The music composed by Gurdjieff and arranged by Thomas de Hartmann for the Movements is one of the most delicate and attractive elements of Gurdjieff's heritage. Among the people who have been interested in Gurdjieff there evolved a moderately sized circle of connoisseurs of this music, who perceive it primarily as an aesthetic phenomenon in a retro style. Their taste for it is enhanced by reminiscences of spiritual practices in various Eastern traditions.

The myths and anecdotes surrounding the founder of the Fourth Way are widely disseminated by tradesmen of pop culture. On the other hand, large groups of Europeans and Americans perceive Gurdjieff's teaching as a sectarian cult and call for saving unsteady and inexperienced souls from its influence.

The Gurdjieff Foundation in the context of the modern world resembles a system of impregnable fortresses in a land controlled by vagrants. As the situation in the world is becoming more grievous and critical, the Foundation is hardening in its position of maintaining its isolation from the outer world.

To sum up our review of the present state of Gurdjieff's tradition, we could say that the overall situation resembles that of a combination of chaos and paralysis.

---

[19] *Views from the Real World: Early Talks of Gurdjieff as Recollected by his Pupils*, E.P. Dutton & C., N.Y.1973, p. 210-211.

All & Everything Conference 2010

What kind of world do we live in now?

The world carnages of 1914-1918 and 1939-1945 have divided the most recent history of Europe into three parts: before World War I, the interwar period and the time after World War II. The final collapse of traditional Europe took place as a result of these two squalls which have descended on it, slaughtering millions of people physically and hundreds of millions spiritually. These horrific sacrifices have taught people the sad lesson of hopelessness and submissiveness before cruelty.

The time period before 1914 was characterized by an accelerating disintegration of the social order, although society was for the most part dominated, at least nominally, by traditional European values. Then the first squall descended, and the weak ones lost their courage. The period between the two wars was a nostalgic one: people tried to forget about the recent war and convince themselves that a lengthy peace had arrived, similar to the one in the pre-war years. However the storm clouds gathered once again over Russia and Germany, and new horrors began looming on the horizon. In 1945, after the end of World War II, the new world order established itself permanently, continuing up to the present day – a new type of tyranny, hypocritically labeled as democracy. From that time on, "democracy" has become a concept which masked a new technocratic brand of dictatorship. In this type of society the submissive masses are controlled by anonymous magicians, who have tightened to the extreme the mechanisms of control over them.

The intelligent spiritual seeker (according to Gurdjieff, "man number 1, 2 and 3"), prior to 1914, had contented himself with theosophy or anthroposophy, showed off his left-wing radicalism and flirted with black magic (if one is to remember Arthur Machen, the author of "The Great God Pan," as well as the main character of Huysmans' novel "Là bas!"). During the inter-war period various talented spiritual seekers (René Daumal and Hans Kastorp from Thomas Mann's novel "The Magic Mountain") turned towards surrealism, Dadaism and mysticism. They had no wish to ponder over the carnage which had just ceased or over that which was approaching. The Western truth seeker of the period after World War II, bewildered by the unprecedented scale of its cruelty, was "pink" in his political sympathies, and simultaneously a cynic and adventurer in his approach to life (such as the heroes of Nabokov's early novels), still dreaming in his heart of the pre-war paradise in which his childhood had passed.

Presently the psychological stagnation is spreading across the world, becoming global and irreversible. In a visible future, our civilization may be destroyed, either totally (due to the inaptitude of the environment for habitation in it) or in part (due to the impossibility of suppressing tensions in society). Distinct symptoms of this approaching catastrophe could already be discerned today. Globalization (read: global standardization and control) is occurring within the spheres of economics, communications and culture. All of these phenomena have had their own proponents and critics, and they threaten us with wars and other disasters. The present-day financial crisis has shown us what kind of chaos could arrive even in such a seemingly common case as an economic recession. We are currently living in the new world, in which the level of entropy has reached the critical point, cherishing in the hearts of millions the old dream of being saved from catastrophe by a miracle. The question is how we can save from this deluge a fragile spiritual tradition?

This grievous situation, in this case considered in regard to the Gurdjieff Movements, was apprehended by one of the matriarchs of the Gurdjieff Tradition Jessmin Howarth: "In a very few years, the older people who have struggled to prevent the distortion of the Movements will be dead. You can continue your dedication to Mr. G.'s teaching by actively setting about the formation of a nucleus. You will try to exchange, share and stay all together, supporting each other's efforts, and so endeavor to preserve purity in teaching Mr. G.'s System of Movements."[20]

Wim van Dullemen also finds this to be a pressing problem. He writes: "There is the well known esoteric principle, "You can't give what cannot be taken," or, "Do not cast pearls before swine." But how to select those that can take them?" He is referring to a particular situation when Gurdjieff presented his Movements in France and in America, these events being open to anyone interested and admission was always free. When Gurdjieff was asked, "Why do you open this to all these people?" he answered angrily, "How can you judge?... We have to let everyone hear. The results do not belong to us." Wim van Dullemen's choice is the middle way: "we didn't want to throw the Work out onto the street at the feet of every passerby, but rather, to open it to those with a real interest." And this meant to him carrying out Work "in smaller subunits, rather than in a "top-down" structure."[21]

Both of those perspectives, Wim van Dullemen's and Jessmin Howarth's, are marked by a sense of uncertainty and pessimism. Neither of them can be viewed with even the slightest degree of hope.

What could be done in the way of improving this grievous situation?

In the following part of my paper I will address directly the problem of transmission of Gurdjieff's Legominism. This brings up once again the question: what is Gurdjieff's Legominism?

The three Legominisms of Gurdjieff, which essentially create the core of Gurdjieff's teaching, are the following. The first Legominism of Gurdjieff is the statement about the "Terror Situation" which demands urgent spiritual effort. The second Legominism is the foremost significance of Conscience which is God's chief representative on Earth. Finally, the third Legominism is the clear distinction between being-knowledge and mental knowledge, and the stress made on the first type of knowledge leading one to the awakening. These three Legominisms of Gurdjieff, which bring in the parallel with three Legominisms of Christianity - total depravity, repentance and salvation – provide us with the reliable direction for spiritual effort and create a criteria for the external actions. The corresponding Legominisms in Buddhism are *dukha* (suffering), *prajna* (distinguishing knowledge) and *bodhi* (liberation).

---

[20] Jessmin & Dushka Howarth, *It's Up to Ourselves*, Gurdjieff Heritage Society, NY, 2009, p.466.
[21] Wim van Dullemen, *The History of Gurdjieff Movements*, Newsletter 1/2002.

In order to revive Gurdjieff's tradition and to make it meet the expectations of forthcoming new generations, serious changes are needed in a number of directions, such as defining objectives, enhancing instruction, encouraging creativity, and developing the language, but first of all, one should think of the creation of an organ, a proto-nucleus capable of administering all the necessary changes.

We must ask ourselves: what is the desirable shape of Gurdjieff's tradition in the present day? In the absence of an enlightened Master, we certainly do not want to see it as an autocracy or monarchy. Should the Gurdjieff tradition be organized in the manner of the 19th century British Empire, in which colonies were ruled by viceroys? Or would it be better if it resemble the European Union of our days, governed by its top officials? We certainly would not like to see that future as inevitable anarchy, ruled by arbitrary choice and incompetence? But is this not our present state? The Christian church during the course of time was divided into several autocephalous churches, which have never been reconciled since. Is the same fate awaiting us too? What will happen with Gurdjieff's Legominism in a situation of schism and chaos? And where, incidentally, it is dwelling presently?

Our best possible choice would be the creation of a Council of competent masters, a nucleus of like-minded persons who would take on the responsibility for the future of Gurdjieff's tradition, and who would determine a strategy for its development. One of the aims of this type of Council might be to gather together all the elements that are healthy and strong in the present-day Gurdjieff Work. This Council must have at its center a person who would highlight the best qualities of all its other members. The leader of such a group could not be merely appointed by somebody at random – he must develop within the circle of other mature and enlightened individuals. The principle of Brotherhoods should be established as the dominating principle of that Council as well as of the other nucleus affiliated with it.

*On the first sta*ge it would be necessary to carry out scrupulous preliminary investigation and planning. Here it is the appropriate time to recall what Gurdjieff wrote about the club of the Adherents-of-Legominism and the speech of the Chaldean sage named Aksharpanziar, who recommended two essential things: first, to preserve the old way of transmitting Legominism through a succession of enlightened beings, and then, to include another way based on concealing elements of Legominism, either in objects created by human beings or in their rituals, both of which should be artificially distorted for this purpose. In the process of embodying this idea, a Media Holding should be created for the purpose of dissemination of the ideas of the Work with controlled distortions, which would enhance the process of enculturation of the teaching.

On the second stage an assault must be launched "against the contemporary world." This Council must focus on gradually turning the Gurdjieff tradition into an active disposition in the modern world, on conversion from a defensive position to an offensive one. The strategy of the Council must be based on spiritual illumination and an offensive against consumerism, pragmatic materialism, and other similar harmful trends. One of its important objectives could be to create conditions for overcoming the anthropomorphism of Western religions and establishing a new openness for the wisdom of the great Oriental traditions. This may introduce a new period of spiritual discourse and disputation, similar to the one which was known to the Western world during the first centuries of Christianity. If Christianity has survived that challenge, Gurdjieff's tradition has no lesser capacity of enduring it.

The creation of Fourth Way Brotherhoods around the world must be encouraged in the manner it had been done by the great saint Ashiata Shiemash. These Brotherhoods should take part in disseminating the three main Legominisms of Gurdjieff. They could participate in a creative manner in the projects of the Council and bring feedback reactions from the experiences of their dealings with the outer world. We could recall that "Ashiata Shiemash has sent the 'great initiates' from… two brotherhoods with appropriate instructions to organize similar brotherhoods in other countries and towns of the continent of Asia". As a result of that care and guidance of Ashiata Shiemash "at that period, particularly on the continent of Asia, the question of Conscience began to predominate". This particular Work should be enacted with the anticipation of the support of youth which is completely disappointed with the perspectives available to them today. This success will be assured by the quality of Gurdjieff's Legominism and by the purity of our intensions.

Simultaneously, an assault should be launched against technological cults, which have been established, basing themselves on distorted elements of Gurdjieff's tradition. We may remember what Gurdjieff wrote about the false 'initiates' and 'robber gangs,' which have greatly multiplied in our time, as they had at the time of Ashiata Shiemash, and whose members had the principal aim of 'stealing' particularly the 'essence-values' from those around them.

We should keep in mind that the main objective of this "assault against the contemporary world" is the spiritual awakening of our contemporaries and securing the transmission of Legominism to the distant generations. Those who would say that the modern world is not ready for such a change and that it is a dangerous undertaking should recall the conditions at the times of all historical spiritual transformation. The world always is ready for the "coming good," and there is no danger for human beings that is greater than the decay and necrosis in the midst of which we live now.

The anticipated course will inevitably produce an explosion of both, creative and destructive forces; however that process will be moderately controlled by the three Legominisms of Gurdjieff. Those who crucified Jesus Christ were concerned with public calm and tranquility, however He has chosen the other way: He knew that Legominism means the continuous reconstruction of the Tradition, its adjustment to concrete historical needs.

Gurdjieff's book *Beelzebub's Tales* has a great amount of potentials for providing us with many additional insights into our future.

© Copyright 2010 - Arkady Rovner - All Rights Reserved

The Gurdjieff Tradition: To Be Continued - Questions & Answers

Speaker 1: From my personal point of view, one of the reasons I like coming to this conference, and being involved, is because it gives a free and open platform for all these various traditions to come and have their time on the soapbox; to share and discuss these ideas. One thing that I like about it is the openness. That there is no-one out there trying impose some sort of dogma, or act as some sort of police, as to what we should do, and should not think about this work. So that's my take on this. Thank you.

Participant 2: I would like to ask whether you believe in addition to the three methods you mentioned for disseminating logominism -

Arkady Rovner: Which three methods? One is the regular method, namely the transmission from an initiate to an initiate...

Participant 2: No, at the end of your talk you gave, you talked about, having a group...

Arkady Rovner: I talked about two types of groups.

Participant 2: You talked about selected masters, you called them, or...

Arkady Rovner: Yes, the Council of masters, and the creation of groups...

Participant 2: Yes, and I wanted to ask you something about legominism. Whether you believe, or whether it is also mentioned anywhere in the Gurdjieffian teachings, that one way by which, what I would call knowledge is perpetuated through the species, is actually though the DNA, through the offspring of people who have been doing the work? Do you believe that is another possibility?

Arkady Rovner: Could you repeat the last sentence?

Participant 2: Do you believe that one of the ways by which what you call legominism, or what I understand is as knowledge, is the way it is perpetuated, through the ages, and through the species, is through the DNA of those people who have been doing conscious work. In other words, do you think that by doing such work, people create faculties which are passed on genetically to the next generation to their offspring? Just like we see in nature, some species passing on what they have managed to achieve to the next generation?

Arkady Rovner: No, I don't believe in natural, automatic, transmission of legominisms. I think that conscious labour and intentional suffering changes the DNA in those who are involved in Gurdjieff practices, but I don't think this can be inherited and transmitted through the genes, from generation to generation. Each time, the personal effort is required. What can pass automatically is mechanical. Legominism dwells on the tops of the mountains, not in ravines or in low places. So only those who reach those places can do it, and a different type of responsibility is awakened in those who do the work, the practise.

Participant 2: Thank you.

Participant 3: I thank you very much for this talk. I believe that the person who never thought about the things that you said, or anything that has to do with them, is really strange. I suspect, to a lesser or greater degree, most people have. Though I suppose very few in the clear way that you formulated your opinions. In fact, I feel your talk like a finger pointed at me: why have you not done anything about it? Like you accuse me of something.

Arkady Rovner: I accuse only myself

Participant 3: It has been my concern ever since I came to these Conferences, which is since the first one, actually, and in fact I saw these conferences as an opportunity, for something like the thing you describe, from the very beginning. I do not know what I did, I do not know what I said, I think I said things like the one you said, like the things you said. But it could have been perceived very differently, or it could have been very different in actuality. The fact is that I came up against a wall, from the people in here. A wall that was ranging from indifference to negativity. To intense negativity. This gave me an opportunity for much thinking. How could it be so? Don't people see problems like the ones that you mentioned today? And why don't they want to talk about it? It has impressed me profoundly that four year of our congregation, I think at the suggestion of somebody from the London Society, there was introduced into our by-laws the phrase "this is not a work situation", which was not there from the beginning. This sort of approach bared this Conference, at least seemingly from any serious reality, that can possibly influence the work, since it is not a work situation... but you know, with the years comes the success of old age, to which unfortunately I am liable, and now, to tell you the truth, I had a thought yesterday, these things that were said in those lectures, some of them were truly marvellous. To put it simply, I envy them. I envy the fact that I wish they were part of my real knowledge, not just my intellectual knowledge, and that they could be put into practise in actual work. And then I said, but this is so strange, all these manuscripts of people who have talked in the past are there, one could read them, why don't I read them with some care, and select the wisdom of things said in the past, to work with. Well, anyway, I have a view right now of the whole matter. I believe that this is the Council - The Conference is the Council you were talking about. It has no power, like Ian said, and personally I do not mind that it has no power. I think that every power elicits negativity.

Arkady Rovner: Yes.

Participant 3: ... and why should it have negativity? Why should it not be open to anybody, with no leader, and people take things offered here and work with them to the ability that they can. There are things that have been said here because in most cases they represent a distillation of thinking over a number of years for many people, what is being said. And a good percentage of goodwill, not fully goodwill, but a good percentage of goodwill. I personally believe that if it was an effort of an actual Council to be put together, with by-laws of a strict nature there would be violent reactions left and right, to that point that it would undergo the danger it being destroyed, not only from the outside. Now, to all the things you said I agree, there is one point to disagree. To the use of the word assault.

Arkady Rovner: Well, this definitely was a sort of exaggeration, an attempt to intensify the idea.....

Participant 3: Yes, to make me wake up, I saw that, yes, ok....

Arkady Rovner: I wanted to make it sound striking. I have apparently borrowed this image from symbolist or romantic literature.

Participant 3: I think that there is nothing to be assaulted about the stupid way of life that we live in. I think that one can be profoundly sorry, but I am afraid of assaults. Maybe this is what I am reacting to. Thank you very much again for what you said.

Arkady Rovner: I thank you for what you said. It has great significance to me, and I would gladly replace the word assault, with the word compassion, borrowing it from Stephen's presentation.

Participant 4: If your question about how to take care, or how to preserve the teaching for the future, if it is a real one, and it has a real meaning in the sense that you were presenting it, my question is, to whom does this apply? And my answer is, that it must apply to those who are working in the tradition that Gurdjieff left to his... to the people that worked with him. Because I believe that it is right... that Pentland points out, that this is an oral tradition, and how can this be conserved by those? I can see only one way, and that is that those people apply these ideas to themselves that is that it can only be taken care of through inner personal work. The consequence will be, that will be something, for somebody, I can't see that it is possible to any way organise this outside the direct inner work, and consequences that this inner work has for individuals. And the basis for this is, to take care of one owns imperfections, because the perfections, they will take care of themselves. The work is... exists, as a potential. We are told how to work with this potential. That is the only way it can be preserved, as I see it.

Arkady Rovner: Well, I fully agree that work on oneself is the foundation of everything, and that the process that I have been speaking about in the last part of my presentation cannot be organised, the way we organise enterprises, hotels, businesses. I have stressed the principles of brotherhood as the proven way of transmitting legominism, and I was referring to the early Christian brotherhoods. I could speak of Buddhist brotherhoods and Islamic brotherhoods, as well. These are not societies organised for the sake of enrichment, or for the sake of gaining and increasing power. Brotherhoods are organised for those who are involved in self-transformation, and the Council of enlightened masters of which I have spoken, which was exactly understood by Dimitri, is not a political authority, it has no power, except the power of presence. And the brotherhoods that might be organised for the sake of Work would have no political authority. They would be brotherhoods in the world, in society, not in the mountains or deserts, like it was with Christian monks in most cases. So I don't see a contradiction between the stress on Partkdolgduty, on work involving Conscious Labour and Intentional Suffering, involving different levels of interpretation, and of practises, and of achievements. I think that according to my project, there will be even such levels where people will worship little statues, as we have seen in the chapter on Abram Yelov, so we will have primitive, naive followers and brothers, but we will have also profound levels of achievements and of understanding within this scheme. One does not exclude the other, and the stress is always on inner work and on inner esoteric tasks. So this will create new hierarchy, as this happened with Buddhism and Christianity. This could restructure society, and revitalise society, and bring new purpose to the world we live in. It is an interesting plan to me, and I need help, and I need friends. I have friends in Russia and in Europe who are trying to make first steps in that direction.

Participant 4: What I am trying to come to, is this that, if one starts to think of the consequences of inner work, in terms of brotherhoods, etc, etc, then one opens up for all kinds of imaginary ideas, and it is possible to escape that, to simply not think about it, because what the world needs, in that sense, is people who are working, and I believe that there is a danger in starting to think in these terms of what it will lead to panels of higher levels, and I don't know what. If those panels are to appear, fine, let's see, but let's not look too far ahead. We have this moment here, what are we doing now? You see, there is a danger I see in imagination here, and the source for this kind of imagination from my perspective is that we try to apply a view which is a part of our common suggestibility, that we want everybody to have a nice and good life, etc. I am not sure if it works like that with inner work.

Arkady Rovner: We can't avoid these distortions that you call imagination. We cannot avoid it. It happens anyway. Dimitri was talking about leaks from Gurdjieff's teaching, and distortions that these leaks end up with. We have to trust that Gurdjieff's legominisms will moderate these dangers, and will control the unruly imagination, that the openness will bring about a sense of freedom and a sense of fulfilment. We cannot restrict it; we cannot arrest Gurdjieff's tradition within this prison of what is correct. But we can do correct things, and be an example for those who want to follow this example. It is a challenge that I think it is worthwhile to accept.

Participant 5: This presentation and discussion is arousing considerable sympathetic nervous system stimulation in me. As Dimitri said, most of us think about this question, I think about it intensively as I get older; where is my responsibility? Particularly this question of finding a new language. This brings to mind Mr. Bennett's discussion of the Law of Hazard, and his use of the words Dramatic Universe. If there is nothing at stake, there is no drama. The more that is at stake, the greater the Drama. One cannot not choose. If one does not act, that is still a choice. Of course, the concerns here that people have raised are profound. The establishment of an organisation to counter the Foundation; don't want that. How to avoid politics? Who would be on this Council of masters? I would suggest as the first criteria that anyone who should volunteer that they should be a master should be disqualified. (applause) Where is Ashiata today? This reminds me of my reading of Plato's *Republic* as a young man. I thought this was a great idea, but where do you start? Everything is already corrupted. And yet, there is the question. But as I have listened to this, some preliminary thoughts have come to me that are very interesting; that I think have potential; that should be contingent to explore. I have an image here of perhaps an internet connected international group, but not as an organisation, but as a group of individuals who share a wish to look into the possibility of this kind of aim. Who could perhaps work together from time to time in an attempt to help each other stay sincere rather than isolated groups working in their own locality trying to produce effects in their local area, which we all do to some degree, we already have that kind of model. The sense that at some point work for the Work should include some external manifestation that might bring some quality B influence into our surrounding community. So in one way I see this as just a larger extension, maybe, of that model. How to come together to think through intelligently what today's culture and language would allow or be receptive to as B influences, whether those be writings, or statuettes, perhaps a central place where all work groups could share their ideas, back and forth, so everybody does not have to re-invent the wheel in their own locality; someway to stop the fragmentation due to geography, not just lineage, but geography itself, and have a sharing house of ideas, and people who had an interest in trying to extend their effort beyond their community, at least in helping supporting those who might have access to printing houses or places that manufacture statuettes, could communicate with each other. We now have the internet, and maybe occasionally would be face to face but provide in that way greater resources to practical efforts. There will always be the risk that at some point this would become an organisation with all of the problems that would then ensue but just because there is that initial danger, I think it's an idea worth pursuing.

Arkady Rovner: Just to comment on what you said. I work with groups and individuals in Russia for the last sixteen years, since 1994. We have groups in Russia, Ukraine, and Lithuania, and individuals. Now we have a sort of a brotherhood of those who live far away from each other. We meet once or twice a year for seminars usually in the mountains or the forest, for about two weeks. But we function as a brotherhood in spite of the fact that we are separated, we use heavily Internet and Skype program to communicate. We have Skype conferences; we help each other in many projects and even in personal matters and affairs. So I don't see these Brotherhoods as limited to the same location. They can be international and they can include people from different countries and continents. What matters is sincerity and common striving to the higher ends.

Participant 1: I'd like to pick up where Steve left off, with some comments about organisational structure and what kind of example of organisational structure - you talked of changing the world, so to speak, or having an influence on the world, and I think that the type of organisational structure one would adopt would have an influence on the world, possibly. I am just wondering what type of organisational structure would be an appropriate influence. In your talk you mentioned two basic types of organisational structure, the pyramid structure, top-down, and the de-centralised structure, and today's world is undergoing transformation from the bottom up, with de-centralised organisational structure. With the infrastructure already in place, the Internet, its grown up under our noses over the last ten years, unnoticed by most people, and most governments, who are now scrambling in retrospect to censure, to take peoples free voice away. As far as I can see, the ideal structure is a de-centralised structure, and that pyramid structures are going the way of the dinosaur, and that we should not have anything to do with that type of structure. We need to be interconnected, each person connected to each person directly, not intermediaries or hierarchies. What do you think would be an ideal organisational structure?

Arkady Rovner: Well I agree with your evaluation of centralised, hierarchical structures and de-centralised communities and I think that your question should be addressed to the Council of masters, not to me. I am not inclined to make detailed elaborations on this plan. It is too responsible question to answer, and there are very serious questions that I don't dare to pronounce my verdict on. But then comes in the problem who is a member of this first proto-nucleus, the Council of enlightened masters. Who are those, I can't answer to this question easily, those who take on initiative of materialising this idea of this Council. You remember in Rene Daumal's *Mount Analogue*, there was a writer who fantasised about the *Mount Analogue* that touches both the earth and the heaven, and then there was a person who called him up and recommended to begin the expedition. So I see myself more as a writer with some imaginable *Mount Analogue* in my paper and in my mind, and I depend on somebody approaching me after this meeting will be dismissed and telling me: well, let's begin. So those who will produce this initiative will have the right to do.

Participant 3: We were talking about structure and structure means, some sort of means of people associating. Rules. And as I speak, I cannot forget Terje and his admonition that we can so easily end up talking about other things. I think that he is absolutely right. Except, in the case where structure is the exercise. The thing that makes the brotherhood is that people practise similarly, at least with the same words, because what is going on inside nobody will ever know, except myself, and I will have nobody to tell it to anyway. So I think these are the bonds that can make some sort of reality out of affiliations and brotherhoods, in quotes, or not in quotes, so if we suppose that we are the masters as it is, and nobody is going to apply for the jobs, we just take it. Then the bonds can be a means, the bonds I am talking about, personal contacts can be the means of putting forth the exercise, the way of thinking, the way of approaching work, and whoever picks up the suggestion is part of the brotherhood who works with this suggestion.

Arkady Rovner: Let us just remember of the so called old heretical groups in early Christian history. There were hundreds of them. Everybody had their own theology and their own rituals and their own visions. Eventually Christianity was divided first into two streams, Eastern Christianity, and Western Christianity, then numerous Protestant, Lutheran, Calvinist groups emerged. Christianity is a multi-layered structure, nowadays it is in a big trouble, but for two thousand years the purpose of Christianity's has been fulfilled and it gave inspiration to many great people, composers, painters, spiritualists, writers, and I can see the ideas of Gurdjieff working and reaching humanity in a similar way, not losing at the same time its profound depth, and that display of different approaches and levels is. Splitting is unavoidable; it's already here. We speak of so many lineages, that started with Ouspensky, Bennett, Rodney Collin, Orage, in the first place, and then this splitting continued. I don't know anything about most of your teachers, and you don't know anything about my lineage and my teachers. But we are indebted to our teachers and we learned to love them, and they shaped us up. So we have to admit that and live with that, and search a common ground, that would not reduce us to a primitive level of sharing common ideology, but will elevate us. It is a creative process, a process of Working, and learning together.

Participant 6: Can I suggest a sisterhood as opposed to a brotherhood?

Arkady Rovner: All Brotherhoods could be parts of sisterhoods, so we...

Participant 6: You are saying though...

Arkady Rovner: ...male could have rights to join Sisterhoods, and sisters can come into masculine Brotherhoods, so I don't think Brotherhoods should imply a sexual discrimination. It's just a word.

Participant 7: The problems in Africa, aid going to Africa, which is being dissipated, and wasted has been taken in hand by women, who are now constructively using money to invest in their own labours and infrastructure, wells, and machines for sewing, and has proved the only successful, as yet, system in operation.

Arkady Rovner: But still I am not inclined to discuss the methods of organisation. If I will have access to the Council of competent masters, and you too, then we will discuss organisational matters, but so far I am very grateful to all of you for attention, and for landing your thoughts to what I was thinking about for many years. In July, July 2nd, 3rd, and 4th, we will be at the European Gurdjieffian Congress, in Czech Republic, not far from Prague, initiated by young men, whom I know for about one year. Ian knows him too. Well, it is again an attempt to bring together individuals and groups from France, from Holland, from Germany, from Russia, from Belgium, think and work together. You are all invited, details can be found on our web-site, which is www.gurdjieffclub.com. It is a web-site that we are working on for one year, its in English, and in Russian, and we have facilities to communicate in four more languages, German, French, Italian and Spanish, and we already began working on the German, third language, which is now a part of our site. It is an open platform for exchange; one can find a lot of videos, music, a lot of books, articles, references, and so on. It is just meeting place for all of us. So just please do explore it and find information about the upcoming July meeting of European groups and individuals in Czech Republic.

Participant 8: I just want to share something which I find, certainly I have found quite amusing, it was when we were discussing changing the world. And then suddenly I recognised that here we are, we are approximately thirty-five people, and I find that quite amusing. I don't know.

Participant 1: Thank you Arkady. I think your sincerity has been noted by all here, and I'd just like to end here by saying I think there is one thing that we all do hold in common, and that is a respect for Mr Gurdjieff and the work he did bring, and so on that note I would like to thank you very much for coming to talk to us and letting us know about the work you are carrying on.
Arkady Rovner: Thank you, all of you. (applause)

Seminar 3: Men N1, N2, N3, N4, N5, N6 and N7: Levels of Beings in *Beelzebub's Tales*

Facilitator: Popi Asteri

Introduction

I find it interesting to discuss this topic, because as I was studying the six descents of Beelzebub upon earth, I realized that there was a certain structure. That for every descent, B. recounts a story where there is a central hero, and that through those heroes and their actions Gurdjieff speaks about people who are at different levels of being.

I think that this structure is not accidental and that one of the ways we can look at the descents is this. That is, that G. describes in A&E the inner development of man. And it is certain that in order to describe the development of man he uses the octave.

As he has said: "The division of man into seven categories or seven numbers, explains thousands of things which otherwise cannot be understood. The division gives the first conception of relativity as applied to man." Therefore, I believe it is very useful to exchange views on this matter.

In *Tales* there is a continuous reference to the terms "three-centered" and "three-brained", and to the fact that human beings - while they are three-brained and have the potential to perfect themselves spiritually - due to the unnatural conditions of their usual existence, do not develop harmoniously. It is also mentioned that the quality of existence of humans and the state of their consciousness depends on the harmonious function of all three centers and that when this balance does not exist, the way we perceive our self and the world is one sided and imperfect.

I will try to specify some of those imperfections of men N1, N2 and N3, as they are described by G. in *Tales*, through certain characters that appear mainly in the first three descents. I will also refer to the qualities of man N4, who is mainly described in the fourth descent, through the inner pursuit and actions of Belcultassi - the founder of the Akhaldan society. Through Belcultassi's progress and his efforts to create an esoteric school, G. shows the way through which man N4 acquires the state of consciousness and the being of man N5, and how he is, afterwards, transformed into man N6. Man N7, who is the man who has reached complete development, is described in *Tales* mainly through the Deliberations and the activities of Ashiata Shiemash, and all the other Messengers sent from Above.

Man N3 - In my view, the description of man N3, whose centre of gravity is the intellectual centre, is given by G. in the first descent, through the story of a young and inexperienced kinsman of his, who got into difficulties with King Appolis. G., through this story, describes how unrealistic the ideas that men have about changing the world are. If we examine the matter deeper we will see that all those images of the young kinsman about what has to be done to change the existing situation, is the function of the intellectual centre. The intellectual centre, on its own, cannot appreciate the situation fully. It proves that it is inept and futile to want to change the mechanical flow of things, without taking into consideration all the consequences that our actions will have. At the same time I believe that through this story G. also shows the way for inner growth of man N3.

His path goes through the contrition he feels when, due to the problems caused by applying his ideas; he experiences the state of consciousness that, in Christian terminology is conveyed with the phrase: "Poor in Spirit". In the case of the young idealist, the realization of reality comes when Beelzebub's young kinsman understands how unrealistic his ideas are. Beelzebub's young kinsman represents every man N3 that has the potential to develop. He undertook the responsibility that, in case of failure of his methods, he would give the money to king Appolis himself. The person who does not have the potential to develop can undertake no responsibility. At the same time, through this story of the young kinsman and king Appolis, G. sheds light to the painful results that this one-sided perception of reality had and will have on mankind. This is the main cause of the procedure of revolution that has been repeated many times on this earth and has caused much suffering.

As he characteristically says:

"And during their revolution of that time, as it has also become proper there to these three-brained phenomena of our Great Universe, they destroyed a great deal of the property which they had accumulated during centuries, much of what is called the 'knowledge' which they had attained during centuries also was destroyed and lost forever, and the existence of those other beings similar to themselves who had already chanced upon the means of freeing themselves from the consequences of the properties of the organ Kundabuffer were also destroyed." (p.118, 119)

Man N2 - In chapter 19 that has to do with the events that took place during the second descent, G. through the description of the actions of the High-Priest Abdil depicts the image of man N2, the man whose gravity centre is the emotional centre. The High-Priest Abdil, who helped B. to eliminate the custom of offering sacrifices, is murdered by the other priests in the end. His sincere wish to do good to his environment, cost him many sufferings, his life itself. High-Priest Abdil is man N2 who acts following his emotions. He preaches and defends his beliefs and he makes dedicated enemies who finally kill him. Man N2 cannot assess the existing situation and draw an effective course of action. He acts exclusively following his emotions. He is the hero who sacrifices even his self for his ideas. In contradistinction to Abdil's actions we have the actions of B., who, during his descents on earth, in order to achieve his goals, uses indirect course of action, drawing, every time, a plan that takes into consideration the circumstances that prevail in every area, the mentality of the people and the prevailing beliefs. And High-Priest Abdil is the man N2 who has the potential of inner development.

Seminar 3

As it is mentioned in the text:

"The function of conscience, fundamental for three-centred beings, which had been transmitted to his presence by heredity, had not yet become quite atrophied in him." (p.188)

When he places himself in the service of a higher cause his path goes through his contrition and grief that he feels, when the other high-priests attack him, when the men that he believed in abandon him.

Man N1 - In his third flight to the earth in the city of Gob in the continent of Asia B. finds another ally in his struggle to eliminate the terrible custom of offering sacrifices, a man who was the owner of a big "Chaihana". B mentions that, although, they became related with close friendship bonds, he did not feel for him the same appeal he felt for high-priest Abdil and he doesn't even mention his name. Through the description of his anonymous friend who believed in the religious doctrine, which B. invented, without even asking any questions, G. gives us the image of man N1, the man whose centre of gravity of psychic life lies in the moving centre. The moving centre learns through imitation. The man, who has as his centre of gravity the moving centre, believes what most people believe and adopts, without question, the views of the society in which he lives. G., through the funny images of the people who believed in the religious doctrine and started bowing before animals and treating them with particular honor, sheds light on the causes of an unnatural peculiarity of the psyche of men, suggestibility, which he considers to be the most dangerous of all, and the cause of its appearance is the fact that men have stopped exercising their "being Partkdolg duties".

Man N4 - From the fourth descent G. begins to refer to the inner humanity, to the people who, with their conscious labour and intentional sufferings pursue entering the "Kingdom of Heaven". The state of consciousness of man N4 is revealed through the inner pursuit of Belcultassi the founder of the Akhaldan society. Belcultassi, through his efforts for the perfection of his self and his efforts to establish an esoteric school he was able to bring the perfecting of his higher being part to the Being of a Saint 'Eternal Individual'. The "Saint Eternal Individual" is the man N6. All his actions reveal the passage from the level of man N4, to the level of man N5 and the level of man N6. There are many references in A&E to the qualities of man N4, let us summarize the main ones:

1 - Man N4 knows the way, in which, through meditation, he can absorb consciously the sacred cosmic substances that constitute the second and third being-food, substances that are necessary for the arising and existence of higher being-parts.

In the chapter " the holy planet Purgatory" G. says:

"The beings of the continent Atlantis then called the second being-food 'Amarloos,' which meant 'help-for-the-moon,' and they called the third being-food the 'sacred Amarhoodan,' and this last word then signified for them 'help-for-God.'"

And further on he says:

"And, namely, in view of the fact that in them, together with the cessation of the intentional absorption of these definite cosmic substances necessary for the arising and existence of higher being-parts, there disappeared from their common presences not only the striving itself for perfection but also the possibility of what is called 'intentional contemplativeness,' which is just the principal factor for the assimilation of those sacred cosmic substances." (Purgatory p. 783).

2 - The man, who works on himself, at the moments he works, is subjected to the "Foolasnitamnian" principle.

In chapter 23 (Fourth descent) at the point where he analyses the symbolism of the statue that was the emblem of the Akhaldan society, which was called consciousness, there are five qualities that man who works on himself has to develop.

The five qualities:

1 - Indefatigable labours for perfection of the self
2 - labors should be performed with that cognizance and feeling of courage and faith in one's might.
3 - That during the said labours and with the mentioned inner psychic properties of self-respect, it is necessary to meditate continually on questions not related to the direct manifestations required for ordinary being-existence
4 - Love should predominate always and in everything during the inner and the outer functionings evoked by one's consciousness
5 - this Love should be strictly impartial
(p.310-311)

Man N5 - It is the stage where the man who works on himself can impartially observe the inner struggle that takes place inside of him between his contradictory parts and be able to find a balance among the active and the passive force within him. G. is referred to the state of consciousness of man N5 in *Meetings with Remarkable Men*: "Only he will deserve the name of man and can count upon anything prepared for him from Above, who has already acquired corresponding data for being able to preserve intact both the wolf and the sheep confided to his care". In this sense one of the main qualities that characterizes the person who is in the state of man N5, is impartiality.

During the Fifth flight to earth B. meets a wise man from Assyria Hamolinadir, who, according to the narration, had received education in Egypt at a school superior to all those existing on earth at the time, which was known by the name "School for the Materialization of Thought".

As he mentions in the same chapter:

"At the age he was when I fist met him he already had his "I" - in respect of rationally directing what is called the automatic-psychic-functioning" of his common presence- at the maximum stability for three-centered beings of the planet Earth at that time, in consequence of which during what is called his "waking-passive-state" he had very definitely expressed being-manifestations, as for instance, those called "self-consciousness," "impartiality", "sincerity", "sensibility of perception", alertness" and so forth." (p. 332, 333)

According to the narration Hamolinadir spoke at a scientific conference, fifth on the row, on the subject: "The Instability-of Human-Reason". We have an additional indication of the status of Hamolinadir in the fact that not only did B. meet him on his 5th descent but he was also the fifth speaker in the conference. G. through Hamolinadir describes the person who realizes that intellectual knowledge is not enough and that the mind is incomplete in front of the great existential issues, like the issue of "soul", or the great mystery of life and death. He knows a lot, he can see the contradictions inside of him, but he cannot stand impartially in front of what he experiences.According to the narration after this conference Hamolinadir was never occupied with "sciences" and that he spent his existence only in planting "choongary". I think that his main effort should be to find a balance between the active and the passive force within him.

Man N6 - In A&E there are references to many people who managed through their conscious efforts and intentional suffering to promote the perfection of their higher being-parts to the being of a Saint "Eternal Individual" and this higher part resides today in the Holy Planet Purgatory. Among others there are Belcultassi, Poundolero and "Sensimiriniko" the two initiates of the brotherhood "Tchaftantouri" etc.At that point we have to point out the following: in the sixth descent there is no mention of a certain person we could describe as man N6. But as G. himself has said, the keys to the understanding of *Tales* are not near the locks. In order to understand that there is this kind of structure in the six descents we have to take into consideration what is mentioned in chapter 26, that is, that he found out about the facts concerning Ashiata Shiemash during his sixth descent. According to the text:

"So, my boy, when, as I have already told you, early in my last descent in person on the surface of your planet I first became acquainted in detail with this Legominism, that is "the Terror of the situation."

"And so, as one of my chief tasks during this last sojourn of mine in person there, on the surface of your planet, I made a detailed investigation and elucidation of the whole of the further Very Saintly Activities there among your favorites of that Great Essence-loving now most High Very Saintly Common Cosmic Individual Ashiata Shiemash." (p. 360-361)

That is the case with S. Buddha as well. He found out about the facts concerning S. Buddha during his sixth descent. (p.241)

I think that through the teaching of Ashiata Shiemash, as for example, the 'being-obligolnian-strivings' and the references to the brothers of the brotherhood Heechtvori, created by himself, who in order to become all-the-rights-possessing brothers of the brotherhood Heechtvori, should initiate a hundred more people, G. shows the way through which man N5 acquires the state of consciousness and the being of man N6.

The state of consciousness and the being of man N6 is the highest level which people can reach through their conscious labor and their intentional sufferings. One of the main qualities characteristic in man N6, is described by the phrase written on the inscription placed over the chief entrance of the Holy Planet Purgatory:

"ONLY-HE-MAY-ENTER-HERE-WHO-PUTS- HIM-SELF-IN- THE -POSITION-OF-THE-OTHER-RESULTS-OF-MY- LABORS." (p. 1164)

Man N7 - Men N7, as mentioned in A&E are all the ones sent from Above, who were sent to earth by our Common Father aiming at regulating, somehow, the existence of three-centered beings and coordinating it with universal harmony.

In the Introduction he mentions:

"Although the solar system "Ors" had been neglected owing to its remoteness from the center and to many other reasons, nevertheless our LORD SOVEREIGN had sent from time to time HIS Messengers to the planets of this system, to regulate, more or less, the being-existence of the three-brained beings arising on them, for the co-ordination of the process of their existence with the general World Harmony." (p. 53-54)

In the chapter "Religion" he mentions that:

"During my observations on the process of the existence of these peculiar three-brained beings, there had been many times actualized from Above, in the common presences of certain of them, the germs of these Sacred Individuals…" (p. 698)

What I gather from those texts and other references is that men N7 come to earth only from Above. That ordinary people through their conscious labour and intentional sufferings can reach up to level of man N6.

The Messengers sent from Above as they appear in A & E (p. 699, 725) are seven:

Saint Ashiata Shiemash	
Saint Krishnatkharna	
Saint Buddha	1) The Buddhistic
Saint Moses	2) The Hebrew
Saint Christ	3) The Christian
Saint Mohammed	4) The Mohammedan
Saint Lama	5) The Lamaist

The teaching of Ashiata Shiemash is on Objective Conscience.
The teaching of Saint Buddha is on Objective Reason.
The teaching of Jesus Christ is on Conscious Love.

Seminar Discussion

Popi Asteri: This was the introduction, if you wish to discuss something or if you need some more information, there are also some relevant extracts from A&E, which support these ideas and we could read them if you like.

MC: I think with the time left, it would be better spent asking questions, for people to ask questions, and the other comments could be included in the proceedings.

Popi Asteri: Ok.

MC: Does anyone have a question or a comment?

I would ask a question, in that case. Is it possible or how would it be possible for one of us, a normal human being, anyone here, as you say to become a man N7, is it possible for any of us, to, at some point in our future, to become man N7?

Popi Asteri: I believe we can reach the point of Man N6 only. Men N7 can come only from above. Gurdjieff says this in the Tails.

Participant 1: So, the answer is yes, but you have to die first.

Participant 2: Could you please repeat the last sentence mentioned in man N6? I didn't catch it.

Popi Asteri: One of the main qualities?

Participant 2: Yes, please.

Popi Asteri: One of the main qualities characteristic in man N6 is described by the phrase written in the inscription placed over the chief entrance of Holly Planet Purgatory: "Only he may enter here, who puts himself in the position of the other results of my labors."

Participant 2: So, what are the other results of His labors? I wonder; can anyone help?

MC: Well, the other results of His labors would be the whole of creation, and everything in it, maybe. Could one put oneself in the position of a man N7, as a man N7?

Participant 6: We have an image here, of six descents, possibly with six points on an enneagram. My urge would be to see if there is any practical advice that Gurdjieff here gives for Work-besides them being stories. Could I extract somehow-how could I extract-in one way or another, ways of working. Can I see these texts as offering the possibility of extracting from them, ways of working? I'm just stating my concern, the question I have. It is a question brought about by Popi's interpretation. This is six levels of men. Do we have, in what it says, practical advice how to work in the groups? Can we truly take this advice to be practical for Work in the groups?

I'm not going to answer my question; I just want to say a joke that Nick told me this morning. He said, spiritual effort is an ascend to a high mountain, and when you get to the top you see two signs, one says toward Nirvana, toward Heavens-to Heaven-and the other one says to lectures about Heaven, and Nick said that all Europeans go to the lectures. I suppose the Americans, as well. It is the god guys that go to Heaven. So, is this lectures about Heaven, or is it somehow we can get to Heaven through extracting ways of working from the text?

Participant 5: Of course it's very complex and there are all sorts of ways of looking at the descents. But Dimitri asked if there is anything practical and I can only try and remember that I have to see in the book myself, on every page, so whether this is man N 1, 2, 3, 4, 5, 6 or 7-I'm not sure about that, but I'm certainly not disputing it-but these descents for me would be, in a practical sense, certain stages in Work. At the beginning, I cannot come within and solve these inner problems that have conditioned me, so I have to create something outside of myself-which I call an 'I'-which will observe me impartially, but this 'I' also has a quality of benevolence, so it has not only an impartial view of me, it has a benevolence towards me; and it wishes to come closer to me, to help me solve some problems connected with my behavior. So initially, at the beginning of the book, Beelzebub is on Mars observing the life on the planet, which is me, my body, and all its movements, and the life within; but after some time I have to come down closer to myself to solve all the tendencies that are preventing me from developing further. And I see these six descents as this 'I' coming closer to me, to draw my attention to my tendencies and my behavior which are unbecoming. So, that's just a kind of simplification about how practical these six descents are, obviously there's a lot more involved in that.

Participant 7: What I found very practical in listening to this presentation is that I could easily recognize parts of myself in it. States of mind, or even certain characteristics, not necessarily of one type of man, but different types of men, as they are described here; I mean I can easily see me twenty or thirty years ago believing that I could change the world just by taking part in a political party or something. And I can easily recognize the contrition and the grief, at some point, when I realized-I started realizing-how futile this may be and that I cannot really do anything else but work on myself and that's the only thing I have, that's the only thing I can somehow change.

Participant 8: In light of negativity, seems to me that the different steps in development also indicate ability to deal with this negativity. Man N4 is not free of negativity, it's not something that belongs only to 1, 2 and 3 and the next step from dealing with negativity, in the sense of being able to digest it and use it, there is needed very long preparation-mainly in self remembering-so that one gets prepared to be able to nourish oneself from the negativity which still is in the machine-the second conscious shock. And I think it is easy to have the idea that man N5 and N6, which we hardly can speak of, I think, especially man N5; does it have this attitude towards, that's free from negativity? I don't think so. It's able to deal with it, to be nourished by it.

Popi Asteri: I think that it is very useful for anyone to know, when he thinks of changing the world or when he wants to sacrifice himself fanatically for some cause, or when he accepts what he hears around him, in the society-and he accepts it without any criticism-that these are one-sided functions of certain centers. That when he is in a state of meditation, and can perceive the second and the third kind of being food, through the perception of energies that go through him, that this is the level of man N4. And when he feels the contradiction inside of him and can continue his life carrying these contradictions and transforming the negative emotions, that this is the state of man N5; and that these levels are not permanent but when I am at these levels, I can understand it. Of course we cannot easily speak about the level of man N6 but we can understand what is said in the texts. And it is explicitly mentioned in the texts that this level can be attained by somebody when he is a member of a school, which in a way has the purpose of transmitting the teachings to the feature. These are the ideas that I want to convey, so I used the text for this reason.

Participant 9: I don't know if I heard right, are there two entrances to the Holly Planet Purgatory? Is this correct?

Popi Asteri: No, he mentions one entrance, the chief entrance. It says in the chief entrance.

Participant 9: So, there might be another one. I think there must be some significance to that. I think there's some meaning there, I don't know what.

Participant 10: I've heard the story several times and I don't know its origins, so perhaps someone here certainly can tell me, but it's the parable of the man who dies and goes to Heaven and comes up to the gate and there is a long line of people-it's these people waiting to get in-a very, very long line and over the gate is the word "Wisdom". And he figures, well he has eternity, but this is a very long line, so he continues walking along the wall and he comes to another gate with a very long line of people and the legend over this gate is "Beauty". Well, he certainly has more than enough time on his hand so he keeps exploring, comes to one gate after another, enormous lines, one virtue after another over the gate and finally after a long walk he notices a gate and there is nobody there and he looks up and over the gate is the word "Humiliation", and he walks right in.

Participant 6: So, in fact, if I am right, Nick, Popi's description about going into different levels within me would cover your point of view?

Participant 3: So, from your description there appeared to be levels of detachment as we are going up the levels of man N1,2,3,4,5,6 and now that I had time to reflect on foot you just read for me, putting oneself in the place of another my fruits of my labor, maybe it's another person, it implies perhaps a sort of sacrifice. And something that ties in with the previous talk that we had with Arcady was this question: How is knowledge perpetuated throughout the ages or how is communication possible between people. And it seems to me that there are many lines of Work;

you have written five of them at least. These lines of Work, as long as one is confined within that particular tradition-with its jargon and way of working-which might be the way of the yogi, the way of the monk, the way of the fakir or even the fourth way, one is still limited as to whom one can convey knowledge because people in the street or people in the world do not share the same language. So, in order to communicate one has to be able to transform that teaching within oneself and let go of the jargon and in a very natural way be able to speak naturally to another person. But the information will carry something of the flavor of the type of work that one has been doing, which involves a certain letting go and sacrifice perhaps of one's personal struggle within the school, so that one can objectively be able to convey something to the outside world in a more impartial way, if I'm using the term correctly, in a more objective way.

Participant 6: I believe you are touching upon a very serious problem, that of language, not only in the sense that Gurdjieff uses, that we should learn a new language, but also in the sense that is used in everyday exchanges, the world language. To what extend are carried away by language? It is the problem, I think, that is under what you said, the question: Does language carry us away from what we really want to say from experience? And, I think, to give an answer, to begin to give an answer to that, we would come to: How direct are we? How awake are we to experience, what is happening right now? If we were to imagine ourselves to be awake to what is happening right now, then both people that want to communicate, that is, maybe they 'd have some difficulty selecting the right word but eventually they would communicate, because there would be a mutual experience. At that very moment there would be communication, direct communication, in the body sense even. So, they could just be naming things that they see inside of themselves and they would be agreeing because the relationship they would be describing would be similar, or identical. The problem of communicating with a language that comes from another school is the minute that you are using words as symbols, as prefabricated references to things that do not have value at that moment, so again communication in that way, through language, is a matter of being awake or being asleep.

Participant 3: And also the significance, the meaning one attaches, so to say. That this chair is brown is something that we might all agree with, but how brown it is and how significant that is to me, that's where a lot of differences, and opinions, and arguments arise. So, one school might say, love is the most important, the other one says no.

Participant 6: No, no, this is completely theoretical, what you say right now. Because love would be meaningful if love was present the moment it was discussed and I was present to my self to see what was there. So, in an awakened state the problem does not exist. It is if we refer to other things, if we talk about Heaven that the problem exists, not if we are in Heaven.

Participant 3: So, if people share experience, if they have the experience they can communicate. If they don't have the experience, then it's theoretical.

Participant 6: I think, in fact, that this is what makes group work so important. Because the group is the natural place where experiences can mature and become identical; and then the problem of communication goes into second perspective, it's not so important, the problem of selecting the right word to communicate, because the reality of experience is identical. And this can only happen in a group situation, as far as I understand. I just haven't seen it ever happening in my life in a situation outside the group situation that experiences mature to be identical. So the problem of communication, the solution to communicate is taken away from language. You do not depend on this prefabricated set of symbols to communicate.

Participant 10: We are talking about levels of being and this reminds me that in the Ashiata Shiemash story the order dissolves, sects disappear, hierarchical levels disappear, and leaders are chosen by the community who sense the quality of the being of certain individuals. In *Meetings with Remarkable Men* we have the two monks, Brother Sez and Brother Ahl, who travel around and lecture. I believe it's brother Sez, who speaks wonderfully and eloquently and everyone thinks his words are wonderful, and the other brother mumbles. And yet, a short while after they depart no one remembers what the eloquent fellow said, but something that came from the quality that the older inarticulate monk resonates. And in *In Search of the Miraculous* a great point is made that in order to be born again, one must die first and that a man must die to himself and see his nothingness. And I say, think about it, conceptualize about it, this sounds like an experience. So, I'm looking at this and wondering, how would we understand or can we have a near understanding of where, in terms of these levels of men, the level of experience of seeing one's nothingness and dying to oneself ought to appear?

Participant 3: So, to me, within words in a language, speaking of the Holly Planet Purgatory, those words mean to me the experiential realization of the fundamental unity of everything.

Participant 8: I have a question, my experience is that my states and my understanding fluctuate, so what I understand in one moment can leave me, and I have to reach it again. I just want to comment on the point that Dimitri is making, the necessity of a group and when an experience is reduced to a concept it is easy then to forget about the whole experience and communication can then take place only on the level of that reduction, concepts, concepts, concepts. I think, this is one important thing with the group, that it can be again and again pointed out that the map and the landscape are never the same. However delicate the map, it's never the same as the landscape. And that is something that can be understood through repetitious situations where it is pointed out.

Popi Asteri: I want to say something. All these ideas are like closed doors that can open only through exercise, through practice in Gurdjieff's groups. What we can do here in a seminar like that is simply to mention which these doors are. And one of these doors is "to feel my nothingness" that was mentioned before, to feel that I am "poor in spirit". One of these doors is when somebody feels the grief because what he expects to happen doesn't happen, as in the case of Abdil. But I believe that this map can help.

Participant 5: I was thinking about the fourth descent, which is of a completely different flavor from the first three descents, and for me the fourth descent, it's such a critical descent that is almost the linchpin or the anchor and I think that the fourth descent is at the far bridge and I introduce something else at that far bridge something outside in order to be developed, but the far bridge itself of Kesdjan, I still have sol, la, si of Kesdjan to go and there is a lot of…We mention, at the top of our heads, in almost every discussion about intentional suffering as it is something we do every day. And this is… "Oh yes, we do this every day". But, for me, intentional suffering is at the state of Purgatory. Purgatory is a state of Work, an emotional state, which has arrived at a very late stage in Work when I have reached the si do of my Kesdjan body. And I am at that time on a level with the far bridge of the soul body, and the far bridge of the soul body, for me, is Purgatory; where then, it's only at that period that I can introduce real intentional suffering, because if I introduce intentional suffering beforehand, I have absolutely no foundation within myself to tolerate intentional suffering. And there are so many different explanations about what intentional suffering is that it's very difficult to talk about it. There are so many differences of opinion but if I am at the "only God can complete the si do of my Kesdjan body", that last semitone is such a concentration of energy that unfortunately being in Work because I've arrived perhaps at that level and I've done all this work myself that I am entitled to complete that octave, and I don't think that that's the case. I think, the case comes when only God can complete the si do of Kesdjan body and that's at the level of intentional suffering and we talked about masters this morning and we are all actually masters, but we are all masters at avoiding suffering, and that's the problem. That's what Purgatory is about, that I've been provided with this planet, that all the beautiful birds, the trees, the flowers, everything is absolutely wonderful, but I have to sit in my cage because all the chemicals of my behavior prevent me from moving to the next step. And it's all these opinions about my life, my needs, my desires my wants; I want two cars, I want four chickens in the pot, all this stuff that prevents us from moving to the next step has to be got rid of and I can't move to the next step until that has taken place. And, for me, intentional suffering is a very profound and courageous step to take, but it can't be taken unless I have a foundation within me.

MC: I think that's a good note to end this seminar. So, I'd like to thank Popi and her crew, her triad, for leading us through this. Thank you.

End of Session

Notes:

We have to point out certain things:

In order to have a more complete view of the events described in the 6 descents of B. on earth we have to take into consideration three different time frames:

- That the actual time frame, during which the narration takes place, is during their journey in the spaceship Karnak, from the planet Karatas to the planet Revozvradendr that belongs to the solar system "Pandetznokh", after Beelzebub's return from exile.

- Everything concerning the Akhaldan society, which is mentioned for the first time during his fourth visit on Earth, had happened 735 years before the destruction of Atlantis, that is, during his first descent upon Earth.

- The same applies to the events concerning Ashiata Shiemash.

The events he recounts had taken place seven centuries before the Babylonian events, that is, before the fifth descent of Beelzebub on Earth.

- That the events concerning Ashiata Shiemash and S. Buddha became known to B. during his sixth descent on Earth.

It would be interesting to mention here that the sixth time B. had come to Earth was a while before he was pardoned and was permitted to return to planet Karatas: It was the year 223 after the creation of the World according to the objective time measurement, or as they would say here on Earth the year 1921 after the birth of Christ.

The six descents of Beelzebub on Earth

First great disaster. - Collision of Earth with the comet Kondoor. - The moon and Annolios break away from the Earth.

The First Descent of Beelzebub upon the planet Earth

City "Samlios", which was the capital of the continent of "Atlantis" - The leader of that great community was "the King Appolis" - The story of a young and inexperienced kinsman of his, who got into difficulties with King Appolis. - In the first descent there was the Akhaldan society in the continent of Atlantis).

Second great catastrophe. (Second Transapalnian perturbation) - The loss of Atlantis

---

Second descent of Beelzebub on the planet Earth

11 centuries after his first descent (Asia, Caspian Sea, city "Koorkalai'- Priest Abdil-his aim was to extirpate a religious custom of Sacrificial-Offerings that existed in all the religions of the three-brained beings of the planet Earth.

All & Everything Conference 2010

Third descent of Beelzebub on Earth
a) Asia, Sea of Beneficence, city of Gob, King Konuzion, descendant of a wise member of the Akhaldan society - Doctrine of Heaven and Hell - His aim, the same as in the second descent. b) Visit to India (Mention to Saint Buddha. c) Visit to Tibet.

Fourth Personal Sojourn of Beelzebub on the planet Earth
(Africa - "The Red Sea" - City of Thebes, which at the time was the capital of what later became Egypt-Mention of Deloultossi founder of the Akhaldan society, which was founded 735 years before the loss of Atlantis.)

Third catastrophe due to powerful winds- the centers of their civilization were destroyed, that is, the main part of the countries of Tikliamish and Maralpleicie in Asia and the area in the center of the continent of Grabontzi (Africa), which is the desert Sahara today- that time was called the time of the Great- trans-migration- of the races.

Fifth Flight of Beelzebub to the Planet Earth
(Persian Gulf, City of Babylon - the aim of Beelzebub was to investigate the reasons of the diminishing duration of existence of the beings on planet Earth-a heated issue of the wise men of Babylon: the issue of the soul-Hamolinadir)

The sixth and last sojourn of Beelzebub on the planet Earth
Asia, Afghanistan - Visit to Russia, France etc. - His aim was to study the strange particularity of their psyche to destroy the existence of other beings similar to them - Beelzebub made a detailed investigation and elucidation of the Activities of the Very Saintly Ashiata Shiemash

Seminar 4: The Implied Mechanical Transformation in *Beelzebub's Tales*

Facilitator: Mike Readshaw

Introduction

To take the wrong road can be almost as long as a short cut, or, what was Gurdjieff really teaching?

1. The mind that wakes up is not the mind that is asleep.

2. The Gurdjieff was not teaching ideas but was initiating in his pupils a transformation, or awakening, that takes place of itself, automatically, by itself, mechanically(Gurdjieff's words! BT p24/25) and which takes place outside the person, without the awareness of the person, and takes about 30 years (my experience).

3. BT consists of a ladder of teachings, none of which appear in any of the established literature, with the bottom rung being the comparison between the 'vices' at the start of this transformation, the ordinary man, (using the words ordinary, abnormal, external) and the 'virtues' at the end (normal man). The second rung consists of the 64 'essences of certain real notions' (BT p24/25). Third rung, Gurdjieff's use of remorseful rhythm, and so on.

Before continuing this first chapter, which is by way of an introduction to all my further predetermined writings, I wish to bring to the knowledge of what is called your pure waking consciousness, the fact that in the writings following this chapter of warning, I shall expound my thoughts intentionally in such sequence and with such logical confrontation that the essence of certain real notions may of themselves automatically so to say go from this waking consciousness, which most people in their ignorance mistake for the real consciousness, but which I affirm and experimentally prove is the fictitious one, into what you call the subconscious, which ought to be, in my opinion, the real human consciousness, and there by themselves mechanically bring about that transformation which should, in general, proceed in the entirety of a man, and give him, from his own conscious mentation, the results he ought to have, which are proper to man, and not merely to single or double-brained animals." (BT p. 24/25)

Mike Readshaw: I am not in any Gurdjieff group. I have never been in a Gurdjieff group. And so I am outside. I have never actually worked on myself, either, so I am outside the Gurdjieff teaching, in that sense, also. In coming to this conference, I asked myself how could I contribute to it, in those circumstances? It occurred to me that being outside the Gurdjieff teaching, as it were, I could provide a viewpoint from outside, on that teaching, that might be perhaps useful for those inside the Gurdjieff tradition. Sometimes it is easier to see something, or one does see something differently, from outside.

I first read BT at university, which is now over thirty five years ago, and I have kept going back to this book ever since. And one of the things I noticed, that stands out, when you are outside, as it were, the Gurdjieff tradition, and don't belong to a Gurdjieff group - one of the things that stands out - is that there seems to be a very big difference between the Gurdjieff/Ouspensky/Fourth Way teaching, which appears in Ouspensky's *In Search of the Miraculous* , it appears in the books - all the books - on Gurdjieff, on all the web-sites, which you can go to, on Gurdjieff, films about Gurdjieff, magazine articles about Gurdjieff, there seems to be - looking from outside - there seems to be an enormous difference between this and what Gurdjieff himself actually wrote. When thinking about this, in the 1980s, I went back to BT, and started to read it with this in mind. And I didn't actually have to go very far, because I got to page 24, and I got stuck. I got stuck on this paragraph, and it is a paragraph in the introduction to BT. It is a paragraph everyone reads. Everyone who even tries to read BT should surely get that far?

Participant: Will you read it for us?

Mike Readshaw: Yes, yes. Thank you. I will.

I got stuck on this paragraph because it seemed to me, and I have chosen this paragraph for this seminar because I will be very interested to listen to what people have to say, or other peoples impressions of this paragraph. As I say, I have been stuck on it. I am hoping that, by listening to what other people will say, I will be able to move on, after twenty five years, - to the next paragraph!

If I could stand up and read it. This is what the paragraph says.

I chose this paragraph because it seems to - there seems to be nothing in this paragraph that bears any resemblance to anything in the Gurdjieff traditional teaching, and there are some words that I found, certainly in the 1980's, and since, very, very unusual.

(NB. The paragraph is from the introduction to BT, entitled: The Arousing of Thought. This title has seven syllables, and so, the paragraph was read by me, in my usual way, between the commas, and with a corresponding seven second pause at each comma. MR.)

"I wish to bring to the knowledge of what is called your 'pure waking consciousness' the fact that in the writings following this chapter of warning I shall expound my thoughts intentionally in such sequence and with such 'logical confrontation,' (*seven second pause*) that the essence of certain real notions may of themselves automatically, (*seven second pause*) so to say, (*seven second pause*) go from this 'waking consciousness' (*seven second pause*) - which most people in their ignorance mistake for the real consciousness, (*seven second pause*) but which I affirm and experimentally prove is the fictitious one (*seven second pause*) - into what you call the subconscious, (*seven second pause*) which ought to be in my opinion the real human consciousness, (*seven second pause*) and there by themselves mechanically bring about that transformation which should in general proceed in the entirety of a man and give him, (*seven second pause*) from his own conscious mentation, (seven second pause) the results he ought to have, (*seven second pause*) which are proper to man and not merely to single- or double-brained animals." (BT p. 24/25).

Now I wondered if you would like to perhaps talk about that. I will point out first one or two of the things that I found rather strange in this. I wondered what were these, or this, essence of certain real notions? Then there were the words 'of themselves automatically.' Of course, Gurdjieff says that our real consciousness here is our subconsciousness, - our subconscious. Then there are the words ' by themselves mechanically?' Now I, a long time ago, I read *In Search of the Miraculous*, and that was the word, - mechanically - I suddenly thought: that is a bit strange. 'Bring about that transformation... giving the results a man ought to have, proper to man.' Of themselves, automatically, by themselves, mechanically.

Now when I read that, I found that rather strange - I don't know whether you agree? And, twenty five years on, I still do.

I am happy to throw the floor open to any comments you might have, and I will be happy to listen.

Seminar Discussion

Participant 2: I have noticed, when I have read the text, that some part of me is informed in another way, that my usual breathing apparatus absorbs, so I am not opposed to what you say. But I think that the book is such a strange and remarkable book that I have a problem in accepting that it is the only purpose, that I go along with it that that is part of what takes place.

Participant 3: There are two things I want to say, at this point. Maybe later on there will be more interesting things to say.

The way I read this, is: there, by themselves mechanically bring about the transformation which should proceed in the entirety of a man and give him - through this transformation, but from his own conscious mentation, the results he ought to have which are proper to man and not merely to single- or double-brained animals. In other words, the way I read this, is that there is something mechanical happening, then, but should pass through his conscious mentation to bring about results. That is one.

The other thing I want to say is that in the chapter of Heptaparaparshinokh, I happen to remember this, not because I remember the book by heart, - by no means - it just happened to be a part of my presentation which I did read, last year, and it has to do with the three wills, the will of man, which I interpreted in the enneagram I showed, as the will of man and woman to procreate, - the will coming from the species - and then the will of cells uniting to form larger organisms, the will of organic life, and then the will of God, when it says that this is a will, this is getting together substances, aggregation of the similar, the name is, if I remember correctly, by which substances can collect within Tetartocosmoses, or within human bodies, and mechanically cause something that, if I remember correctly, is to create higher bodies, and then, that is said in one chapter 39, and, which is the chapter on Purgatory, on the thirtieth chapter, it repeats that, as if it created some sort of shock, to the ears of Hassein, and he comes back and says: I ought to explain to you about this mechanical thing, the way substances in a mechanical fashion. And, I do not remember the entire paragraph, I don't know, maybe you have it as some part of your presentation here? The idea is that all the things necessary are placed there, like, a kernel, - that was the word, I think - kernel, placed in man, all the, he calls them, active elements, as a matter of fact, and they are placed in man, for this kernel - yes, for this kernel - to sprout. So, yes, he definitely wants to say that there are certain things placed there in man, mechanically, but still the way I understand it, in that paragraph as well, never is the idea of conscious mentation taken out of the cycle necessary to fulfil.

Now, of course, the idea is, the way that I understand it, that higher forces have a vested interest in man acquiring higher being bodies - it is not that he has to do all the work himself - they wish for him, they do everything for him, to acquire higher being bodies. Unfortunately, he also has to do something about it.

Participant 1: Unfortunately, Mike, I have twenty two pages of notes... (laughter)

Mike Readshaw: Well, come on then.

Participant 1: I don't have time, so I will give the salient points.

Mike Readshaw: That's what we need.

Participant 1: I should preface what I am saying. I think it's, what he says, in this paragraph, is actually an experience. And, it is, depending on certain qualifications, and Dimitri mentioned one, that the important thing is conscious mentation. And what is conscious mentation? And what is 'logical confrontation'? And he tells you that it is written to deliberately, and to select one sentence, that can cause within you an internal cacophonous effect. It has a cacophonous effect, and this is a very interesting statement he makes, amongst many others in this chapter, and what he is leading up to saying, to me, is that the way you read this paragraph - and you didn't read it mechanically, you hesitated at every comma, practically, like you described the other night, and that is something I have an experience with - and that really does create a tremendous friction, internally, because one part of me wants to and objects strongly from me reading this book mechanically, and the other part wants me to hurry it up and get this over as fast as I can. That is yes and no. But for me the real effect, what he is talking about there, is that I have to introduce a third element. And it is the third element which gives me the transformation. From this paragraph, what he is describing, that that third element is the reconciling factor impartiality, because the yes and no only create friction, which is destructive. But if I can add impartiality, I can then create, as he describes it in the chapter on form and sequence, because here Gurdjieff elaborates this whole problem, which you have just stated, in the chapter on form and sequence, and it is said exactly what you said, it is the law of three. There has to be the affirming, the denying, and the reconciling. Then will the certain notions, the essence of certain notions, even if I can't introduce the reconciling principle, if I ponder some of those notions - and the pondering takes place in a different part of my brain - then I am absolutely positive that certain things will go into my subconscious, but the full transformation really can't take place without including all the other elements, of which there are so many that we can't take them all out. But, basically that is how I feel about it. Even the fact that I see the book on the table and one part of me says: I must read the book, but another part hates me reading the book, but if I can introduce the third element, I don't even have to pick the book up to have the result which he is talking about.

Participant 8: Yes, this is an interesting paragraph you have picked out here.

Mike Readshaw: I thought so as well, after twenty five years.

Participant 8: What I see in this is that there is a kind of like a two step process. There is the automatic transformation and then comes the conscious mentation. And, what I see here, I see it reflected in the process of the enneagram, where on the right side, we have the mechanical shock, and then later, after that has been processed, you have the conscious shock. So, what we have here, really, is an enneagram with the right and the left sides. That is what I see. We have the harnelmiatznel on the right side and the further harnelmiatznel on the second side, and that completes the enneagram.

Participant 1: He describes the friction as Zernofookalnian-friction.

Participant 4: I have a simple question. When you are referring to reading it mechanically, well, what do you exactly mean: is it just reading without any kind of reflection, as if it is just letters?

Mike Readshaw: No. Let's be clear. I am not reading it mechanically. I think, it's just that the word 'mechanical' is there. I'm not quite sure what you mean by that.

Participant 4: How do you read it?

Mike Readshaw: I read it as I read it to you.

Participant 4: Do you ponder upon it?

Mike Readshaw: No... but inevitably one tries to make sense of it. The technique that I use to read it I think I have described to you elsewhere.

(NB. I had earlier explained that to read the book the second time, it was necessary to read it 'between the commas,' that is, pausing slightly at each comma, for it to sound, almost, as a piece of music. Then, when reading it a third time, for understanding, it was necessary to pause, at each comma, an appropriate number of seconds, according to the part of the psyche destined for each chapter, indicated, in my opinion, by the number of syllables in the chapter heading. MR)

My understanding of it is that when he says 'of themselves automatically' I allow the time for it to, as it were, resonate, when I am reading it, in me.

Participant 4: Where does it resonate?

Mike Readshaw: Oh, I couldn't say exactly for that. I am not that conscious ! But I read it, more or less, as I have read it to you. I have puzzled about this matter which is why I have introduced it here. I am very interested to see all the comments.

Participant 4: Sorry, if it sounds stupid but I just try to understand how you read it. When you, for example, have been reading your chapter, do you, at any time, sit down and ponder what you have been reading? What these things mean? Do you?

Mike Readshaw: I do ponder what it means, but usually this just happens. So, I am not quite sure what you are asking. I don't ponder it when I am reading it. I simply read it, as I have done, slowly. Later on, ideas might come back to me, as they do, when you read any book. I then might ponder various ideas, yes.

Participant 4: So, if there is a reflection afterwards, at some time, it is not some kind of reflection that you intentionally seek, to go to. It is as if it just comes.

Participant 5: Thank you, Mike. If I understand you correctly, what your understanding of this paragraph is, simply reading the book will cause some kind of internal reaction

Mike Readshaw: Well, to be honest, Alistair, I wasn't going to say that. I was hoping you would discuss this amongst yourselves, But, yes, that is my view. My view is that, if you read this book properly, the essence of certain real notions pass into your subconscious, and there, mechanically,...

Participant 5: That's what the chapter says.

Mike Readshaw: That's what it says.

Participant 5: That's what the paragraph says. That something will happen.

Mike Readshaw: To me, that's why Gurdjieff wrote the book.

Participant 5: Well, in fact, it doesn't say that something will happen. It basically says that certain real notions will pass into the subconscious ...

Mike Readshaw: And there, by themselves, mechanically, will bring about that transformation...

Participant 5: But would normally require conscious mentation to achieve that result.

Mike Readshaw: Well, conscious mentation in the sense that the true consciousness is the subconscious, which is what Gurdjieff says there. So these ideas are going into the subconscious, and there, by themselves, mechanically, they are transforming us. I wasn't going to say that, because I do not want to put my views too strongly, but, since you ask.

Participant 5: It's difficult because I had to sit and read the paragraph about ten times since you read it.

Mike Readshaw: Well, that's great.

Participant 3: I have a question, a general question. Does the subconscious function in terms of language, or is it above or beyond language in its functioning? Does anybody have any ideas?

Participant 1: I don't think it has anything to do with words.

Participant 3: Wait a minute. We just want to carry this through, Gabriel. Excuse me. You don't think the subconscious works in words?

Participant 1: I don't think so.

Participant 3: Okay. You know, reading, one wonders what language should you read it in, because, quite obviously, when you read it, you are reading language. So, to read, you are using a tool, that the subconscious is not using.

Participant 1: Well, for me, that is a very big question, because he tells you that we read it and we allow the consonances of these words to flow past us, so my main language is English, but, I realised, a sum of years ago, that I did not know what these words meant. So, I have to make an effort to find out what these words really mean.

Participant 3: So you can't be passive. You have to think.

Participant 1: It is worse than that, because, I have to have, beside me, a dictionary, now, because there are many, many key words in this book which require me to look in the dictionary to find out what the real essence, or the foundation, or the root of the word, really means. And if I find out what the root of the word means, it is much closer, and it is actually quite alarming to find out a certain word which I use in everyday language is now, in Beelzebub, I see that that word has absolutely nothing whatsoever to do, as I understand it passively. So now, I have to take these words and make an effort, a real effort, to understand what he is talking about, and I have to ponder that. I am 'logically confronted' by all these notions, and if I just read them mechanically, it is going to give absolutely nothing for me. I have to find out what he is talking about. And, many times he gives references that he is going to learn Greek, or he is in Babylon, to learn Greek. I think he mentions this in several chapters, and often, you find out, if you look at some of the words which occur throughout the book, it is the root word - more often than not, the Greek word - which gives you the solution to what he is talking about in the book.

An example, for me, would be, in Heptaparaparshinokh, when he is talking about the apparatus, Alla-attapan - well, I know what an apparatus is, some device for doing this, that and the other - but if I look in the dictionary 'apparatus' and I look at the Latin, the root of this word, it means 'be prepared.' So, 'apparatus Alla-attapan' now takes on a completely new insight: 'be prepared' because 'Alla', God, is 'pan', everywhere. So, all this stuff that is in the book, unless you make an effort to read and study what these words mean, then it is just 'gobbledegook.'

So, this is what Terje is saying, that I can't read it passively, and hope that something is going to happen to me. It is not possible.

Participant 6: Just a response to your question. What language does the subconscious talk, which is a fascinating subject? I thought about it. I think our consciousnesses, our intellect, our rationality, speaks written and spoken language, whereas, one thing gives the meaning of itself. There is a different layer of communication which is metaphor, and analogies, where one thing resembles something else, like the sound of a certain word, or the combination of certain words. We don't understand the metaphoric language but I believe that our subconscious talks in this language. This is what grows in me as a response.

Participant 5: I am just having my own, it may be unfair to call it ignorance, highlighted to me. Having read this paragraph ten times, on maybe the eleventh or twelfth read, I spotted another word which actually says 'may, of themselves, automatically.' So, he is not actually saying that there is a certainty that reading the book will alter you, he is saying 'it may, of themselves, automatically' cause a change, without the conscious mentation.

Participant 1: I think the language of the subconscious is intuition.

Participant 7: From what I see, your approach seems to be more like reciting the book like a big mantra, where you are repeating it, bypassing the conscious mind, and - I don't know - hoping or intending or trusting or having faith that something will be revealed to you at another level. And, I was reading, this very morning, in fact, from the first chapter of Gurdjieff, in BT, and he is asking himself: which language should I write the book in; should it be Russian, or should it be Greek, or Armenian, or English. He says, English is very good, but good for the salon, so he is actually struggling with this question as to what is the appropriate language for us, so maybe he is implying that there should be conscious effort on the readers part to understand what is actually being said and to struggle with the concepts as well as following the writers rhythm, of this book, which is very idiosyncratic, I must admit.

Participant 8: A question for Michael. You are a mathematician. You plug numbers into an equation, to give an automatic result, and there is no question about that result. May I ask what result the reading of this book has automatically given to you then, if that is not too personal. If you feel like sharing it.

Mike Readshaw: I am happy to try and say a little bit. I think that the difficulty in answering the question, Ian, is that Gurdjieff says that, in maybe the following paragraph, or a couple of paragraphs after this, he says something about the two minds of man, the two consciousnesses of man, and he says that our ordinary consciousness - we have an ordinary consciousness and we have the subconscious - and he says that, I think, that in his opinion the subconscious should predominate in the common presence of man. So, I see this transformation as making the subconscious predominate in the common presence of man. But I think he also says, and again and again, in BT, in different chapters - linking it to these two consciousnesses - he says that the two consciousnesses have almost nothing in common, and in another section, and I think in the chapter we actually examined the other day, he says that the two consciousnesses have nothing in common. So, I have been reading BT for nearly forty years, so, I think that what happens is that the subconscious does develop, but that we know nothing about it. It is not part of our common presence. It develops completely outside of us, as it were, and it is only after a long period of time that we, sort of, gradually become aware of quite subtle changes in ourselves; subtle changes in what I might describe as the origins of our behaviour, that instead of initiating actions from the person that I think I am, I am able to initiate actions from somewhere else, and I find myself able to do things that previously I would have been completely unable to do. I think it is a very long process. It is a very subtle process, because these two consciousnesses have nothing in common, but to my mind, it is a definite something.

Participant 9: Hopefully, this might add something. The word 'mechanically' is the word that really jumps off this page, with all of the associations it has within this Work. By thinking about Claire's presentation this morning, we see how the process of digestion happens mechanically, automatically. But, we have to make a contribution. We can't digest the food unless we eat it. The air comes in automatically. Our contribution is to be present in the breath. And, then another process takes over. But, we don't guide those stopinders in between the shocks. Impressions come in mechanically. But, if I make the effort to be present to those impressions, another process begins. Gurdjieff talks about the two rivers - this analogy of the two rivers, and that the river of ordinary life flows in one direction. But there is another river: smaller, narrower, that goes to the great sea. And, if we are alert, once in a while those rivers may come close together, and we may be able to jump from one river into the other. And then it takes us, the current takes us, we just have to know how it went, to make the jump. So, whatever has happened to all of us, Mike included for reading this book, is because it was not left undigested on the bookshelf. We made an effort to go to it again and again and again. And, in that effort, something different happened that would not have happened without that effort. So it seems to me that digestion will occur, and that growth of some type will occur, but, from what perspective, what attitude, what place do we approach what we are going to eat? Because how that ingestion and digestion is begun seems to lead to different processes that have their own automaticity, but they go in different directions. Our small, but absolutely necessary contribution, is to learn to be there at the right moment, with the right attitude, the right approach, so that what comes in goes off into the second stream.

Participant 4: I have found myself many times in a situation, when I read the book, suddenly I become aware that I am reading, and that I have been reading for maybe a minute, maybe more, without paying attention at all. And if I see this now in the perspective of centres, it is the formatory apparatus which is engaged, and I am just reading with my moving centre. The times, or sometimes, when I go to the book in order to look for something, and I can sort of sense that it is there, to try to make an effort, and there comes up resistance, that it is difficult. And if I go on, now and then, something happens. And that is that I see some meaning. Then I am not reading with my mechanical parts. All the mechanical parts, they are on one line, and they are connected, if you like, with thick heavy wires. I mean, between all parts and centres there are wires, but between each emotional part of centres, each intellectual part of centres, there is a thicker wire than in those criss-crossing. And when I make the effort to try to go against my instinctive centre, for example, I then find it tiresome to continue. If I try to hold my attention and try to seek out what I am looking for, then there is the possibility of an emotional situation inside when I find it. I have never experienced contact with my intellectual part of emotional centre when I am just reading words. It just hasn't happened. But it has happened to me several times that I am connected with the intellectual part of my emotional centre when I really make the effort to try to understand. And what is the difference between these layers of centres. Here, you operate on almost no attention. And, yes, it is there, but it is just floating, in the emotional part of centres. My attention is there as long as there is some kind of interest in what I am reading, not on my behalf, but in the inner part of centres, or the intellectual part of centres. I have to go against some kind of second force in myself to be able to hold that attention, but, my main thing is this: I have never experienced an appreciation of what I have read if I just read letters.

Participant 3: I just did a thought experiment. Perhaps some of you are familiar with the notion of thought experiments? Putting yourself in a situation imaginarily thinking about it. Okay, I put myself into the situation: I am a guy who just walked in here and knows nothing about Gurdjieff. And I find all these weird people here talking about very peculiar things with words I know nothing of, initially. And then some kind people start to stand up and explain to me what it says in that book that they all respect so much. And I begin to understand that there is something that we might call, that you might call, the Work, which promises things to me. Something good will happen if you partake in this work. So I say: What do I have to do? Should they begin to say intentional suffering, and effort, and being in a group. And I say: Wait a minute, you mean to say that this work is like a meat machine, a minced meat machine? And I am not perfect so my meat will be thrown into this machine and this machine will kind of work on my meat and mince it out and make it into nice hamburgers or something? Round, and perfect? Whereas I was not before? And now I am perfect. I will be perfect with your machine. And then somebody stands up and says: Look, you don't even have to do that ! All you have to do is just read this book. Is this what I want? Yes, this is exactly what you want. You will become better. In what way? Well, in a way that maybe I do not know so well but this Gurdjieff knew. So I imagine myself taking off for the nether world, in front of the gates of heaven - the real heaven not the lecturers one - and they say stop ! You cannot go through. And I say why? Because you did not do what you were supposed to do. But I read this book which said everything about Beelzebub in it ! And they promised me that if I read the book everything is going to be alright. So, in view of this, I don't just stop and read the book, but I throw myself into the mince meat machine, of the Work. It sounds like a better chance, to be processed by a big machine rather than my thought and my reading. And I become a hamburger, and the hamburger goes back, and they say: Stop ! And you can't go through because... Well, what do you mean, I can't go through? I went into what Gurdjieff said this work would get me someplace. Can you imagine if I get the answer back: Mr Who? That would be something. Anyway, there is no way, in front of judgement, that I can push on my conscious responsibility, and divert it to somebody else. What I would need, in walking in here as an ignoramus, would be for somebody to suggest a way, which would awaken my own responsibility. Not the way to acquire values that somebody else put in a book. Whom do I know he was? And who is the guy who is telling me to read the book? Or who is telling me to throw myself into the mince meat machine? I cannot trust all these guys. I have to trust my judgement, my critical faculties - and he who has no critical faculties, his place is not here ! - to awaken my own responsibilities. That is the kind of program I would buy. I would never buy a program that depends on some weird sounding guy, who is a matter of voting if he was a charlatan or not. So this is how I would face the Work in general, if I was to just walk into this room for the first time.

I think there is something really strange in believing, in having this image of the Work as being a machine that will process you, and change you from meat to a hamburger. Something very weird, like an attitude. How could I ever possibly speak to somebody to join the Work if my proposal would be: Come be a hamburger next to me. The only thing I can speak in the name of is maybe this Work will awaken the responsibility in me. And I think that this is what the Work is about. It is not to make better humans, according to the values of anybody. It is to awaken one's responsibility inside you. And if somebody was to say: Don't worry, this is the place for that, then I would negotiate the terms of being here. I would accept it as a possibility.

Participant 2: I don't disagree with you. In the beginning of the book, it is stated that we have to read it many times, and he specifies, he says three times. I think that is only one way of stating that we have to approach it in three different ways. And what I understand from your presentation is that you demonstrate the second meaning, but not all the readings

Participant 8: Another question for Michael.

Mike Readshaw: I thought so.

Participant 8: Where, or what role, do you see for personal initiative in this work then? Or in your understanding of what you have said here about the mechanical side of it. Do you see a necessity for any type of individual effort?

Mike Readshaw: I think the key to the question is that question, Ian - about initiative - where that initiative comes from, because - as Gurdjieff says - we have our conscious mind, which is a 'fictitious' one. It is asleep and always will be asleep. And, we have the subconscious mind, which is our true consciousness. And, I think, in terms of - I think Gurdjieff says that our growth as individuals depends upon initiatives and understanding coming from the subconscious mind. So, it is a question of where does the initiative come from? And I think it is a mistake, in my opinion, to divide the conscious mind, the 'fictitious' mind - to dived it against itself. We have to allow the subconscious to act through us, rather than try to act from our conscious mind. Sometimes it is best to switch the conscious mind off, to act and perceive through the subconscious mind. Now, that could be regarded as the Work that you are doing.

Participant 8: Well, yes. Probably a lot of people here have had experience doing Movements, and would agree.

Mike Readshaw: That's interesting, yes.

Participant 9: I think that is one of the big questions in what you just said is who would make that decision to switch off the conscious mind and work with the unconscious? I found myself, a moment ago, realising that during much of this awareness of being in the room that attention was mostly tracking thoughts: people's words, my words. And then there was a more waking up and sensing into the body, and the words were still going on. And then trying to come back behind the words, and watch the words in my head responding to the words coming out of everybody else's head. So, the words are really - they are the most exterior manifestation of what goes on inside of my psyche. So this question, what is and where is the subconscious - well, if the words and the images are on the surface in what we call our normal consciousness, but are really quite mechanical, where do we stand in relation to that constant flow, that river of words? We stand right in the middle of the stream. We are in the middle of the railroad tracks. They just take us. If we can stand back from them, perhaps anchoring some of our attention in the body, and watch them go by, they may very well contain some useful information. But one does not have to be taken by them. And then there is the experience of a very deep awareness into which real understanding appears, and epiphanies appear, that has nothing to do with the words. Perhaps a word will trigger something, that will then come into that space? But, the words are not really what we are looking at. I tried to express that, not very artfully, a little while ago when talking about levels of being, that I would say that there is a language of words, but there is a language of being, and the quality of what someone is, the quality of their presence, doesn't require words. It is most eloquently expressed without them. So all of us, I think, can find, in a practical way, this direct experience of something inside of us which is much richer than the words, and maybe have an experiential sense of these two different levels we are struggling with, right here, as part of us wrestles with these words and concepts, but we must also be present behind them, and not get lost, and then maybe we have a sense of what he is talking about.

Participant 1: There exist several pages of a diary by Katherine Hulme, floating around in various groups. And, in there, she is talking - she gives a day where she is talking to Gurdjieff, and

Gurdjieff says, "active mentation, conscious mentation, when real 'I' is present." So, to me, there is no mistake about it, conscious mentation is when the 'I' is present, and this is the theme of the whole book, and outside of the book, it's reinforced in the book in the subtitle of the book. The book gives the subtitle, which was the original title of the book, saying 'An Objectively Impartial Criticism of the Life of Man.' But what is an objectively impartial criticism? And that is one of the most important questions because only the 'I' has the possibility of being objective and impartial towards me. So this is a much more serious problem than just sensing the body. Because, where does that 'I' exist in me, that has these qualities, which are not of this Earth? And that is what he is asking me to do, to try and find this 'I', which exists within me, so that that can become my guide - assuming that I work on myself to develop this 'I' that becomes the guide for my life.

Participant 5: Going back to this paragraph that Mike has placed in front of us, it has begun to strike me that Mike has simply drawn our attention to the obvious. I say the obvious because if the book didn't automatically shock us all, we wouldn't be sitting here. And this is why we are all here, because the book gave us such a shake, simply by reading it. It didn't take us to heaven. It didn't take us to the end of the road. It just put us on the road, and then it is up to us all to navigate that road - to find a way, to work on it every day, and it becomes - it becomes life. And there is a lifetime's work for everybody in this book. And I think that is the reason largely why we are sitting here today, because we have all been so influenced by this wonderful work.

Mike Readshaw: Alistair, I have spent twenty five years on this paragraph. I have worked out that, if I skim a bit, I will have finished this chapter in about seven hundred and seventy five years. It is going to be a long lifetime.

Participant 4: I have got two questions. When he is speaking about the sun, which neither shines nor heats, how do you see this not shining, and how do you view this that it can shine? What would it mean if it shone?

Mike Readshaw: Are you asking me a question?

Participant 4: Yes, I am asking you two. What does it mean to you, after reading the book, that the sun neither shines nor heats? And the second question is: if it should shine, what does that mean?

Mike Readshaw: I think when it comes to questions about the sun, Terje, it is beyond my competence. It is beyond my competence. I don't know.

Participant 4: I think this touches upon what he is saying. You know, I can sit here and I can also have the same experience and then boom, and then I try to, I recognise that I actually am something, and something happens in me, and then I can hear what people are saying.

Mike Readshaw: What is the connection with the sun?

Participant 4: Well, at that moment, my sun is shining. And when I am lost in thoughts, or whatever, it is not shining.

Participant 11: What I have been thinking all this time is that you have taken the book out of the context of the Work. You have read just the book. You have no connection with the oral tradition of the Work or anything that has to do with it and you have reached some conclusions that are completely different from the ones that we believe we have reached, which is not strange, of course. But, I have just realised that we have been given some tools that can help us read this book, which is a very special book. And, you can not ignore those tools, otherwise it will be very difficult for you to understand it as Gurdjieff meant it to be understood, because, of course, this is not the only thing he did. He did not write just that book. He taught the movements. He had groups. He had so many things. He wrote music. So, you cannot just take one thing and analyse the whole Work based upon that. I think this is something that will take you to a road which is obviously half the cake, and not even one tenth of the cake.

Participant 12: I actually have a question which is related to what you just said. And I have been sitting here with that question for quite a while. If your interpretation of this paragraph should be a fact, then, my question is: why did Mr Gurdjieff leave us all the other tools related to Work? Why did he leave us the possibility to work with movements, exercises, working together with other people, which is, in my opinion, a very important tool, in order not to get lost in one's own subjectivity? And, I have this question, why did he leave us the practical tools of the Work?

Mike Readshaw: I think, in terms of the movements, Gurdjieff was a specialist in the physical body and movements. I think that everyone has a specialism, and that was his. He was an expert in that. My impression, from what I know of the Gurdjieff tradition, is that once Gurdjieff had written BT, the focus of his teaching became, essentially, just read the book, and he encouraged people, at all times, to read what he had written. A lot of the ideas about group work and remembering yourself, and self-observation, a lot of that comes from the period before BT was written. I get the impression.

Participant 3: After I heard Ulrike, and myself, and other people, attack Mike, so viciously, compassion arose in me, and I feel I have to take his side, I am sorry to say. I think that he should be left with some breathing space, to change his mind. If you keep on pushing the issue onto him, what do you want him to do, he will just clam up, and defend his ideas. There is no other way for him to do, nothing else, thus closing him off, sealing him in a tighter and tighter way, into this little cubicle, of paranoia, you say, but it is not! He has to be left free. We cannot create a scapegoat. And, after all, if he considers himself to be a Gurdjieffian, he might be an odd cousin, but a cousin non-the-less.

Mike Readshaw: I might one day find a group that will accept me.

Seminar 4

Participant 8: I think, on that note, that we should bring this session to a close. I would just like to say a couple of things before you all get up and leave. First, thank you Mike for coming and raising these questions.

Mike Readshaw: Thank you. It has been a great honour.

Participant 8: You came with questions. You brought up those questions. You have all examined those questions, to a certain degree, and I think it is always important that we always do question ourselves and our beliefs, no matter how strongly we believe them. There is always opportunity, or necessity, that we should question our beliefs. So thank you very much for bringing those and deciding to come here, and bringing us these questions, and challenging us.

End of Session

Banquet Speaker - Democracy, Idiocy and the Esoteric Schools

George Kazos

Less than a hundred kilometers from here lies Athens, the city where some hundred years before Christ, art, philosophy, theater and science flourished in a way probably never met before or after.

Now why on earth did all these achievements took place in this city, what was so special about it? Why there and then? What was the key element that made all these things possible?

It is commonplace that it was its unique political system called "Democracy", which made it possible for Athens to unleash all the potential its citizens had.

Well, that raises another question. Why was democracy born in Greece and especially Athens?

Back in 1992 I spent some months in Moscow for a project. I was impressed by how different Russia was from Greece. Flat land stretching everywhere. You need to travel for almost 1.400 kilometers to get to the Ural Mountains and 1.000 kilometers to reach the Baltic Sea. So easy for a powerful clan or ruler to control and dominate. No place to hide if you are in the opposition. And look at the climate also. Winter came, covered everything with snow, nights became long, everything stood still. So difficult not to accept your fate.

Now take Greece. Fragmented by mountains, countless little islands lie off the coast. The world for anybody living here is a place so full of surprises. You move along and it is constantly changing. It is not easy to accept there is only one God (many gods must inhabit this place) or that you should obey one ruler. It is also a hard place to make a living. You need to cooperate, trade, communicate in order to survive. So back in the ancient times, the 6th, 5th and 4th century BC Greece was a bubbling pot where all kinds of government were tried: monarchy (the rule of one - monos), oligarchy and aristocracy (the rule of the few - oligoi or of the best - aristoi) and finally democracy (the rule of the people - the deme). All this took place in the many small independent city states in which Greece was divided, but above all in Athens.

One can easily see that Athens is positioned at a key point of Greece. It is practically where the mainland meets the islands. The breeze that came from the islands was always one of freedom and equality. The wind that would come from the plains of Sparta or Macedonia would be much colder, with a smell of oppression and control. So eventually it was here where everything would come together.
After the mythical years when heroes reigned, round the end of the 7th Century BC monarchy had given way to aristocracy. There were already steps taken towards the democratic way of

government we will see in detail later on, but the nine archons which administered the Athenian state were elected annually on the basis of noble birth and wealth. There was an assembly of Athenian citizens, but the lowest class was not admitted and the procedures were controlled by the noble. From time to time there were violent clashes between the people of Athens due to rivalry either economic or regional. For that reason at the year 594 BC, a well respected Athenian citizen and poet called Solon was asked to propose a constitutional reform that would bring peace to the city.

According to Aristotle, Solon legislated for all citizens to be admitted into the assembly (the Ecclesia) and for a court (the Heliaia) to be formed from all the citizens. He gave the common people the power not only to elect officials but also to call them to account. Solon broadened the financial and social qualifications required for election to public office. He divided citizens into four political classes defined according to their property. The citizens of the higher class had access to higher office, either in piece or in war where they could participate as generals, cavalry, infantry or auxiliaries.

In the years to come various "aristoi" (noblemen) managed to seize power and become "tyrants", that is rule the city as they saw fit, but without abolishing the existing laws altogether. One of them called Hippias became a tyrant in the year 508 with the help of Athens greatest enemy, the Spartans. That eventually led to a revolution by the people, who without having any leader managed to drive Hippias and the Spartans who held the Acropolis, out of Athens and free the city.

What happened next was rather unique. They called another well respected nobleman called Cleisthenes who was in exile not to rule but to assign to him a special task: That he would come up with a detailed form of government that would secure for the years to come that the people of Athens will govern themselves. Cleisthenes agreed and elaborating on Solon's laws introduced reforms that led to what he called isonomia ("equality vis à vis law", iso=equality; nomos=law) and what was later called demokratia (democracy).

The city was governed by the following political institutions:

The Ecclesia of the Deme - the assembly of all citizens which voted the laws and took decisions on various matters.

The Vouli - a governing body for preparing and proposing the laws. It was a legislative body with 500 members chosen once a year by lottery among the citizens older than 30 years of age. This body was preparing the bills to be voted as laws. Any citizen could come to the Vouli and propose a law or decision to be taken by the Ecclesia. The bills proposed could be rejected, passed or returned for amendments. The Vouli held daily meetings and also looked after the correct application of the laws voted. Each day of the year a different member of the Vouli was appointed as "chief of state". He held the keys to the treasury, the stamp of the state and he presided in the Vouli and the Ecclesia.

The Dikasteria (the law courts) or The Heliaia. It had 200 members over 30 years of age, chosen by lottery each year and it was a public court where citizen addressed their complaints and the cases were tried.

Apart from the above ten Generals were appointed by the Ecclesia each year, to be chiefs of the army and navy. They were over 30 years of age and should have special skills, knowledge and. war experience.

The Ecclesia of the Deme

The main governing body was the Ecclesia of the Deme, the assembly of all active citizen, those being all male adults (over 20 years old) with parents from Athens. There weren't any restrictions having to do with the economic status of the citizen.

Athens population at that time (5th - 4th century BC) is estimated round 250.000-300.000. The citizens eligible to vote must have been from 30.000 to 60.000. That was a big number compared to most other contemporary Greek cities where the numbers would be round 1.000. Corinth which was a significant and rich city had less than 15.000 citizens.

The Ecclesia decided by voting about the laws to be applied, about important decisions such as Athens going to war and appointed some key officers of the state.

The procedure was the following: One or more citizen would speak for or against a law prepared and proposed by the Vouli to the assembly. Than the voting would take place. That was done usually by raising hands and some people specially assigned would estimate the result. Sometimes it was mandatory to have a minimum number of citizens present and their votes actually counted. For example if it was proposed that a stranger would be given citizenship a minimum of 6.000 votes was necessary. Then each voter would throw in a big pot either a white or a black pebble, in favor or against the proposal. The pebbles would be counted and the decision would be taken accordingly. If a citizen was proposed to be exiled from the city for a period of time (usually ten years) because he was considered to be a threat for democracy, those in favor would write his name on a piece of pottery (ostrako) and throw it in a pot. If more than 6.000 "ostraka" were gathered he would be ostracized.

Although there could be groups formed in favor or against a decision there were no organized political parties and certainly no government and opposition.

There were practically no limits to the power of the Ecclesia. If the Ecclesia after some time took a decision that opposed a previous one, the only thing that could happen was that the citizen who had proposed this could be somehow sanctioned for "misleading" the Ecclesia.

The assembly took place at Pnyka near the Acropolis approximately every nine days, but that could vary. The participation wasn't mandatory, but there were measures to discourage non participation. Slaves carrying ropes dyed red, patrolled the city and if they spotted somebody, for example working in his shop, they whipped him so his clothes would be painted red. That was considered a great shame so he had to change his clothes and join the Ecclesia. Those not participating were called "idiotes" that is looking after their own matters only. Eventually the negative aspect of declining to take active part in the city matters gave the word its other meaning that is of an idiot, a fool.

Interestingly enough the Ecclesia of the Deme decided also about religious matters, that is about what is considered to be the official religion, accepting foreign deities, building temples, changing religious ceremonies, defining the salary of priests etc.

Esoteric Schools

So, what happened with non official religions, esoteric schools, philosophers and mystics?

Mystic is a Greek word coming from MUO which means, "to shut the eyes or mouth." MUO is closely related to the verb MUEO, "to initiate into the mysteries." The closed eyes and mouth in this context do not signify blindness or muteness, but secrecy and silence, and the order not to reveal the secrets of the initiation and revelation that one had received. These Greek root-words have given the words "mystic" and "mysticism," "mystery" and "mysterious," as well as "mute."

It seems as if the mystic is the exact opposite of an active citizen, as if he is a kind of "idiot".
One can very easily see the implications of that.

On the one hand democracy being the most open and tolerant form of government, allows people to form and express their opinions and beliefs, to communicate and cooperate, to form esoteric schools and practice as they wish.

On the other hand mysticism can be seen as leading to "idiocy" and raising suspicions that the great Greek mystical philosophers such as Socrates and Plato could be a threat to democracy itself.

This tension seems to be present throughout the history of the Athenian democracy.

In year 322 BC the Macedonian general Antipater ended democracy and imposed oligarchy upon Athens. The philosophic schools were finally abolished by a Justinian law in 529.

© Copyright 2010 - George Kazos - All Rights Reserved

Where Do We Go From Here?

After considering input from the 2010 Conference attendees and evaluating the venue proposals put forward, it was decided that the 2011 Conference would be held in Prague, Czech Republic.

Appendix 1: Concert Programme

The Gurdjieff Foundation
And the music group of

present
a unique concert based on

The Sacred Music

# of Gurdjieff-de Hartman

Friday, March 26, 2010
8:30 p.m.

www.rodatheater.gr
www.gurdjieff.org.gr

In his travels in the Far and Middle East Gurdjieff collected an enormous volume of musical patterns and melodies. Returning to the West he adapted them to the piano with the collaboration of the famous Russian musician Thomas de Hartman, who was one of his followers.

The variety of Gurdjieff's music style is particularly rich. It is based on traditional songs, dervish dances, prayers and hymns found in various monasteries and other holy places that he had visited.

Later on he gave his music its final form so as to be played in appropriate circumstances, mainly to accompany the "Movements", the sacred dances, which constitute an integral part of Gurdjieff's teaching.

Appendix 1

RODA aims at the presentation of Gurdjieff's music to the public, using as a fundamental axis the practice of ideas that the great teacher brought to the West, ideas that became known as the "Work on The Self".

"Ears are not good for this music.
The entire presence should open."
G. I. Gurdjieff

1. Religious Ceremony
2. Armenian Song
3. Persian Dervish
4. Sayyid Chant and Dance No 10
5. Dervish Dance
6. Marche Alerte
7. Asian Song No 40
8. Kurd Melody for two Flutes
9. Religious Ceremony
10. Sayyid Dance No 18
11. Caucasian Dance
12. Sayyid Dance No 31
13. Religious Ceremony

Musicians
Takis Paterelis: piano, flute, saxophone
Pia Pierrakou: voice and keyboards
George Dounis: drums, bells, voice
Dimitris Gasparatos: voice, guitar, bass guitar, drums
George Tabakis: guitar, didgeridoo, drums, voice

Music arrangement and art direction by Maria Peretzi

Appendix 2: List of Attendees

Thomas Anemos - GREECE
Mircea Ardeleanu - GREECE
Stephen Aronson - USA
Popi Asteri - GREECE
Eva Avlidou - GREECE
Paul Bakker - NETHERLANDS
Nikolas Bryce - CANADA
Maria Calderisi - CANADA
Eleni Choremi - GREECE
Anestis Christoforides - GREECE
Colin Clark - UK
Gloria Cuevas-Barnett - USA
Mary Davidson - UK
Dimitri Dobrovolski - RUSSIA
Athanasios Drakopoulos - GREECE
Alistair Edwards - UKRAINE
Angelo Giannatos - GREECE
Stavros Kappas - GREECE
George Kazos - GREECE
Triga Keratso -GREECE
Panagiotis Kokolis - GREECE
Thomae Komliki - GREECE
Kostas Levetas - GREECE
Ian MacFarlane - UK
Wayne McQuillen - CANADA
Kostas Mertzanis - GREECE
Clare Mingins - UK
Dennis Newton - USA
Julieanne Nielson - USA
Dimitri Peretzi - GREECE
Maria Peretzi - GREECE
Gabriel Raam - ISREAL
Michael Readshaw - UK
Arkady Rovner - RUSSIA
Oyvind Ruud - NORWAY
Peter Salapatas - GREECE
Terje Tonne - NORWAY
Ulrike Tonne - NORWAY

All & Everything Conference 2010

Fotis Traganoudakis - GREECE
Nikos Troullinos - GREECE
Mariette Ysselmuiden - NETHERLANDS
Andreas Zarkadoulas - GREECE
Byron Zeliotis - GREECE

Index

A

Abdil, 200, 201, 209, 211
Abrustdonis, 174
Absolute, 83, 106, 127, 129
active, 22, 36, 37, 52, 56, 73, 87, 140, 143, 144, 145, 147, 154, 155, 156, 157, 158, 160, 162, 175, 184, 190, 202, 203, 216, 225, 230, 231
Adrenaline, 104, 105, 107
Advaita, 180, 181
affirm, 109, 213, 214
affirmation, 185
affirming, 155, 217
Afghanistan, 212
Africa, 198, 212
Ahoon, 20, 45, 70
Aieioiuoa, 22, 34, 42, 57
Aim, 17, 19, 21, 23, 25, 28, 31, 91, 111, 119, 133, 134, 140, 141, 145, 161, 164, 182, 183, 191, 196, 211, 212
air, 98, 143, 148, 149, 150, 151, 154, 157, 160, 161, 162, 163, 164, 173, 174, 179, 221
Aisors, 86, 88, 90
Akhaldan, 21, 41, 182, 199, 201, 202, 211, 212
alcohol, 159
Salzmann, de, Jean; Michel, 15, 96, 186
Alla-attapan, 220
allegorical, 123, 126
allegory, 45, 75
Amarhoodan, 201
Amarloos, 201
America, 15, 85, 86, 95, 118, 122, 186, 189
Amygdala, 108, 114, 115
Anderson, Margaret, 125
Angel, 22, 83, 136

Animal Magnetism, 149
Ansanbaluiazar, 155, 168
Anulios, 155, 168
Archangel, 22, 71
Aristotle, 229
Armenian, 220
artery, 110
ascend, 206
ascending, 129, 130, 144
Ashagiprotoehary, 155, 168
Ashiata Shiemash, 67, 110, 111, 123, 124, 183, 191, 199, 203, 204, 205, 209, 211, 212
Ashish, Sri Madhava, 14, 117, 118, 119, 120, 122, 124, 125, 127, 130, 131, 132, 133, 134, 135, 136, 137, 138, 139, 140, 141
astral, 130, 134, 135
Astralnomonian, 148, 149, 174
Atlantis, 77, 182, 201, 211, 212
atman, 135
Atom, 20
Attention, 16, 17, 20, 22, 28, 29, 60, 65, 89, 97, 98, 99, 101, 102, 118, 120, 124, 125, 133, 140, 142, 143, 162, 176, 178, 198, 206, 222, 224, 225
Autoegocrat, 21, 106, 115
awareness, 18, 19, 20, 21, 23, 28, 33, 68, 70, 77, 80, 99, 126, 127, 132, 213, 224
axis, 42

B

Babel, 63
Babylon, 182, 212, 220
Beekman Taylor, Paul, 13, 171
Beelzebub, 3, 16, 20, 21, 22, 23, 24, 42, 44, 45, 46, 59, 60, 61, 65, 67, 68, 70, 71, 75, 80, 82, 84, 94, 95, 98, 100, 102, 103, 106, 108, 109, 110, 113, 116, 119, 123, 124,

129, 132, 133, 134, 137, 139, 141, 143, 144, 146, 147, 148, 149, 150, 151, 152, 153, 154, 155, 156, 157, 159, 160, 161, 162, 163, 164, 165, 166, 167, 168, 169, 170, 171, 177, 180, 181, 182, 183, 184, 191, 199, 200, 206, 210, 211, 212, 213, 219, 223

Beelzebub's Tales
  The Tales, 31, 32, 33, 34, 35, 39, 40, 41, 42, 43, 44, 51, 56, 140, 172, 175

Being, 16, 17, 20, 21, 22, 23, 24, 26, 27, 29, 32, 34, 36, 38, 41, 42, 43, 45, 46, 50, 51, 52, 56, 58, 62, 63, 64, 65, 69, 71, 72, 73, 74, 76, 77, 78, 79, 83, 84, 85, 86, 87, 88, 89, 90, 91, 92, 93, 98, 100, 103, 110, 111, 114, 116, 117, 118, 120, 121, 123, 124, 125, 126, 127, 128, 129, 130, 131, 132, 133, 134, 135, 136, 138, 140, 141, 143, 144, 145, 147, 148, 149, 150, 151, 152, 154, 155, 156, 157, 158, 160, 164, 165, 166, 167, 168, 169, 172, 173, 174, 175, 176, 178, 179, 180, 182, 183, 185, 186, 188, 189, 192, 193, 198, 199, 201, 202, 203, 204, 205, 206, 207, 208, 209, 210, 213, 216, 221, 222, 223, 224, 225, 230, 231

being-bodies, 130, 131
being-effort, 133, 149
Belcultassi, 41, 57, 182, 199, 201, 203, 212
Bennett, John G., 116, 120, 140, 143, 144, 145, 147, 149, 150, 151, 152, 153, 155, 158, 161, 164, 165, 166, 168, 169, 171, 172, 175, 185, 186, 187, 195, 197
Blavatsky, Helena P., 116, 117, 120, 121, 122, 131, 135, 136, 137, 138, 139
Bliss, 127, 135, 136
Bodhisattva, 116, 120, 126
Brahma, 126
Brahman, 126
Brain, 66, 93, 99, 102, 103, 104, 105, 106, 107, 115, 136, 139, 141, 162, 166, 170, 177, 183, 217
breath, 16, 20, 98, 99, 115, 135, 176, 221

breathe, 149, 157, 160, 162, 163, 179
breathing, 99, 108, 113, 160, 161, 162, 163, 179, 215, 226
brother, 171, 195, 203, 209
Brother Ahl, 209
Brother Sez, 209
Brotherhood-Olbogmek, 183
Buddha, 24, 67, 125, 203, 204, 205, 211, 212
Buddhism, 25, 70, 90, 117, 189, 195
Buddhist, 67, 194
Buzzell, Keith, 13, 43

C

Canada, 4, 13
carbon, 153
carriage, 86, 87
Castaneda, Carlos, 187
center, 48, 49, 58, 60, 63, 65, 69, 91, 102, 103, 109, 113, 133, 140, 150, 151, 152, 153, 155, 162, 163, 164, 165, 167, 168, 172, 176, 177, 180, 181, 185, 186, 190, 200, 201, 204, 212, 222
Cerebellum, 150, 151, 172, 176
Cerebrum, 150
cherubim, 128, 129
child, 24, 26
children, 14, 78, 95, 119, 126, 134, 141
China, 111
Chinese, 97, 98, 159
Christ, 67, 191, 204, 205, 211, 228
Christian, 96, 190, 194, 197, 200, 204
Christianity, 70, 90, 117, 180, 181, 189, 191, 195, 197
coat, 176
  coated, 38, 124
  coating, 144, 164, 165
comet, 211
Communion, 161
compassion, 3, 16, 23, 24, 25, 27, 65, 67, 71, 120, 194, 226
concentrate, 102, 106, 128, 129, 135, 144, 148, 150, 156, 210

Index

concentration, 102, 106, 128, 129, 135, 144, 148, 150, 156, 210
Conscience, 17, 25, 42, 57, 61, 79, 88, 101, 110, 111, 163, 183, 189, 191, 201, 205
conscious, 16, 20, 21, 23, 24, 25, 37, 52, 61, 62, 65, 100, 101, 102, 110, 115, 116, 119, 120, 122, 124, 125, 126, 127, 133, 135, 141, 154, 156, 157, 161, 165, 183, 192, 195, 201, 203, 204, 205, 213, 215, 216, 217, 218, 219, 220, 223, 224, 225
Conscious Labor, 133, 135, 154, 183, 192, 195, 201, 204
consciousness, 15, 19, 21, 22, 23, 24, 42, 50, 52, 61, 64, 95, 97, 101, 109, 110, 111, 113, 119, 127, 128, 130, 135, 153, 155, 161, 199, 200, 201, 202, 204, 213, 214, 215, 219, 221, 224
contemplate
    contemplativeness, 202
Coombe Springs, 171
Cornelius, George, 91
Cortex, 107, 108
cosmic, 21, 22, 33, 38, 48, 49, 52, 103, 106, 119, 123, 127, 128, 129, 135, 140, 155, 156, 159, 163, 165, 168, 201, 202, 203
cosmogenesis, 121, 125, 139
cosmology, 20, 124
Creation, 20, 23, 29, 33, 34, 37, 44, 45, 46, 48, 49, 50, 67, 80, 111, 114, 117, 127, 128, 129, 160, 169, 170, 176, 180, 190, 191, 192, 205, 211
creative, 4, 23, 127, 130, 135, 153, 165, 174, 175, 176, 191, 198
Creator, 126, 168, 187
crystallize, 75
    crystallization, 52, 109
    crystallized, 123, 155

D

Daly, Tom, 150, 171
Daumal, Rene, 188, 197
death, 36, 38, 41, 93, 117, 121, 123, 130, 136, 161, 162, 163, 164, 185, 203
deflections, 144, 155
Defteroehary, 147, 148, 149, 151, 154, 177
Denying, 155, 217
descending, 20, 21, 129, 130, 131
descent, 67, 77, 123, 129, 199, 200, 201, 202, 203, 209, 211, 212
Descent, 211
die, 49, 50, 85, 205, 209
digest, 163, 164, 206, 221
digestion, 22, 105, 108, 144, 149, 151, 154, 156, 160, 169, 175, 221
dimension, 20, 28, 42, 50, 92, 94
disharmonized, 109
Djartklom, 163, 175, 176
DNA, 192
    genes, 192
dog, 33, 42, 46, 51, 140
Dramatic Universe, 195
dream, 96, 118, 120, 124, 125, 133, 139, 141, 188
Dullemen, Wim van, 181, 189
dying, 98, 113, 209

E

Earth, 24, 44, 45, 59, 61, 62, 64, 65, 67, 68, 71, 78, 88, 102, 123, 126, 132, 155, 164, 182, 183, 184, 189, 197, 199, 200, 201, 202, 203, 204, 210, 211, 212, 225, 228
Ego, 3, 16, 20, 21, 22, 23, 24, 25, 62, 67, 89, 127
    egoism, 3, 16, 17, 20, 21, 22, 23, 28, 95, 145, 153, 156, 164, 168, 169
    egoistic, 20, 23
Egoaitoorassian, 21
Egypt, 85, 91, 157, 182, 202, 212
Egyptian, 60
electromagnetic, 66
element, 22, 36, 37, 52, 72, 73, 74, 78, 99, 101, 143, 144, 145, 147, 153, 154, 155, 156, 157, 158, 160, 162, 164, 175, 176, 180, 181, 182, 185, 187, 190, 191, 216, 228
emanation, 22, 149, 155, 163, 164, 179

emotion, 69, 70, 97, 98, 99, 103, 106, 107, 135, 147, 150, 151, 153, 154, 162, 172, 175, 176, 200

emotional, 17, 21, 29, 58, 63, 69, 91, 106, 107, 108, 113, 114, 143, 145, 151, 153, 161, 162, 172, 176, 200, 210, 222

Endlessness, 20, 21, 22, 23, 24, 46, 81, 106, 117, 123, 126, 128, 129, 130, 131, 132, 133, 136, 141, 142

England, 14, 122

Enneagram, 43, 46, 51, 53, 72, 83

entropy, 188

esoteric, 3, 4, 15, 36, 38, 40, 42, 63, 70, 82, 85, 86, 94, 95, 105, 116, 117, 119, 120, 122, 124, 125, 126, 127, 141, 189, 195, 199, 201, 228, 231

Essence, 16, 17, 19, 20, 24, 49, 58, 77, 98, 100, 109, 117, 118, 141, 142, 150, 167, 168, 169, 177, 183, 191, 203, 213, 214, 215, 217, 218, 219

Eternity, 76, 207

Ether, 97

Etherokrilno, 128, 155

Evolution, 105, 114, 120, 127, 130, 131, 135, 136, 143, 144, 154, 165, 167
   evolutionary, 132, 154

Evolve, 105, 133, 166, 169

Exercise, 27, 28, 42, 81, 90, 126, 133, 138, 162, 197, 209, 226

Exioehary, 144, 145, 150, 151, 152, 153, 154, 155, 165, 166, 167, 168, 174, 177, 179

exoteric, 41, 119, 120, 141

F

Faith, 21, 24, 27, 75, 88, 110, 153, 167, 202, 220

father, 45, 61, 168, 204

feeding, 37, 162

Feeling, 18, 20, 21, 26, 27, 56, 79, 92, 94, 102, 103, 106, 107, 202

Fire, 83, 98

first being-food, 144, 149, 157, 162

Fludd, Robert, 83

Food, 3, 14, 41, 42, 56, 95, 105, 133, 134, 143, 144, 145, 146, 147, 148, 149, 150, 151, 152, 153, 154, 155, 156, 157, 158, 159, 160, 162, 163, 169, 172, 173, 174, 175, 179, 207, 221

force, 21, 24, 37, 53, 56, 67, 87, 147, 148, 167, 169, 202, 203, 222

Formatory, 89, 113, 172, 222

Foundation, 15, 186, 187, 195

Fourth Way, 45, 46, 180, 181, 186, 187, 191, 214

France, 69, 189, 198, 212

friction, 27, 101, 216, 217

G

Germany, 69, 188, 198

Ginsburg, Seymour, 1, 2, 13, 14, 116, 118, 119, 121, 124, 125, 126, 133, 134, 135, 137, 138, 139, 140

gland, 108
   Endocrine, 107
   Ovaries, 173
   Testicle, 173

Gob, 201, 212

God, 19, 20, 29, 30, 32, 39, 45, 46, 47, 49, 50, 56, 58, 66, 83, 126, 129, 135, 155, 157, 170, 183, 188, 189, 201, 206, 210, 216, 220, 228

Good, 36, 38, 82, 184

Gornahoor Harharkh, 123

Gospel, 94, 147, 150, 151, 152, 153, 154, 156, 165, 171

Grabontzi, 212

gravity, 33, 36, 38, 109, 133, 144, 152, 163, 164, 180, 181, 185, 200, 201

Great Nature, 109, 116, 133, 157

Greece, 4, 13, 14, 15, 228

Greek, 20, 32, 67, 104, 135, 220, 230, 231

Gurdjieff, G. I., 3, 4, 14, 15, 16, 17, 18, 19, 20, 21, 22, 23, 24, 25, 26, 27, 28, 29, 31, 32, 33, 34, 35, 39, 40, 42, 43, 45, 46, 48, 51, 52, 53, 55, 56, 59, 60, 61, 62, 64, 65,

66, 67, 68, 70, 72, 73, 74, 75, 76, 77, 78, 80, 81, 82, 84, 85, 87, 88, 89, 90, 91, 92, 93, 94, 95, 98, 100, 101, 102, 103, 105, 108, 109, 110, 111, 114, 115, 116, 117, 118, 119, 120, 121, 122, 123, 124, 125, 126, 127, 128, 129, 130, 131, 132, 133, 134, 135, 137, 138, 139, 140, 141, 143, 144, 145, 147, 148, 149, 150, 151, 152, 153, 154, 155, 156, ☐157, 158, 159, 160, 161, 162, 163, 164, 165, 166, 167, 168, 169, 170, 171, 172, 173, 174, 175, 177, 178, 179, 180, 181, 182, 183, 184, 185, 186, 187, 188, 189, 190, 191, 192, 194, 195, 197, 198, 199, 205, 208, 209, 213, 214, 215, 217, 218, 219, 220, 221, 222, 224, 226
  Mr. G., 189
Guru, 138

H

Hamolinadir, 202, 203, 212
Hanbledzoin, 48, 49, 149, 150, 162
Hands, Rina, 159
Harnel-Aoot, 156
Harnelmiatznel, 147, 150, 153, 154, 165
Hartmann, Thomas and Olga de, 161, 171, 187
Hasnamuss, 22, 52, 168
Head-Brain, 99, 103, 149, 150, 174
heart, 16, 20, 58, 67, 70, 86, 97, 104, 107, 108, 115, 136, 144, 151, 153, 161, 172, 174, 176, 188, 215
heaven, 24, 201, 206, 207, 208, 212
Heaven, 197, 223, 225
Hebrew, 135, 204
Heechtvori, 183, 203
Helkdonis, 174
Hell, 212
Heptaparaparshinokh, 33, 34, 43, 45, 46, 52, 55, 127, 128, 147, 151, 155, 156, 157, 163, 215, 220
Heretical, 197
Heropass, 106, 129, 132

hierarchical, 197, 209
hierarchy, 31, 44, 46, 52, 119, 195
higher being-bodies, 71, 184, 185
higher being-body, 52
Hindu, 14, 117, 126
Hoffman, Maude, 122
Holy Reconciling, 21
Hope, 24, 25, 27, 59, 81, 100, 110, 117, 153, 164, 189, 220
hormone, 149, 176
Howarth, Dushka, 189
Howarth, Jessmin, 189
Hulme, Kathryn, 158, 171, 224
hydrogen, 133, 147, 148, 149, 154, 158, 166, 167, 173, 175
Hypnosis, 90, 185
  hypnotised, 24
  hypnotism, 71, 108, 109
Hypothalamus, 107, 108, 114

I

I Am, 122, 137
Identification, 23, 24, 68, 133, 141
Idiot, 49, 50, 61, 125, 144, 156, 159, 171, 231
Illumination, 190
imagination, 25, 30, 97, 150, 153, 176, 195
impartial, 64, 113, 202, 206, 208, 225
Imperishable Being, 116, 117, 136
impressions, 17, 23, 143, 150, 151, 154, 157, 161, 173, 174, 176, 179, 214, 221
In Search of the Miraculous, 31, 50, 70, 75, 86, 95, 98, 117, 118, 119, 120, 123, 137, 138, 140, 141, 145, 147, 148, 149, 150, 151, 153, 154, 157, 158, 160, 166, 168, 171, 184, 209, 214, 215
  Fragments, 55, 184
incarnation, 20, 123, 124, 128
India, 117, 118, 119, 122, 137, 138, 141, 212
Individual, 4, 20, 21, 22, 23, 33, 36, 37, 48, 68, 71, 105, 125, 132, 136, 161, 182, 185, 201, 203, 223
inexactitude, 42, 173

initiation, 19, 136, 137, 231
insight, 120, 124, 125, 220
Instinctive, 18, 63, 91, 113, 222
Institute, 14, 111
Intellectual, 63, 69, 96, 107, 113, 121, 130, 140, 150, 151, 153, 172, 176, 177, 185, 187, 193, 200, 203, 222
Intention, 37, 52, 156, 161, 185
interconnected, 197
intuition, 21, 41, 185, 220
Involution, 73, 143, 145, 154, 165, 167, 177
  involutionary, 168
Involve, 55, 73, 154
Iraniranumange, 37, 155
Islam, 70, 90, 117, 161
Itoklanoz, 18, 19, 23, 27

J

Jesus, 81, 90, 119, 125, 191, 205
Jew, 91
Jewish, 91
Jung, Carl G., 127, 128, 137, 142

K

Kabala, 117, 130
Karatas, 67, 168
Karnak, 175
Keschapmartnian, 168
Kesdjan, 38, 130, 131, 134, 149, 152, 210
King, C. Daly, 150
Koan, 27
Konuzion, 212
Krishnamurti, 122, 123, 139
Kundabuffer, 124, 167, 200

L

ladder, 24, 213
laugh, 167, 168
laughter, 81, 167, 168, 216
Law, 3, 26, 31, 32, 33, 34, 35, 36, 37, 38, 39, 40, 41, 42, 45, 46, 50, 51, 53, 54, 56, 75, 94, 120, 127, 163, 193, 194, 229, 230

Law of Seven, 34, 50, 94, 180
Law of Three, 34, 50, 56, 57, 78, 94, 101, 127, 128, 217
lawful, 18, 34, 42, 163, 173
Legominism, 110, 180, 181, 182, 183, 184, 185, 186, 189, 190, 191, 192, 193, 194, 203
libido, 134
Life is Real, 68, 122
light, 19, 22, 34, 36, 37, 41, 42, 43, 46, 47, 55, 56, 57, 89, 115, 125, 136, 181, 182, 200, 201, 206
Litsvrtsi, 33, 34, 35, 36, 37, 54
Love, 24, 37, 79, 81, 110, 119, 128, 136, 153, 154, 165, 167, 179, 197, 202, 205, 208

M

Macedonia, 228
machine, 88, 90, 206, 222, 223
magic, 83, 84, 188
magnet, 63
  magnetic, 28, 48, 49, 58, 63
maintenance, 19, 127, 157
Maralpleicie, 212
Mars, 45, 123, 206
material, 4, 16, 19, 24, 69, 78, 85, 88, 143, 145, 146, 147, 149, 151, 157, 164, 176
matter, 25, 29, 56, 62, 64, 73, 75, 78, 86, 88, 95, 96, 108, 111, 113, 129, 149, 193, 199, 200, 208, 216, 218, 223, 227
maze, 136
Mdnel-In, 149, 154
mechanical, 24, 43, 63, 76, 113, 119, 141, 193, 200, 215, 216, 217, 222, 223, 224
mechanicality, 94
meditate, 202
meditation, 65, 81, 105, 111, 112, 113, 114, 115, 119, 120, 124, 125, 133, 135, 139, 141, 201, 207
Meetings with Remarkable Men, 3, 82, 96, 165, 168, 171, 202, 209
Megalocosmos, 47, 106, 128, 129

mentate, 167
mentation, 100, 101, 110, 166, 213, 215, 216, 217, 219, 220, 225
mesoteric, 119, 120, 141
Mexico, 96
Microcosmos, 47, 48, 49
mind, 15, 16, 18, 19, 20, 35, 53, 57, 58, 61, 62, 63, 67, 69, 71, 77, 81, 88, 89, 97, 100, 101, 111, 112, 120, 125, 133, 135, 153, 154, 160, 164, 166, 170, 180, 184, 191, 193, 195, 197, 203, 206, 213, 214, 220, 221, 224, 226
Mohammed, 204
monastery, 184
monk, 14, 49, 50, 114, 117, 208, 209
Monochord, 83
Moon, 97, 140, 155, 164, 168, 201, 211
Moore, James, 122
Moral, 90
   Morality, 26, 161
Moscow, 15, 122, 185, 228
Moses, 204
mother, 69, 79
Movements, 180, 181, 185, 186, 187, 189, 224
Moving, 16, 17, 23, 26, 60, 63, 82, 91, 103, 113, 176, 201, 210, 222
Mullah Nassr Eddin, 66
music, 13, 81, 92, 94, 157, 181, 185, 186, 187, 198, 218, 226
mysticism, 15, 188, 231
myth, 24, 67, 117

N

Nature, 2, 22, 56, 58, 59, 68, 69, 78, 92, 97, 103, 104, 117, 130, 132, 133, 164, 169, 178, 192, 194
Negative emotion, 87, 97, 114, 161, 163, 207
Neocortex, 114
Neologism, 16, 21
nerve, 102, 103, 104, 110, 150
nervous system, 18, 66, 102, 103, 104, 105, 106, 107, 108, 110, 111, 114, 115, 195
   parasympathetic, 102, 104, 105, 108, 110, 112, 113, 114, 115
   sympathetic, 102, 103, 104, 105, 107, 108, 110, 112, 114, 115, 195
neural, 107, 108, 110
Neurology, 106
neurotransmitter, 177
Neutral, 64, 65
   Neutralising, 56, 88
   Neutralizing, 65, 70, 73
Newton, Issac, 237
Nicoll, Maurice, 125, 137, 139
nine, 34, 35, 39, 41, 63, 84, 94, 96, 229, 230
Nisargadatta, 118, 119, 134, 141
nitrogen, 153
nothing, 27, 42, 56, 66, 76, 79, 89, 90, 94, 95, 98, 99, 125, 126, 127, 130, 131, 135, 138, 139, 140, 144, 169, 174, 177, 194, 195, 214, 220, 221, 222, 224, 226
Nothingness, 209
Nott, Stanley and Rosemary, 32, 51, 133, 134, 137, 161, 171
Nyland, W, 185

O

Objective, 52, 56, 60, 64, 67, 68, 81, 95, 97, 110, 127, 129, 178, 180, 181, 182, 183, 191, 205, 208, 211, 225
Obligolnian, 203
Occasion, 59, 60
octave, 43, 45, 54, 55, 60, 127, 128, 144, 145, 146, 147, 148, 149, 150, 151, 152, 153, 154, 155, 157, 160, 173, 174, 175, 199, 210
Okidanokh, 22, 64, 155, 165
Omnipresent, 22, 155, 165
Opium, 43, 55, 72, 75, 78, 79
Orage, Alfred, 97, 122, 143, 144, 145, 146, 147, 148, 149, 150, 151, 152, 153, 154, 156, 162, 164, 165, 166, 170, 171, 174, 175, 176, 185, 197

Oragean Version, 63, 140, 143, 144, 145, 148, 149, 150, 151, 154, 158, 166, 171, 172
oral teaching, 122, 123, 134, 143
organic, 39, 52, 56, 64, 65, 86, 88, 154, 216
Ors, 204
Oskianotsner, 19
Ouspensky, P. D., 15, 31, 50, 62, 70, 75, 76, 83, 86, 88, 92, 94, 116, 117, 119, 120, 122, 123, 126, 130, 134, 137, 138, 139, 140, 143, 146, 147, 149, 151, 155, 171, 172, 173, 175, 184, 185, 186, 187, 197, 214

P

Parable, 207
Parabola, 129, 130
paradise, 188
Paris, 15, 76, 156, 159, 164, 171, 184
Partkdolg-duty, 154, 156, 166, 167, 201
passive, 56, 73, 99, 109, 202, 203, 219
Pentland, John, 15, 91, 185, 194
Peretzi, Dimitri, 1, 13, 14, 15, 31, 55, 56, 57, 58, 102, 237
Persian, 77, 168, 212
personality, 18, 20, 28, 36, 38, 41, 42, 48, 49, 58, 67, 84, 85, 90, 117, 133, 136, 141, 186
physical, 16, 18, 29, 36, 38, 41, 42, 113, 120, 126, 130, 131, 160, 176, 226
physics, 33, 36, 147
Piandjoehary, 150, 151, 152, 153, 154
Pinder, F., 133, 134
planet, 19, 22, 37, 38, 45, 48, 49, 51, 59, 60, 66, 67, 75, 102, 110, 118, 123, 124, 126, 132, 135, 140, 141, 144, 155, 162, 163, 164, 168, 182, 183, 201, 203, 204, 206, 210, 211, 212
planetary, 34, 38, 66, 86, 103, 109, 124, 157
Plato, 195, 231
Pogson, Beryl, 139
politics, 195
ponder, 78, 85, 93, 145, 160, 161, 163, 188, 217, 218, 220
pondering, 17, 63, 93, 217

Positive emotion, 153
Poundolero, 203
Prayer, 161, 170
Prem, Sri Krishna, 117, 119, 124, 125, 136, 137, 139, 141
presence, 17, 23, 28, 52, 92, 101, 103, 106, 114, 120, 123, 127, 130, 144, 161, 163, 166, 179, 182, 194, 201, 203, 221, 224
Priest, 86, 200, 201, 211
Prieure, 122, 160, 161, 163
Prime Source, 162, 168
Protocosmos, 47, 49
Protoehary, 147, 148, 149, 151, 154, 155, 160, 177
psyche, 66, 68, 81, 110, 120, 135, 154, 160, 161, 164, 166, 167, 168, 169, 201, 212, 218, 224
psychological, 16, 17, 18, 22, 23, 69, 126, 127, 128, 162, 188
Psychological Commentaries, 137
psychologist, 100
psychology, 14, 16, 20, 33, 61, 89, 93, 97, 100, 106, 107, 110
Purgatory, 32, 33, 35, 36, 38, 42, 43, 46, 47, 99, 102, 106, 144, 145, 146, 147, 148, 149, 150, 151, 152, 155, 156, 163, 167, 172, 173, 174, 182, 201, 202, 203, 204, 205, 207, 209, 210, 216
Pyramid, 196

Q

quintessence, 158

R

radiation, 48, 49
Rascooarno, 130
Ray of Creation, 31, 43, 45, 46, 47, 48, 49, 50, 155
Real, 20
Reason, 23, 39, 41, 51, 52, 56, 64, 67, 69, 72, 93, 100, 110, 129, 130, 141, 147, 155, 172, 185, 186, 203, 205, 207, 225, 229

Reciprocal, 59, 60, 61, 64, 74, 128
Reconcile
   Reconciliation, 23, 33, 67
   Reconciling, 64, 101, 102, 155, 169, 216
Relativity, 20, 21, 41, 42, 45, 46, 199
religion, 76, 88, 204, 231
Remember, 27, 28, 62, 63, 70, 75, 76, 77, 78, 79, 86, 90, 94, 96, 98, 100, 113, 133, 140, 147, 168, 172, 173, 175, 179, 188, 191, 197, 206, 215
   Remembering, 73, 93, 100, 111, 226
Remorse, 16, 17, 22, 34, 36, 37, 41, 42, 57, 100, 163, 164
Remorse-of-Conscience, 34
Repentance, 161, 189
resonance, 23
resonate, 86, 91, 141, 218
Resulzarion, 152
Russia, 4, 15, 71, 72, 88, 90, 96, 123, 126, 185, 188, 195, 196, 198, 212, 220, 228

S

Sacred, 22, 27, 33, 37, 52, 95, 109, 110, 111, 123, 127, 128, 130, 153, 155, 157, 163, 165, 183, 201, 202, 204
Sacred Individual, 123, 204
sacrifice, 207
   sacrificial, 211
Saint Lama, 204
Science, 14, 32, 55, 56, 68, 102, 103, 108, 113, 114, 115, 177, 178, 179, 228
Scientific, 102, 104, 106, 107, 178, 203
Sea of Beneficence, 212
second being-food, 144, 145, 162, 163, 175, 179, 201
Second Conscious Shock, 31, 154, 206
seeing, 25, 28, 54, 68, 73, 78, 209
Self, 19, 21, 22, 23, 24, 100, 110, 126, 133, 135, 136, 139, 181, 186
Self Observation, 100, 226
Self Remembering, 28, 100, 133, 141, 206
Self-consciousness, 19, 20, 203
sensation, 16, 18, 29, 99, 115, 135, 173, 177, 178
senses, 24, 90, 91, 99, 101, 103
Sensimiriniko, 203
Sensing, 29, 58, 93, 118, 165, 224, 225
Sensory, 19, 21
seraphim, 128, 129
seven, 32, 72, 101, 129, 130, 144, 157, 164, 182, 199, 204, 211, 214, 225
seventh, 151, 152
Sex, 3, 143, 144, 147, 150, 151, 152, 153, 154, 160, 165, 166, 167, 168, 169, 171, 175, 176
   sexual, 36, 37, 134, 140, 144, 153, 154, 165, 166, 167, 168, 169, 173, 174, 175, 176, 177, 179, 198
   sexuality, 134, 140, 169
Shiva, 126
shock, 43, 66, 148, 161, 178, 216, 217, 221, 225
Sianoorinam, 150
siddhi, 138
singing, 14
sister, 198
Sitting, 29, 64, 98, 120, 124, 225, 226
Skull, 36, 38
Sleep, 24, 78, 105, 125
snake, 114
Society, London, 193
solar plexus, 69, 97, 103, 149, 150
son, 117, 124, 126, 127, 128, 130, 131, 132, 135, 136, 139, 183
Soul, 78, 143, 168, 169, 170, 203, 210, 212
sound, 20, 27, 33, 43, 55, 194, 218, 220
sounding, 223
sperm, 173, 176
spinal column, 176
spine, 150, 173
Spirit, 78, 118, 120, 124, 125, 129, 136, 141, 200, 209
   spiritual, 16, 19, 20, 24, 76, 89, 95, 114, 126, 127, 130, 133, 139, 147, 149, 150,

152, 153, 165, 166, 169, 171, 177, 180, 181, 186, 187, 188, 189, 190, 191, 206
spirituality, 71
Stopinder, 37, 52, 128, 144, 149, 151, 152, 153, 155, 156, 175
subconscious, 20, 61, 62, 91, 93, 101, 102, 109, 110, 111, 213, 215, 217, 218, 219, 220, 221, 224
subconsciousness, 111, 215
subjective, 16, 18, 19, 20, 21, 37, 52, 95, 101, 127, 156
substance, 72, 128, 147, 149, 150, 152, 155, 160, 161
Suffer, 24, 25, 66, 104, 164
   Intentional Suffering, 52, 133, 135, 154, 183, 192, 195, 201, 203, 204, 210, 222
   suffered, 186
   suffering, 16, 17, 20, 24, 25, 161, 164, 189, 200, 210
Sufism, 180, 181
suggestibility, 24, 59, 60, 61, 74, 75, 90, 163, 185, 195, 201
Sun, 22, 47, 49, 71, 83, 97, 99, 103, 106, 128, 129, 140, 155, 162, 164, 225, 226
Sun Absolute, 22, 47, 49, 71, 106, 128, 129, 155
Symbol, 42, 43, 51, 91, 94, 177
   symbolic, 120, 125
   symbolism, 141, 202
Synchronicity, 142

T

Table of Hydrogens, 179
Tail, 21, 158
Tarnotoltoor, 34
Tazaloorinono, 55
Tchaftantouri, 183, 203
telepathic, 120, 130
telepathically, 120, 124
telepathy, 119, 120, 138
Tenikdoa, 35, 36, 38, 40
Tescooano, 45
Testosterone, 176, 177
Tetartocosmos, 31, 36, 37, 45, 47, 48, 49, 50, 51, 152, 216
Tetartoehary, 149, 150, 151, 153, 154, 158
Tetetzender, 35, 36, 38
Thalamus, 114, 115
Theomertmalogos, 20, 155
Theosophical, 14, 116, 117, 118, 122, 123, 125, 136, 137, 138, 139, 140
Theosophist, 120, 121, 122, 123, 138, 139
Theosophy, 118, 122, 136, 139, 188
third being-food, 166, 201
Third Force, 23, 45, 46, 126, 128, 169
three-brained, 16, 17, 33, 71, 102, 103, 110, 111, 123, 126, 132, 133, 134, 141, 182, 183, 199, 200, 204, 211
Tibet, 119, 212
Tiflis, 89
Tikliamish, 212
time, 17, 27, 40, 41, 43, 46, 48, 49, 56, 57, 58, 59, 65, 67, 68, 70, 71, 72, 73, 76, 77, 78, 80, 81, 82, 86, 90, 92, 93, 94, 95, 99, 101, 103, 108, 110, 111, 114, 120, 123, 128, 129, 130, 133, 135, 138, 140, 148, 155, 158, 160, 169, 173, 177, 178, 181, 183, 184, 185, 186, 187, 188, 190, 191, 192, 196, 197, 200, 202, 203, 204, 205, 206, 207, 210, 211, 212, 215, 216, 218, 221, 223, 226, 229, 230
tolerance, 27
Transapalnian, 182, 211
transform, 17, 18, 77, 100, 159, 162, 163, 164, 166, 172, 208
transformation, 3, 16, 23, 88, 100, 110, 133, 134, 143, 144, 145, 146, 147, 148, 149, 150, 152, 154, 155, 157, 159, 160, 161, 162, 165, 166, 173, 174, 176, 191, 194, 196, 213, 215, 216, 217, 219, 221
transmutation, 134, 147, 163, 166
transmute, 145, 166
transpersonal, 133
Transubstantiate
   Transubstantiate, 111
Travers, Pamela, 15

Index

Triad, 45, 56, 58, 73, 84, 88, 126, 210
Triamazikamno, 22, 33, 34, 43, 45, 46, 78, 127, 128
Triangle Editions, 137, 171
Trimurti, 126
Trinity, 34
Tritocosmos, 47, 49
Tritoehary, 148, 149, 151, 154
Trogoautoegocrat, 21, 44, 45, 105, 106
    Trogoautoegocratic, 103, 144, 148, 155
two-brained, 134

U

unconscious, 167, 224
understanding, 16, 19, 21, 22, 23, 26, 27, 32, 37, 43, 61, 63, 67, 68, 69, 71, 74, 75, 80, 81, 86, 93, 100, 117, 119, 120, 135, 145, 163, 174, 176, 180, 195, 203, 209, 218, 223, 224
Union, 190
universe, 20, 21, 42, 50, 64, 66, 83, 91, 93, 99, 103, 126, 127, 128, 130, 131, 139, 140, 144, 155, 183, 200
Urdekhplifata, 35, 36, 38, 40
USA, 13, 237

V

Vedanta, 180, 181
vein, 110, 157
vibration, 33, 36, 38, 128, 147, 156, 167, 173, 182
Views from the Real World, 125, 137, 149, 171, 180, 187
Vishnu, 126
vivifyingness, 37, 52, 156

W

Washington, 171
Water, 29, 95, 98, 160, 166
Welch, William and Louise, 15
Will, 17, 27, 28, 132, 143, 165, 169, 214
Wine, 95
Wisdom, 67, 116, 120, 121, 124, 125, 136, 137, 139, 191, 193, 207
womb, 131
Word, 155
Word-God, 155
Work, 4, 14, 15, 17, 28, 31, 32, 34, 36, 38, 41, 42, 45, 46, 49, 50, 60, 67, 69, 70, 72, 73, 77, 82, 85, 95, 102, 110, 111, 114, 115, 134, 169, 181, 185, 186, 189, 190, 191, 194, 196, 205, 206, 207, 210, 221, 222, 223, 224, 226
world, 4, 14, 15, 16, 17, 18, 19, 21, 22, 23, 24, 25, 26, 27, 29, 31, 32, 33, 34, 36, 41, 43, 44, 45, 46, 47, 48, 49, 50, 51, 58, 59, 61, 62, 67, 70, 78, 79, 80, 83, 89, 90, 91, 98, 99, 101, 105, 115, 117, 118, 121, 123, 127, 129, 133, 135, 155, 158, 160, 165, 169, 171, 180, 181, 184, 186, 187, 188, 190, 191, 195, 196, 198, 199, 200, 204, 206, 207, 208, 211, 223, 228

Y

Yelov, 68, 82, 85, 86, 88, 89, 91, 94, 96, 195
Yoga, 115, 136, 137
    Mantra, 97, 98, 220
    Pranayama, 115

Z

Zen, 27
Zernofookalnian, 101, 217
Zoostat, 108

www.ingramcontent.com/pod-product-compliance
Lightning Source LLC
Chambersburg PA
CBHW080334170426
43194CB00014B/2560